SECRET NARCO

WENSLEY CLARKSON has investigated numerous crimes across the world for the past thirty years. His research has included prison visits, surveillance operations, police raids and even post-mortems. He and his family have received death threats from criminals and he has also worked alongside homicide detectives. There is no one more qualified to tell this story. Clarkson's books – published in more than thirty countries – have sold more than two million copies. He has made numerous documentaries in the UK, US, Australia and Spain and written TV and movie screenplays. Clarkson's *Sexy Beasts* – about the Hatton Garden raid – was nominated for a prestigious Crime Writers' Association Dagger award.

www.wensleyclarkson.com

SECRET NARCO

WENSLEY CLARKSON

AD LIB

First published in 2020 by Ad Lib Publishers Ltd
15 Church Road
London, SW13 9HE

www.adlibpublishers.com

Paperback ISBN 978-1-913543-99-0
eBook ISBN 978-1-913543-91-4

A CIP catalogue record for this book is available
from the British Library.

Every reasonable effort has been made to trace copyright-
holders of material reproduced in this book, but if any have
been inadvertently overlooked the publishers would be
glad to hear from them.

Printed in the UK

10 9 8 7 6 5 4 3 2 1

*To the many old faces who helped me with this book down the years,
but are no longer with us.*
RIP

Praise for other books by Wensley Clarkson

'Reveals a fascinating life, albeit savage and ultimately wasted.' *Killer on the Road, Loaded*

'One of the best crime books I have ever read in thirty years of reading crime books.' *Killing Goldfinger*, Mark Lester, Amazon

Sexy Beasts
'Makes you wonder if the writer was in on it.' Amazon

'Brilliant. Another great read from Wensley Clarkson.' Joe Steed, Goodreads

Bindon
'This is a lurid tale ... yet Clarkson tells it in a way that makes it nothing short of fascinating.' *Independent on Sunday*

'Bindon emerges from Clarkson's portrait as a true gent, if a ferociously violent one, with an unsettling sense of humour.' *Daily Telegraph*

Hit 'em Hard
'Utterly compelling.' *Evening Standard*

'There is no doubt that Spot was a nasty piece of work but in this well-judged biography Clarkson brings him to life ... BRILLIANT.' *Time Out*

'A thrilling glimpse into a hidden world of money, power, glamour and violence.' *Killing Charlie*, the *Sun*

'Jack Spot's legend is still frighteningly alive in Wensley Clarkson's hands.' *Sunday Express*

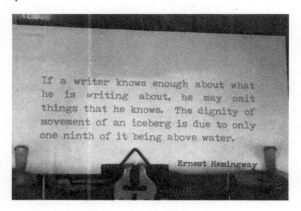

If a writer knows enough about what he is writing about, he may omit things that he knows. The dignity of movement of an iceberg is due to only one ninth of it being above water.

Ernest Hemingway

CONTENTS

Two thousand escudos of silver
They will give for his head alone
Many would win the prize
But nobody can succeed
Only a comrade could.

OLD SOUTH AMERICAN PROVERB

AUTHOR'S NOTE

It was inevitable that I would upset certain people by writing a book about Charlie Wilson.

One of the chaps I came across on the Costa del Crime warned, 'A lot of people have been chopped up round here. You should be careful doing a book on Charlie. Last bloke who tried it gave up after a few days.' That was fifteen years ago, when the original version of this book was first published.

More recently I found myself working on an in-depth TV documentary about some of Charlie's oldest associates and came across information that takes this story to another level. It includes new revelations about Charlie's involvement with the most infamous narco of all time and how Charlie came to be the ultimate dead man walking. I've had to trust the judgement and recollections of individuals, many of whom would rather not have their names reproduced in this book. Memories are fallible and contradictory, touched by pride and capable of gross omission. It was a risky business. But there are no hidden agendas in this story because Charlie is no longer with us. I relied on a long series of interviews and conversations, as well as recollections supplied at times unwittingly by dozens of individuals all over the globe. Naturally, some important names are missing and that will frustrate those who were involved in Charlie's world.

The story you are about to read may not be the one that most criminals would have preferred to be told. But it is the nearest to the truth about an underworld that has left a mark on everyone it has touched, from the hard-pressed police forces of three nations to the families of the victims of crime and even the criminals themselves.

During the course of research I've been taken into the confidence of many people who, for obvious reasons, would prefer to remain anonymous. I have respected the wishes of those individuals and I need only say that my decision to do so was as much to protect both the guilty and the innocent as it was to ensure the safety of close-knit communities.

As a result, some scenes represent a combination of facts reconstructed to reflect events as they were told to me. Certain characterisations, incidents, locations and dialogue were composited for dramatic purposes and to help protect the identity of my sources.

Ultimately, however, I have tried to recreate a life story that twisted and turned from the mean streets of south London to harsh prison corridors and the heated, manic, cocaine-fuelled Costa del Sol via the killing fields of Colombia to end in what some might think was an inevitable outcome. It was a bizarre, risky journey that I hope you enjoy and relish as much as I did.

Wensley Clarkson, 2020

CAST OF CHARACTERS

BUSTER – train robber whose life took a tragic turn

KING OF CATFORD – Brink's–Mat suspect who got too flashy

THE COLONEL – loyal childhood pal turned train robber

EL DOCTOR – the twentieth century's richest and most murderous drug baron

FREDDIE FOREMAN – ex-robber and Kray twins associate

FRENCHY – former war hero who saved Charlie's skin

THE GREY FOX – workaholic detective who never gave up

THE LUMP – west London hardman out for revenge

MAD MICKEY – short-fused south Londoner on a mission to destroy

THE MILKMAN – Kilburn Irishman with a finger in every pie

PADDY THE SMUGGLER – Charlie's old pal who needed a big favour

PAT – wife who feared the ultimate knock on the door

LA PATRONA – Medellín's London boss

THE PIMPERNEL – the most artful dodger of all

POPEYE – Medellín's number one killer

THE PREACHER – cold-blooded Amsterdam kingpin

THE PROFESSOR – graduate Scotsman who worked both sides of the Atlantic

SCARFACE – thought he was invincible

SKINS – escaped convict on a mission

THE TIGRESS – ETA's deadliest brunette

THE WEASEL – pint-sized train robber whose thoughts turned to gold

PROLOGUE
23 April 1990

Urbanización Montana, Marbella, Costa del Sol, southern Spain

No one took much notice of the pale-faced man with badly dyed, spiky blond hair.

He sunned himself on the mini-roundabout close to an estate of detached haciendas. A yellow mountain bike lay beside him as he sat nonchalantly on the grass, a big, overhanging eucalyptus tree providing some shade. He stayed for hours, occasionally swigging from a bottle and rolling himself a few joints. Enjoying the sunshine. Watching and waiting.

Two hundred yards away, the spring sunshine was beating down on the immaculate lawn of the back garden of a detached whitewashed house. A gentle breeze blew in from the pine woods behind the property, causing a slight ripple on the surface of its swimming pool. In the far corner of the garden, a man in his late fifties, wearing shorts and a polo shirt, had just finished lighting a barbeque. Looking immensely pleased with himself, he crouched down to pick some thyme from a neatly trimmed bed of herbs. He was preparing a very special dinner to celebrate his thirty-fifth wedding anniversary.

Less than 2 miles away, another pale-skinned man was speaking in a hesitant voice into a payphone in a petrol station forecourt on the N340 coastal road. It was known locally as the Road of Death, having claimed the lives of motorists and pedestrians over the years. The man slammed the phone down, got into a white van and drove onto the dual carriage before taking the next exit and heading towards the mountains.

Back in that immaculate garden, the middle-aged man in shorts was gently whistling to himself as he sprinkled some thyme and salt on two raw, blue steaks laid out on a plate next to the barbeque. Then he broke into Frank Sinatra's 'Come Fly With Me' as if he didn't have a care in the world. The song took him back nearly thirty years, when he and eleven others created history by pulling off the most daring train robbery in criminal history. In the sunshine of southern Spain, as his Alsatian Bo-Bo snoozed at his feet, all those memories must have seemed a million miles away. The days of professional, gentlemen villains were long gone. Now the Costa del Sol's chilling drugs underworld was filled with trigger-happy characters settling scores with a bullet.

By now the white van had reached the mini-roundabout where the man with the yellow mountain bike waited under the shade of that big eucalyptus tree. He nodded briefly at the van driver, who parked his vehicle just beyond the roundabout and got out. Separately they walked up a quiet side street dotted with ornate streetlamps and houses on one side, faced by a huge plot of land. They passed number seven, a white house, then numbers nine and eleven. Instead of a number on the next house there was the name 'Chequers'. They'd been here before, so they knew it was the one they wanted. Bougainvillea and carefully cultivated shrubbery covered much of the front of the property. The middle-aged man was still in the back garden when the doorbell rang. Bo-Bo barked briefly but settled down as soon as his master told him to. The owner's wife answered the door to find the pale-faced man standing on the doorstep in a grey tracksuit. A baseball cap pulled low on his forehead. His yellow mountain bike was leaning against a wall.

With a distinct south London accent, he asked the woman, 'Is he in?'

She nodded and told him to put his bike in the porch in case someone tried to steal it.

The middle-aged man was busy cutting up tomatoes and cucumbers for a salad when his wife called. He put down a knife he'd been using and greeted the young man with a grimace and nodded towards the patio area next to the pool. Bo-Bo remained quietly curled up in a shady corner of the garden. As the two men walked across the patio, the homeowner's wife heard raised voices but decided to stay in the house while they talked business.

Five minutes later, the visitor suddenly karate-kicked the other man in the testicles. He doubled over, struggling for breath. His nose was broken by a crunching karate chop. Bo-Bo, leaping to his master's aid, received a vicious kick in the chest that snapped his front leg and shoulder bone like a twig. The assailant produced a gleaming silver Smith & Wesson 9mm pistol from under his tracksuit top and fired at point-blank range. The first bullet pierced the carotid artery of the older man's neck. The second entered his mouth and exited from the back of his head.

In the kitchen his wife heard two loud bangs. At first she thought they'd come from a building site behind the house. Then she heard Bo-Bo screeching and rushed to the garden to see the faithful dog wounded on the ground while her husband staggered towards the pool, blood spurting from his neck. She later said, 'There was blood, blood, blood everywhere. He was desperately trying to stand up. He stared at me, but could not talk.' Her husband held his finger to his open mouth. Blood was streaming. He then tried to point to the back wall, over which the gunman had escaped. The shooter could easily have waited and turned his gun on his target's wife.

Contract killings on Spain's notorious Costa del Crime were two a penny. But this was the cold-blooded murder of 'Narco' Charlie, who thought he could thrive in the deadliest underworld of all. And his violent end would eventually lead investigators to the door of the world's most famous criminal, Pablo 'El Doctor' Escobar.

PART 1 – CHEEKY CHARLIE

In each of us, two natures are at war – the good and the evil. All our lives the fight goes on between them, and one of them must conquer. But in our own hands lies the power to choose – what we want most to be, we are.
Dr Jekyll and Mr Hyde, USA, 1920

1/

Some say that murder victims have a moment of clarity in the moments before they die. They experience a flashback to the pivotal points that shaped their lives.

In the case of Charlie Wilson in the back garden of his Marbella home, it must surely have been the bombsites of wartime London that he saw. After all, they'd first set him on his path to self-destruction. They'd been like playgrounds to him and his gang of young friends back then. This left an indelible mark because they'd all learned to fend for themselves from a very early age, ducking and diving to avoid the long arm of the law, as well as stealing whatever took their fancy to enjoy the sort of luxuries that rich folk took for granted.

One of Charlie's first childhood memories was a clip round the ear from a policeman who – wrongly – accused him of trying to drown a pony in a waterlogged bombsite. In fact, eight-year-old animal lover Charlie had been trying to save the stricken animal from the mud. He later said, 'That bastard copper never even gave me a chance to explain what was happening and that poor horse drowned because he wouldn't let me back on that bombsite to save him.'

Wilson believed, as did many of his contemporaries, that the police were the sworn enemy. He hated the way local coppers would bully and taunt him and his mates. There were even rumours that one or two of them abused some of the kids who lived on his south London housing estate.

It was into this harsh, urban environment that one of the most notorious outlaws in British criminal history, Charles Frederick Wilson, had been born, on 30 June 1932. Wilson grew up surrounded by dire poverty and misery. Living in that environment convinced him to have one priority in life – to make money. The names of London's big-time criminal legends– Jack Spot and Billy Hill – would dominate his early years but

Wilson's own underworld achievements would eventually outstrip them all.

Wilson was born to a hard-working family caught in a poverty trap from which there seemed no escape. As a small boy, his mother Mabel was the strongest influence in helping shape his later attitudes towards life. She found herself cursed by powerlessness through poverty and despite her wisdom the fate of her children was out of her hands. The Wilsons lived in a low-level tenement flat close to the river in Battersea. Charlie's dad worked long hours on the buses to provide his family with the basics. The pressure of surviving would lead to clashes between Charlie and his old man as Charlie had an aversion to all rules and regulations.

Battersea was light years away from being synonymous with comfortable streets full of upwardly mobile professionals. In the 1930s and '40s it was a collection of drab, cobbled streets lined with rundown terraced houses and tatty redbrick tenement blocks. Most of the housing had been built more than fifty years earlier for servants who worked in the big houses north of the River Thames.

The Wilsons eventually scraped together the deposit to buy their own house for the princely sum of £250, most of which came from a building society loan. The house had electricity but the only hot water came from a smelly gas boiler in the kitchen. An old tin bath was brought out no more than twice a week and everyone in the Wilson family was expected to share water to save money.

With cash so scarce, it was hardly surprising that most of Charlie Wilson's schoolmates were up to no good from a very early age. Wilson soon grew to appreciate the thrill of grabbing a bar of chocolate from the corner shop counter and dashing out the door. It was a buzz he'd spend the rest of his life trying to replicate.

On the streets of London during World War II, rationing was in place while most adult men were away fighting on two battle fronts. No wonder the heavily blitzed streets of south London became one big adventure playground for Charlie and his tearaway friends. Unexploded bombs, condemned buildings and lumps of shrapnel were all ample evidence of Hitler's bombers. Boys like Charlie soon learned to identify German aircraft by the noise they made and he'd often count them in and out as they buzzed loudly through the breaks in the moonlit clouds above him.

Bill and Mabel Wilson found it difficult to keep tabs on their young son, so they were relieved when Charlie was evacuated to stay with a family on the south coast of England. Charlie lived by the seaside for a year and childhood friend Bruce Reynolds remembered meeting him for the first time shortly after they'd both returned to south London. He recalled, 'We used to sit in the Anderson bomb shelter at the back of his garden smoking Woodbines and discussing the mysteries of women.'

The Wilsons' terraced house contained three bedrooms and one reception room. Charlie's bedroom – which he shared with his brother – was at the back and he'd often slip out of the house by climbing down the drainpipe, hopping over the back fence and running down the badly lit alleyway behind the terrace.

Policemen and local youths were involved in regular clashes. The police station at Nine Elms, near what was to become the New Covent Garden fruit and vegetable market, was a familiar place to both Wilson and Reynolds. One night Charlie, aged ten, was arrested and an officer drove to tell his parents. But the copper didn't give his father a ride to the station, which was 3 miles away. Wilson's irate father walked to the station to take his young son home with a face like thunder. The boy knew he was in for a beating. That usually meant a belt was brought out and the punishment would be followed by a lot of yelling, but no actual tears from the proud boy. He'd dust himself down and walk away without a word of remorse. Wilson understood that more often than not he deserved to be punished, but what upset him the most was that his father rarely explained what he'd done wrong. He tried his hardest to please his father but by the time he was twelve, their relationship had deteriorated to the point where barely a word was exchanged at meals.

At school Charlie was constantly pulling pranks in class and being kept in at the end of the day for detention. Yet despite frequent absences, Wilson thoroughly enjoyed reading books, although he was lazy about writing essays. He was a cocky, strong-willed child who took out the frustrations and violence of his home life on other kids by extorting money in exchange for protection from other bullies. Wilson didn't make himself very popular but few had the courage to stand up to him. 'Even then he had these piercing blue eyes that used to challenge you. They made Charlie seem a bit mad and scary,' recalled one friend.

His mates included two young tearaways called Jimmy Hussey and Tommy Wisbey, who both worked at Covent Garden fruit and vegetable market every weekend with Wilson. All three would hump crates around to earn a few extra bob. They often went to a youth club at the Elephant and Castle on Friday and Saturday nights. Wilson also hung out with Joey Pyle and others at a mobile snack bar on the south side of Albert Bridge, next to Battersea Park. During the hotter summer months, hundreds of south London youths would turn up there until the police moved them along when their presence caused major traffic problems.

South London's postwar youths were emerging as a restless, rebellious generation determined to make a mark for themselves. And although Charlie and his mates undoubtedly committed numerous petty crimes, they still retained certain standards and abided by codes. Targeting a man walking along the street and stealing his watch was frowned upon, while raiding cigarette wholesalers or shops was totally legit. 'The fat cats were there for the taking but you don't rob your own – ever,' explained Pyle.

Every youngster on the streets was fascinated by guns. Most had their own air guns and a few had even managed to find real weapons through fathers or grandfathers who had been fighting.

Charlie longed to find out what it was really like to fire a gun and kept his eyes and ears peeled for an opportunity to steal one when the moment was right.

By the age of thirteen, Charlie had little need for education. He was a bright, quick-witted teenager with an eye for the main chance and he'd already started earning a crust. Most Sunday afternoons, Charlie and his south London pals, including Reynolds and another, gangly kid, Gordon Goody from nearby Putney, would go to the pictures at Clapham Junction. The majority of teenage boys back then still wore suits and although Charlie wasn't flush with cash, he somehow managed to afford to buy a smooth mohair suit that greatly impressed the girls.

At weekends, Charlie and his pals went dancing at the Lyceum Ballroom in the West End, the Hammersmith Palais and the Wimbledon Palais. Charlie was one of the many who carried knives. Wilson even practised stabbing motions on old cabbages when he was working at the fruit and veg market. At that time incidents of 'shivving', or scarring, opponents with knives were numerous among petty criminals and the racetrack gangs admired by Wilson and his friends.

Wilson emerged as one of the leaders of a bunch of tearaways who specialised in smash-and-grab raids on phone boxes, as well as grabbing handbags from unattended cars.

One popular meeting place was a coffee stall in front of the Plough pub on Clapham Common. Wilson, Reynolds, Gordon Goody and Freddie Foreman all adored the meat and onion pies sold from the stall. 'Then we'd go on to the Clapham Manor dance hall because all the town halls back then were turned into dance halls at weekends,' explained Foreman.

In the daytime on Saturdays, Charlie went shoplifting in the big department stores in posh areas such as Knightsbridge and Kensington. One favourite shop was men's outfitters Cecil Gee. Reynolds never forgot the time he was buying two shirts for three pounds each when one of their friends, a stocky character called 'Buster' Edwards, grabbed ten or fifteen ties and ran out of the shop. When Reynolds eventually found Edwards further up the street he'd already sold the ties for a pound each to a local stallholder.

It was in the summer of 1948, as Heathrow was developed to replace Croydon as London's main airport, when legendary London crime boss Jack Spot masterminded a robbery that was supposed to confirm his status as one of the kings of the underworld. Ten raiders, all wearing nylon stockings over their faces, targeted three hundred thousand pounds of loot at an airport customs warehouse. One of Spot's team grassed them all up and all roads leading to the airport were under police surveillance. Thirteen Flying Squad detectives lay in wait in the customs shed and ten more were hiding in a van round the back. As Spot's team crashed in, a bloody battle ensued. Three of Spot's mob got away, but the rest of the battered robbers were dragged off in waiting Black Marias. They were all convicted and received up to twelve years' imprisonment each.

Up-and-coming tearaway Charlie Wilson knew a few of Spot's team. He swore then that he'd 'do' any grass who cost him his liberty. 'They're scum and should be put down,' he told a friend.

Youngsters like Charlie Wilson began to flex their muscles. In one dance hall in Brixton, south London, he got caught up in a gang clash involving razors when a couple of young hoods smashed their pint glasses on the bar counter and challenged all-comers to a fight.

As Charlie's self-destructive personality continued to emerge, family members noticed how fearless he had become and the way he'd try to manipulate situations to suit himself. He also often seemed incapable of realising when he'd hurt other people's feelings. Out on the streets, Charlie carefully hid his own feelings. Joey Pyle said, 'Charlie was always laughin', always good for a giggle, if you know what I mean. We even nicknamed him "Cheeky Charlie".'

Some Sundays, Wilson and his crew organised road trips to Brighton using stolen cars driven by kids in their mid to late teens who were already specialised motorists. They included a small kid called Roy James, nicknamed 'the Weasel', a cheeky youth called Mickey Ball, from Fulham, and a budding racing driver called Ritchie Bristow (who later died racing cars in Belgium). One time, James and Ball raced each other down to Brighton in two stolen 4.2-litre Jaguars. Charlie and his pals all put heavy bets on who would win before the two high-powered vehicles set off into the Surrey and Sussex countryside. A big statue on the seafront at Brighton was the prearranged winning post.

Pyle said, 'I can't remember exactly how long it took but Roy James won by more than a mile.'

Wilson and his mates decided pint-sized James, a sometime racing driver, would make a superb getaway driver if they ever started robbing banks and security vans. Wilson had begun fencing stolen goods when he worked the odd day in a scrap-metal yard near Battersea Bridge. He soon got a reputation for finding a home for all sorts of stolen property.

In 1950, aged eighteen, Charlie was called up for National Service. It came as quite a shock since he was already earning a decent wedge ducking and diving around the streets of south London. The army taught Wilson the importance of being fit, even though he had a lot of problems obeying orders. It was no surprise that when he emerged from the army in 1952 he immediately linked up with all his dodgy old south London pals again.

Many of Wilson's contemporaries may have been petty thieves, but to become a real outlaw you had to do everything your own way. Nobody and nothing else mattered, apart from your loved ones, of course, and that made you more feared and respected. No one could get away with pulling a fast one on Cheeky Charlie. Beneath that wise-cracking exterior lurked a cold, calculating individual capable of making split-second decisions that would one day mean the difference between life or death. Some people saw villains like Wilson as budding Robin Hoods, striking blows against the traditional enemy – the police or the filth, cozzers and all the other derogatory names they went by. Even at that early stage, Wilson's crimes were celebrated and talked about in the local pubs because they represented getting one back on the Establishment.

Wilson played up to his growing reputation. When he walked into certain pubs the place really did go quiet, as if he were starring in his own western. But Wilson wanted to be more than just a bit of local muscle. He saw himself as a leader of men, an artful criminal capable of taking on and beating anyone.

Cheeky Charlie was a quick learner and observer. He'd watched his older contemporaries getting out and about, wheeler-dealing in everything from coffee to nylons. He understood the potency of money and he'd decided from a very young age that he would be rich, come what may.

2/

While Cheeky Charlie was undoubtedly a cold-blooded thug, he also had a social conscience and showed great loyalty to those he liked. He knew when to help rather than hinder.

He was shrewd and arrogant and wanted wealth so badly that he was prepared to use his own popularity. He was, in the words of one of his contemporaries, 'a strange combination of hard heart and soft mind. Capable of beating a man, but also just as likely to help an old lady cross the street.'

Wilson and his pals had been burgling and carrying out raids on the nearby docks and it was inevitable they'd graduate to bank robberies – 'blags'. As Joey Pyle said, 'When you're on a blag, it's like being part of a football team. Each person has their role and you count on the rest of them to pull their weight. It's a fantastic feeling. We'd get tip-offs about likely targets and the normal percentage for that kind of information is ten per cent of whatever you get. It's all a game.'

Once Wilson and his gang had picked a day to commit a robbery, they'd work on getting all their tools together with a stolen car for a fast getaway. A classic target was the man collecting takings from the illegal betting clubs that were known as spielers. They soon graduated to much bigger jobs. Pyle recalled, 'We started blowin' safes in them days. We also did smaller things like jumpin' over counters in banks and grabbing a handful of cash. We also hit post offices because their security was rubbish. Some companies left wages in the safe overnight and of course there was no cheques or monthly salary slips back then. It was a weekly thing, always with cash.' Pyle recognised Wilson's abilities even then. 'If you went across the pavement [committed a bank robbery], Charlie would be the first one out of the car and the first one in to grab the dosh.'

With a few bob in his pocket, Wilson began visiting the clubs, dives, spielers, pubs and hotels of Soho, in what was then the sleazy West End. But he was careful to avoid involvement in the lucrative vice trade, something he considered to be a distasteful profession. Instead he got himself work as an enforcer for some of the violent and unscrupulous characters who ran West End protection rackets. Charlie was renowned for his relentless pursuit of cash on their behalf. Favoured tools of the trade in Soho included razors, broken bottles, revolvers, hammers, hatchets, coshes and knuckledusters. Charing Cross Hospital employed a special staff of medical seamsters to deal with the resulting gaping wounds. Victims seldom complained but instead harboured their urges to get even.

The London underworld was ever-shifting, people moving backwards and forwards across the capital. The West End thrived because there was a need to enjoy oneself, even in the poor times after the war. Drug-dealing and blackmailing tactics were added to an already potent mix. They were used alongside 'long firms', fake businesses set up by villains who persuaded the gullible people to invest in them before disappearing.

One of the most powerful criminals to emerge after the war was smooth-talking former smash'n'grab merchant Billy Hill.

He was a real West Ender, born in 1911 at Seven Dials on the Holborn side of Leicester Square, which was then a Dickensian area of poverty and beggars just a stone's throw from the vice dens of Soho. Many younger villains like Wilson noticed that Hill and his arch-enemy Jack Spot were making a fortune working as bookies at the big horse race meetings across the country.

It was no surprise when smalltime crooks like Charlie Wilson started working as illegal bookies themselves. Sometimes, Wilson spent entire weekends laying off bets at point-to-point races that were not so well policed. Charlie would stand on a couple of boxes beside a post with a bookie's name on it and use a board for writing on the odds. This was known as a bookmaker's joint. It could be put up in seconds. Villains had to pay other spivs for the pitch and the chalk – even for the water to wipe the board clean between races.

During the race meetings Wilson also attended illegal bare-knuckle boxing bouts in fields well away from the prying eyes of police and racing officials. Carloads of villains would turn up with their favourite bruiser. One Derby day, renowned race-track hardman Albert Dimes oversaw a fight to the death between one of his boys and a gypsy at their Epsom Downs camp close to the racecourse. The two fighters smashed each other to pieces for a hundred-pound prize. More than ten times that amount changed hands in bets. In the early 1950s, Wilson – who prided himself on his fitness and fighting skills – entered at least half a dozen such contests himself. He eventually retired unbeaten having made a small fortune betting on himself.

Wilson was well-known at a fairground in north London where he often fenced stolen goods for the gypsies who ran the site. A friend said, 'Charlie was always flogging lots of Tom he'd got up at Barnet.' 'Tom Foolery' was slang for 'jewellery'. 'He told me he knew the gypsies wouldn't grass him up.'

Police corruption always coloured Wilson's attitude towards the authorities. His argument was simple. 'How can you trust a copper if most of them want a backhander? They're the enemy but most of them are less honest than we are.' He didn't recognise anyone in authority, apart from the occasional underworld name, as he climbed the criminal ladder on the streets of the capital. He developed a penchant for stealing flash cars such as Jaguars and the Rovers that had more legroom for his well-built, 6-foot frame. 'Fuckin' Jags are for midgets,' Charlie told one friend. 'Great motor but just not right for me, unless we're on a blaggin' of course.'

Wilson had a violent clash with south London villain Tony Routger – brother of a feared character called Peter Routger – that seemed a big risk, considering Charlie was still a relative upstart at the time. Pyle said, 'The Routgers were two flash bastards but Charlie laid into Tony at a pub on Camberwell Green. They went out back and had a scrap. Few minutes later Charlie walked back in and Routger was never seen again. That incident made people realise just how strong a character Charlie was.'

By this time Wilson was tall, with a fresh complexion. He had dark-brown, well-greased hair, blue eyes and a scar on the knuckle of the first finger of his left hand. He also spoke with a strong Cockney accent and could break into entire sentences of Cockney rhyming slang at the drop of a hat. His favourite drink was a light and bitter and he was a regular at the Mason's Arms pub in Lambeth Walk. It was often filled with characters such as the powerful Richardson south London crime family.

Wilson's friend Nosher Powell said, 'A press photographer was in there one time and I saw Charlie disappear into the toilet because he definitely didn't want his photo taken. It was the type of place where you went to meet "the chaps".' Being described as one of the chaps meant a villain had well and truly arrived in criminal terms.

In the middle of all this frenzied activity, Wilson still found time for romance. He developed a soft spot for a girl called Patricia Osborne, the pretty blonde sister of his friend Georgie Osborne.

Wilson began courting Pat a few months after being demobbed from the army, although the couple didn't marry until 1955. He was twenty-three and Pat was twenty-one. They moved into a small flat in south London, but Wilson promised Pat he'd soon buy them a proper house. Within a year the couple's first child, Cheryl, was born.

Cheeky Charlie definitely wasn't afraid of hard work. He helped run his new in-laws' fruit and vegetable business in Penge, south London. Pat earned fifteen pounds a week working from home as a dressmaker, while Charlie was up at four each morning to buy produce from Spitalfields market. He often also did the buying for other shopkeepers, who trusted him implicitly and relied on his good judgement.

Pat later insisted she had no idea Wilson was involved in any criminal activity. She said, 'Charlie was always cheery, with quick-witted jokes tumbling from his lips. People in our road used to say they could set their clocks by him he was so punctual getting home for his 7 p.m. supper. Charlie was proud of that side of his character.' Cheeky Charlie would often tell Pat, 'Never keep anyone waiting in life. Not only is it bad manners but it shows bad management on your own part.'

When Wilson got in trouble with the police, Pat finally realised that her husband was 'up to no good'. She said, 'It was a minor offence concerning a car and he was given a conditional discharge, but I was deeply upset.' Pat begged Wilson to give up his underworld friends. But all he said was, 'My friends are my friends, love. Don't interfere. It has got nothing to do with you.'

Pat said, 'So he continued to bring home men who frightened me. They never said or did anything to cause an upset. But it was obvious what they were.'

Wilson was soon able to afford to buy the family a comfortable, ten-thousand-pound, three-bedroomed house in Crescent Lane, Clapham, just around the corner from a bookmaking business he ran with Pat's brother Georgie. The Victorian terraced house had a downstairs bathroom, a yellow front door and a neatly trimmed hedge at the front. Pat had been brought up in a tiny house in the East End and was delighted.

Wilson struggled to keep a clean sheet. Shortly after the family moved, Pat and their daughter returned after a weekend away to find the whole place was a shambles. There had been a police raid and Wilson was in a police cell. 'Don't worry, love,' he said. 'Everything will be all right.'

There was more bad news. Baby daughter Cheryl was taken to hospital seriously ill with tonsillitis and doctors discovered she had a hole in the heart. Wilson mentioned this in his application for bail but he was turned down as police and prosecutors poured scorn on his lawyer's claims about the medical problems. Wilson saw their cold-hearted attitude as confirmation that the police were 'scum'. He ended up serving eight months of a one-year sentence for receiving stolen property. The couple's second child, Tracey, was born five weeks after Charlie was imprisoned. Cheryl, thankfully, survived.

Not long after his release, Wilson was again locked up, this time for handling a small amount of explosives that had been found during yet another police raid on his home. Police alleged the explosives were intended for safe-cracking. In Maidstone prison, Charlie befriended a likeable young ducker and diver from Bermondsey called Paddy. They got talking about how their fathers hadn't handed down jobs to them and they'd just had to go out and earn money by whatever means possible. Both men shared a love of money and keeping fit. Later that friendship between Charlie Wilson and Paddy would be put to the ultimate test. For now, prison was reinforcing Charlie's desire to get active again. He and Paddy discussed numerous crimes they intended to commit on release.

By 1960 Wilson had a share in at least two bookies with Pat's brother Georgie Osborne. He got involved with south London friend Joey Pyle in running a gambling club called the Charterhouse in the old Smithfield market area. It was owned by master criminal Billy Hill and well-known car dealer Johnny Matthews. Wilson got his jailhouse pal Paddy a job as a croupier on the roulette table and employed an up-and-coming, wisecracking Irish teenager called Brian Wright from Kilburn.

That same year, a young gangster was gunned down and murdered in a highly publicised incident at the notorious Pen Club in east London. Joey Pyle was present. Scotland Yard finally woke up to the fact they needed to know much more about their enemy. The CIB (Criminal Intelligence Branch) was formed to coordinate information about organised crime in the capital. The police had little or no idea who they were up against. Young gangsters like Charlie Wilson were already giving them a run for their money.

3/

In 1960, Charlie teamed up with childhood pal Bruce Reynolds, who'd just got out of prison after serving time for robbing shops in south London.

Charlie was already working with their old friend Buster Edwards and Gordon Goody from Putney, known as 'Footpad' because he often wore a long, check-patterned coat that gave him the appearance of a street mugger. The four gangsters saw themselves as professional criminals – in Reynolds' words they were 'high-class jewel thieves'. His nickname was 'the Colonel'. He liked to think he was in charge of the gang.

Bank robberies and theft from armoured vans carrying wages were booming at the time. Gangs used the latest technology such as the argon arc gun, a high-powered electric torch that could cut its way through metal. The devices had to be ordered, to make it easier for the police to trace them. Charlie and his friends found a factory in Staines, to the west of London, that stored the argon guns and broke in and stole six of them.

The gang heard the news that railwaymen's wages were paid out from a London office to all the sidings and marshalling yard workers of the western region of railways. The cash was delivered by security van to a single-storey office next to sidings. The clerical staff locked themselves in their office using a bolted door while they sorted the money into wage packets and then paid out at a small window. Late on the night before a delivery, Edwards and Goody let themselves into the office with a skeleton key. They examined the bolt and noticed it ran through the jamb of the door into the concrete of the wall. They unscrewed the lock from the door, cut the screws short and snapped off the end of the bolt so that it only just went into the clasp before putting everything back into place.

The following day a five-man team equipped with their state-of-the-art tools waited in a stolen van in the street outside the entrance to the sidings until they saw the security van drop off the cash and leave. The gang pulled down their stocking masks and drew out their coshes and Goody drove up to the office. One kick smashed open the door with its sabotaged bolt to reveal five men and one woman; the men dived straight to the floor but the woman came flying at the blaggers. Edwards grabbed her and they fell to the floor where she was knocked unconscious while the other robbers began packing bundles of banknotes into a holdall. The gang locked the door behind them and broke the key in the lock. They scrambled into their getaway car and were soon back at their 'flophouse', or hideout. The team counted out £26,000. Wilson was upset with Edwards for hurting the female wages clerk, 'but in the end he let it pass,' said an associate.

Next up was the audacious hijacking of an armoured van, after one of the drivers provided inside information that at least seventy thousand pounds was on offer. The Colonel was keen that the team remain quiet and thoroughly professional throughout the operation and Cheeky Charlie was told beforehand to 'keep it buttoned'. The gang pulled in front of the armoured van, turned around and rammed it head on. The terrified guards flung open the doors and were immediately hauled out and coshed by the group of masked men. Reynolds later insisted, 'They were only glancing blows, designed to mark, not injure them.'

Charlie jumped in the back and ripped open the wages compartment. The gang formed a chain and slung boxes from hand to hand into the boot of their getaway car. Within a few minutes they were finished and quickly swapped their first vehicle for another half a mile away. The haul totalled more than sixty thousand pounds in cash.

The London underworld sat up and took notice of this young, fearless band of robbers, although they weren't without their failures. The burglary of a millionaire's mansion was abandoned after a policeman on a bicycle saw the gang's stolen 4.2 Jag getaway car parked on the street outside, keys still in the ignition.

It was a few weeks later when Reynolds mentioned that legendary London gangster Billy Hill always told his boys, 'Trains are the thing.' Hill had even sent his men to check on the movements of certain trains that carried bundles of readies but nothing ever came of it. In the middle of 1962, Buster Edwards came up with a way for Wilson's gang to test Hill's theory for themselves. He was tipped off about boxes carrying wages for railway workers in Swindon, Wiltshire, loaded under tight security onto the Irish Mail train each week at London's Paddington station. Wilson and the rest of the gang jumped the train and got to the boxes, but failed to open them. They leapt off after the alarm was raised. Only Gordon Goody managed to grab a box that contained just seven hundred pounds.

The gang didn't give up. They hatched a plan to rob a train carrying gold bullion that had been shipped from South Africa by Union-Castle Line boat to Southampton. The bullion would be taken by rail to Waterloo and met by an assortment of police, officials and security guards before being escorted to the Bank of England. The plans were abandoned after Wilson pointed out that this security was so excessive that their chances of pulling off the job were virtually nil. But the idea of hitting a train stuck. Surely there was one out there that they could rob?

4/

The two sides of Cheeky Charlie's character were clearly defined. If you saw him out with his wife and daughters on Clapham Common on a sunny Sunday afternoon you'd never guess he was a ruthless criminal already responsible for many robberies across the capital.

Around this time, Nosher Powell spotted Charlie in Foyles bookshop on Tottenham Court Road, London. 'He was going through a load of maps. I asked him what he was up to and he said, "Just browsing." Next time I looked he'd disappeared in a puff of smoke. Typical Charlie, always keeping a low profile.'

Whether it was a map or a blueprint, Wilson was renowned for being a man with a plan. One of his oldest south London friends said, 'Charlie loved the planning stages of any job. He mapped things out very carefully and often came up with something a bit different that would catch people off-guard.'

On 14 August 1962 Wilson's team, including Gordon Goody, employed a fake blind man as a lookout standing near the National Provincial bank in Clapham High Street. It was less than a mile from Wilson's family home. Three of the raiders, in their twenties, calmly walked into the bank where one of them leapt over the counter and struck a twenty-one-year-old male cashier with a pickaxe handle. Wilson grabbed a tin box at the cashier's feet containing £9,150 and threw it to one of the others and all the raiders ran to a stolen blue Ford Zodiac.

Neighbouring shopkeepers thought the bank alarm was a jammed car horn at first. The getaway car was found abandoned nearby, the blind man was not there by the time police arrived and detectives were amazed by the incredible speed and precision of the raid. None of the people inside or outside the bank had time to stop the robbers. This implied some careful planning.

The coshed cashier later visited Scotland Yard to look through photographs in a rogues' gallery album of known criminals. And there, police claimed, the cashier hesitatingly identified Charlie Wilson as one of the robbers. Less than three hours later Wilson was arrested, although no one else had fingered him. On 13 December at South Western magistrates' court the cashier pointed at Wilson in the dock and said, 'I think that is one of them, but I am not at all certain.' Wilson's defence counsel, Mr John Mathew QC, immediately pointed out the hesitancy. The charges were dismissed, Wilson was immediately freed and was granted forty pounds costs. One of Charlie's oldest south London friends said, 'Either the old bill tried to fit Charlie up or some of Charlie's people lent on that bank clerk.'

Wilson returned home and persuaded Pat, expecting their third child, to join him on a holiday to celebrate his release. The family flew to Jersey, where they stayed in a five-star hotel and spent money like water. Wilson was in his element. This was the loving, doting husband and father never happier than when helping his daughters dress their dolls or making them toys with his own fretwork set.

The other side of Charlie Wilson craved excitement, danger and the profits that big-time crime could provide. Naturally, Pat had her suspicions, but she chose not to deal with the issues most of the time. When a group of heavy looking men called round at the house one evening, Wilson told her they were just part of a betting syndicate, 'It's nothin' illegal.' No matter how hard she tried, Pat could not get her husband to admit what he was up to. His loyalty to his associates was almost as strong as his devotion to his wife and children. When keep-fit fanatic Wilson turned his garden shed into a mini-gym complete with weights, chest expanders and a punchbag, Pat jokingly asked him, 'Going in for the next Olympics?'

'Nah, love, just keeping fit for my job,' would come Cheeky Charlie's response. But it was a different job from that which Pat wished he'd been referring.

His obsession with keeping fit had started in his teens when he was enlisted and had been fuelled by his prison terms. He had a genuine belief that a healthy body equalled a fit, clear mind and that he was much less likely to make costly mistakes while he was on a robbery. Wilson had even offset the teenage breathing problems caused by early stage emphysema, although his doctor warned that the condition was likely to reoccur.

There seems little doubt that fears over his health helped drive Charlie Wilson forward to make a fortune as quickly as possible.

5/

Charlie Wilson's growing reputation as a real 'pro' sparked an invitation from an acquaintance to meet a man who worked in BOAC's airline administrative offices, Comet House, at Heathrow.

The office was separated from the passenger terminals by the two main runways and was the largest building on the south side of the airport. The A4 road from London to the West Country ran along the opposite side. Having made the introduction, Wilson's fixer tactfully retreated and left the two men alone to discuss the movements of BOAC wages. A security van ran from the bank to the Comet building every Tuesday morning with two guards who unloaded a box that Wilson and his gang were led to believe would contain between three and four hundred thousand pounds.

In an early reconnaissance trip, Wilson and Reynolds realised they'd have to grab the money after it was taken out of the bank and after it had reached Comet House to stand any chance of getting away safely. Wilson's creative contribution was to suggest the entire gang should disguise themselves as city gents in suits and bowler hats. At least three gang members would enter the building and hide in the second-floor men's toilet, where they'd watch for the security van. Skilled drivers Roy James and Mickey Ball would be waiting in the gang's stolen getaway vehicles.

Wilson met a man known as Frenchy when he was out at a West End nightclub. Frenchy would eventually play a pivotal role in Charlie's life and had a resonant, well-educated voice with, as his name suggested, a very slight French accent and a penchant for wearing black berets. He came up with some much-needed financial backing for the airport job through a group of old-time London gangsters.

Frenchy claimed he'd been awarded honours for his work with the French resistance during World War II and had been personally thanked by Winston Churchill. His speciality had allegedly been coordinating daring raids to destroy German ammunition and troop trains. He also helped organise the escapes of resistance fighters held by the Germans. Wilson's wife Pat recalled, 'Often I'd hear him talk about his love of horse racing. And on many occasions he'd recount stories of how he had been associated with the French resistance movement during the war but apart from that no one knew much about him.'

Pat blamed Frenchy for encouraging Wilson to become a reckless player of the card game baccarat and its variant chemin de fer in London gambling clubs. Wilson was a skilful and, sometimes, lucky player. On occasions, he'd arrive home, toss a huge roll of five pound notes on the table and then say to Pat, 'Guess where I got that from?' Pat would go completely pale and he'd put an arm around her and exclaim with a laugh, 'It's straight money, love. I won it gambling.' To mark a family birthday, Charlie would go off and play a bit of roulette and put a hundred-pound chip on the same number as the date of the birthday in question.

In the run-up to Heathrow, Wilson spent more time using his weights in the garden shed. He also had conferences with groups of heavy-looking characters at the family house. Pat was content to accept they were discussing betting and even told Wilson, 'All the horses will be dead before you make your betting coup.'

Wilson just laughed, 'D'you want a bet, love?'

Behind the smiles, Pat was irritated that the family home in Clapham was being invaded by a bunch of hoods. She could never fully come to terms with Wilson's profession. It would lead to many problems in their marriage but ultimately Pat loved him. He was her rock. He was the one who would always look after her. 'Don't worry, love,' Charlie told her. 'They won't hurt you. Neither will I.'

Wilson came up with the ingenious idea for Heathrow of lining the gang's bowler hats with steel so they didn't have to carry coshes (similar headwear was later used to great effect in the 1965 James Bond movie *Thunderball* by Bond's arch-enemy Oddjob). Specially made umbrellas were also ordered – they didn't keep off the rain as they were also made of solid steel.

In the final two-week countdown to the Heathrow robbery, Wilson and three members of the gang visited the men's toilet in the Comet building from where it was confirmed they had a perfect view, 50 feet above street level, of the security van. They devised a split-second time schedule for washing their hands and faces while peering through the windows over the sinks.

At 9 a.m. on Tuesday 17 November, 1962, a group of men dressed in natty City suits, all wearing bowler hats and equipped with false moustaches and neatly furled umbrellas, entered the BOAC building. The bowler hats concealed stocking masks. One witness later said he thought they were solicitors. Two other members of the gang were positioned at a nearby bus stop. Most of them carried weaponry in addition to their steel-lined headgear and brollies. Wilson himself had a length of cable, bound with tape, down his trousers and Gordon Goody carried a truncheon he'd bought in Madrid from a member of the Guardia Civil. Buster Edwards had a foot-long piece of one-

and-three-quarter-inch pipe spring, filled with lead and bound with tape.

'Buster was a fuckin' liability,' one of Wilson's associates recalled. 'He was the one who usually lashed out, went a bit OTT, if you know what I mean.'

At 9.45 a.m., on the third floor of Comet House, the five smartly dressed men separately entered the room marked: 'CL31 – Gentlemen'. Toilet attendant Bill Turner noticed the new arrivals all wore their bowler hats except for the one who had a Robin Hood-style trilby. Two of the strangers gazed out of the window by the basins, two were inside the cubicles and one more, Edwards, stood by a urinal. Goody, Wilson and Harry Booth washed their hands, combed their hair and straightened their ties to distract the elderly cloakroom attendant who was intrigued by Edwards standing for so long at the urinal. Edwards at last spotted the security van men coming out of the Barclays bank up the street, zipped up his trousers and winked at another team member who slipped out of the gents to call the lift.

One hundred yards down the street, a big black box containing a fortune in cash was being loaded into the armoured security van. The van moved off, escorted by a security car in front and another behind. It headed up the street towards the BOAC building. At 9.59 a.m. the five men who'd been in the gents were waiting by the lift. On the next floor down, three other smartly dressed men – all in bowlers, one carrying a dispatch case – headed towards the stairs. They then stood near a door marked 'Staff Vacancies' as if waiting their turn for an interview. The one with the dispatch case spent most of his time looking out of the window.

Outside Comet House the wages' convoy drew up. Brian Howe, aged twenty-six, a security officer with BOAC, unlocked the rear of the armoured van. Arthur Smith, a security officer from the car that travelled in front of the van, stood guard as Ronald Grey, the forty-four-year-old pay officer, and his assistant loaded the big black box onto a trolley. They began wheeling their cargo across the pavement.

Upstairs, Wilson and the other team members – all breathing heavily – scrambled into the lift. As the doors shut, they pulled down their stocking masks. The security men pushed the trolley into the entrance hall and approached the lift. Grey pressed the elevator button. The indicator light told him the lift was already descending. At precisely 10 a.m., the lift passed the second floor on its sixteen-second journey to ground level. A few yards away, three smartly dressed men ran down five flights of stairs – fifty-five steps in all.

The security men waited patiently.

The three men reached the ground floor by the stairs at the exact moment the lift containing their five associates came to a halt. Just sixteen seconds after ten o'clock, the lift doors opened and the robbers leapt out, pulling out coshes, iron bars and sawn-off pickaxe handles from under their jackets. They stormed towards the security guards yelling like warriors. The raiders from the other floor dived towards the pay clerks.

Guard Howe explained: 'I turned round and saw just one big melee going on. One man attacked me and hit me over the head with what I think was a sawn-off pickaxe handle.' Howe managed to hit one robber with a truncheon when another tore into his side and knocked him flying. He was smashed hard on the head. Another security guard was hit at least twice as he tried to get his truncheon out. Staff members Grey and Harris were struck on their heads and bodies.

At 10.03 a.m., two 4.2 litre Jaguars were being expertly reversed towards the front doors of Comet House by gangsters disguised as chauffeurs. Wilson and another gangster, carrying the wages box, came running out. The rest of the team followed, brandishing their weapons. The money was thrown in the back seat of one Jag while Charlie headed for the second. The cars screeched off at high speed across the grass embankment towards an emergency gate locked with a chain and padlock on the perimeter road of the airport. The raiders had snapped it open earlier with bolt cutters. Edwards leapt out and pulled at the gates that fell open. The gang were off the airport within 250 yards of Comet House. Once again, planning had provided a vital advantage.

Mickey Ball's Jag was the first one out onto the Great West Road but hesitated when he spotted a little Austin A40 in his mirror reversing to block off the other getaway vehicle driven by the Weasel, Roy James. He just managed to swerve before squeezing through the gap. Moments later, James accelerated past Ball. Both drivers were still disguised as chauffeurs. In case of a roadblock the men had removed a back seat and hidden the wages box in the space. It was covered with a grey rug and the effect was to make it look like a normal seat on which three of the blaggers sat.

The Jags continued at high speed to a garage in Hounslow, 2 miles from the robbery. They transferred the money to a minivan which Ball drove to a flophouse set up by Reynolds in the south London suburb of Norbury. The others made their own way to the hideout. James had a getaway motorbike standing by that would not start and passenger Gordon Goody eventually gave up waiting and headed to the nearest underground station. Edwards took a bus to Vauxhall. Wilson wandered off in a southerly direction. They all knew the most important thing was to split up before the police got them. The police eventually found the gang's identical metallic blue Mark 2 Jaguars with discarded chauffeur uniforms, bolt cutters and three blue balaclava masks.

The 'City Gents' gang, as Fleet Street's crime reporters would dub them, had just pulled off one of the most dramatic robberies of all time.

6/

At their Norbury flophouse later on the day of the robbery, the gang were bitterly disappointed to discover they'd only managed to steal £62,500. It had already been agreed that everyone should get the same share, no matter what their role, so there'd be no temptation to grass up the others. Each man was given four thousand pounds to tide him over until the next big job, while the remaining £22,500 was kept in reserve to finance upcoming 'projects' and provide retainers for new recruits.

Wilson and the rest of the gang had proved beyond doubt they had the bottle to carry out spectacular jobs in broad daylight. The only disappointment was the money, which fell so far short of expectations. Around this time, Bruce 'the Colonel' Reynolds mentioned a night train from Glasgow to London that 'might be worth a tug' but he didn't elaborate any further.

Pat Wilson was sitting at home watching television when the raid was covered on the news. 'I'll never forget how my heart sank. I knew immediately that Charlie had deceived me with that betting coup story.' A voice in her head kept saying over and over again, 'Charlie and Frenchy must have planned it.' When Wilson finally arrived home in Crescent Lane later that same night, Pat plucked up the courage to confront him. 'I've just heard there's been a big robbery at London airport. It was on the news.'

Cheeky Charlie didn't blink an eyelid or show any sign of surprise. He flashed Pat one of his brightest smiles, 'Good luck to 'em – such planning deserves every success.' Wilson admitted that everyone was talking about the job and even told her the gangsters believed they were going to get two hundred thousand pounds rather than a mere £62,000. 'It was hardly worth the trouble for the risk involved,' he said. 'D'you know? I hear the actual bowler hats those robbers used at the airport were lined with steel.'

Pat was infuriated with Wilson for so blatantly ignoring her original remark, so she asked him outright if he was involved. Charlie took a deep breath and replied very quietly, 'Darling, don't worry. I won't let you down. Just don't ask questions.' There was a steeliness to his voice and Pat knew only too well what might happen if he let his Cheeky Charlie happy mask slip.

Pat later said, 'On those occasions, I dissolved into tears under the weight of his verbal lashings.' There was no doubt Pat suffered because of Wilson's life of crime. She dreaded every knock on the door. It would either be the police or a criminal. It must have made her feel so vulnerable and over time it had an inevitable effect on her own personality.

The Heathrow raid sparked a blaze of publicity because of its daring and bizarre nature. Police quickly established that the well-dressed villains had taken it in turns over several weeks to recce the location of the robbery. Finger smudges were uncovered on the windowsills in the toilet from which the gang had watched the money being delivered. A reward of £6,500 was immediately offered for information leading to the arrest of the gang. Few expected any results.

Wilson's only real concern after the raid was a story in the *Sunday People* newspaper claiming that Scotland Yard had received an early tip-off about the robbery from an inside source. It was for this reason that security guards were carrying far less cash than was expected. This meant someone inside the gang might be a police informant, a grass. Charlie told another gang member if he found out who it was 'I'll ring his fuckin' neck.'

The police came to ask Wilson about his movements on the day of the robbery. He was so confident they had no evidence that he went to Cannon Row police station three times to 'try and clear up any misunderstandings'. Driver Mickey Ball and Gordon Goody were also pulled in. The police seemed to have more evidence against them. All were asked to appear in identity parades. Charlie agreed to wear a city suit, bowler hat and false moustache the first time. None of the security guards brought in for that first parade recognised any of the three suspected robbers until the time came to finish, when a guard saw Gordon Goody in profile and put the finger on him. At a second parade, all the suspects were put up without make-up or particular outfit. All thirty-eight supposed witnesses failed to pick Charlie out. Then Scotland Yard recruited – much to the amusement of Fleet Street – real City gents from Whitehall to take part in a third parade.

This time Wilson and his airport heist mates found it hard to keep straight faces. He, Goody and Ball were once again made to wear moustaches, dark suits and bowler hats. It was only then that all three were positively identified. While being interrogated, one of the gang asked, 'What you gonna do when the really big one takes place?' The officer involved thought the comment was just sarcasm. It wasn't until many months later they realised they'd stumbled upon a clue that the gang might be planning a much bigger crime.

On 17 December 1962, Wilson, now aged thirty and described as a turf accountant, Goody, aged thirty-two and described as a hairdresser, and Ball, twenty-seven, were charged at Harlington police station with robbery with violence and stealing £62,500 at Heathrow airport a month earlier. The police pulled in other suspected members of the gang but failed to make any charges stick. None of the three men made any statements to police, even after they'd been charged. It was a typical response. Wilson later claimed he was told, 'once a few bob had been thrown in the right direction', the suspects would be given bail, despite the serious nature of the robbery.

The following morning at Uxbridge magistrates' court, all three were given bail totalling thirty thousand pounds. A senior detective told the court, 'They have on three occasions voluntarily come to the police station to attend identity parades and under these circumstances we don't think they would abscond.'

At their Crown Court trial two months later, also in Uxbridge, the jury was told that make-up, false moustaches and chauffeur's hats were found at Goody's home in Putney, west London. The court heard he'd told police, 'I bought them for a Christmas fancy dress party.'

The court was also told of a similar find including chauffeur's caps, greasepaint, false moustaches and sideboards at Ball's home in Lambrook Terrace, Fulham. Wilson insisted they'd been planted by desperate police. The case seemed to be based on circumstantial evidence, not least when two witnesses said they'd seen Wilson at different places but the same time. Judge Sir Edward Anthony Hawke directed the jury to acquit Wilson on the grounds that the evidence was 'of such a doubtful character that it did not justify proceeding against him further'.

The jury couldn't agree on Goody's verdict. A retrial was ordered before which Wilson 'persuaded' a bent copper to swap a hat Goody had worn during the robbery for one that was three sizes bigger. When Goody was directed to try on the sabotaged piece of evidence in the dock it fell over his ears and eyes. The judge freed him and fellow gang-member Edwards.

Wilson celebrated by purchasing himself a well-cut black suit, a bowler hat and an expensive silk umbrella. He'd wanted to take Pat off on another fancy holiday but she wasn't keen on going abroad, so instead he set off alone on a tour of Europe's finest hotels and casinos. He returned a few weeks later, bronzed and fit, ready to buckle down to work. He knew that Pat was fed up with his criminal activity and once again got up at four every morning to get fruit and vegetables from the market for her family shop in Penge. She prayed he'd keep out of trouble. 'I thought two major acquittals would surely have taught him a lesson,' she later recalled. She still harboured dreams that he would give up his lifestyle for ever and they could live together happily ever after.

But Charlie Wilson loved the good things in life and was generous with his family and close friends. His regret was that he had been estranged from his father since he went to prison in the late fifties. He dearly wished he could reconnect with him before it was too late, but at the same time he needed crime to pay for his extravagant lifestyle. He bought himself a gleaming, maroon, four-door Rover 3.5 Coupe. It was his pride and joy. He spent two hours each weekend polishing the vehicle and refused to allow Pat to get into it without taking her shoes off first.

Wilson began staying out for two or three nights a week, provoking uncharacteristically angry words from Pat. She'd already been through so much. How much more could she take? 'Trouble was, he was not a man to lie and he never gave me excuses. He simply refused to say anything.' The truth was that as well as Wilson being hard at work planning new heists and gambling in all-night spielers, he was occasionally getting involved with ladies of the night in Soho. He knew how to skilfully split the two distinct sides of his life down the middle.

Nosher Powell later said, 'Charlie was essentially a loner and although a lot of people knew him as the opposite, Charlie rarely got too close to people. It's a funny thing to say, but he was a great family man who didn't like or trust many other people. As he once said to me after a spell inside, "The bird [sentence] was easy but the absence of the wife and kids was sometimes too much to take."'

Wilson relied on having the security of a stable home to return to after days and nights of partying and thieving. He knew he couldn't survive in the underworld if he didn't hold on to part of the good world as well. The Wilsons' third daughter, Leander, was born in 1963 and there was no question of Charlie going off the rails – getting a divorce and going downhill. He liked his life the way it was and had no intention of changing.

The only disappointment for him might have been that he hadn't yet fathered a boy. But in other ways he was relieved Pat only had girls because he didn't want to end up falling out with a son the way he had with his own father. Their poor relationship left Wilson deeply untrusting of most men.

7/

An immense cancer had grown inside the detective force of the Metropolitan police by the early 1960s. Bribery and planting false evidence was endemic.

Many villains, including Wilson, believed that bail and evidence-tampering could always be bought for a price. A middleman, often a figure well-known to the police, would hand over such bribes while a deep channel of suspicion flowed between police and professional criminals. Corruption commonly manifested itself in charging for bail, suppressing previous convictions and the dropping of more serious charges such as bank robbery, drug offences and involvement in obscene publications. Some officers believed the justice system was weighted against them and that they were justified in 'bending' the rules. Wilson and his criminal associates simply assumed they could always buy themselves out of jail.

As one of Wilson's oldest pals said, 'There was hundreds of ways to bribe a copper back then and that was part and parcel of your business and you accepted that. You even built it into your finances.'

Wilson was one of many to claim that 'verballing' – police inserting words into a suspect's statement – was frequently used to secure arrests. He said, 'Once they had our names as suspects from a grass, we knew we was in trouble because they'd falsify the evidence to secure convictions without hesitation.' The practice had been commonplace since the late 1940s. A fabrication in a statement was designed to infer the suspect had committed a crime because of his use of certain words. Some honest detectives referred to their corrupt colleagues as 'a firm within a firm'. Corruption inside the London police force truly was endemic.

One spring night in 1963, Pat and Charlie were watching television when Frenchy arrived. Pat's heart sank because she knew this meant another job was on the horizon. Wilson and Frenchy went straight into the dining room. Pat was irritated that her husband was up to his old tricks. Their straight businesses were prospering, with a joint income in excess of three thousand pounds a year. Why was he doing this?

Frenchy's visit heralded the start of planning the 'Big One', which Wilson believed would send him into lucrative retirement.

Frenchy was soon calling three times a week, often with as many as four other, burly men. They'd be closeted with Charlie in the front room for hours in thick clouds of cigarette and cigar smoke. Every ashtray was filled to the brim and there would also be three or four empty bottles of Scotch left on the table after each meeting. Wilson always left the house with the other men and sometimes didn't return home for days.

Pat begged Wilson to tell her what they were planning. 'I even threatened to leave him unless I got a reasonable reply.'

Charlie simply looked at his wife and said softly, 'Wait and see, love. What you don't know can't harm you. If this business deal comes off I will be set up for life.' Wilson paused. 'I know you'd never let me down, love.' He was right. Pat never had any intention of deserting him. Despite all her misgivings, she believed that the only people he truly cared about were her and the girls. It was them against the world.

Wilson and the other men had been discussing the Glasgow to Euston TPO (Travelling Post Office), known as the 'up special' or the 'up postal' among staff. It left Glasgow at 6.50 p.m. every evening and arrived in London at 3.59 a.m. The TPO consisted of a diesel engine and twelve coaches with seventy-seven employees. It was packed with hundreds of thousands of pounds every night.

The hardcore of what would become known as the Great Train Robbery gang was an utterly loyal clique. The 'Fulham Team' consisted of Wilson, Reynolds, Ronald Arthur Biggs, Goody, James Hussey, Roy John James, Robert Welch, Thomas William Wisbey, Brian Arthur Field, Leonard Dennis Field, Jimmy White, William Boal, Roger John Cordrey and John Denby Wheater.

The gang also handpicked another man, known only as 'Stan', who'd worked on the railway and was commissioned to create a blueprint to beat the complicated railway signalling system. He taught the gang how to uncouple carriages when it came to the actual robbery. Dressed in railwaymen's clothing – supplied by consultant Stan – Charlie and seven others visited the New Cross rail goods yard, south-east London, for a rehearsal. The gang received a hundred pounds a week on the understanding that they did not undertake any other 'work' ahead of the big day. They later all insisted they were never told the source of this finance.

They had an overriding fear of informants: everyone knew that loose words sank ships. Each member of the team had so little trust in the others that most of them were even armed at those early meetings, Charlie among them, although none would ever admit it.

Charlie and the chaps met in the front room of his house on one occasion when he asked Pat to bring in tea. The five men had carefully drawn the curtains and were sitting in darkness. Frenchy sat at the table, fiddling with a small film projector. As Pat put the tray down, he said, 'That's got it.' The machine whirred into life, showing a film of the countryside that seemed innocent enough at first. Pat later recalled, 'Then there was a train coming down a railway line. Frenchy passed it off by saying, "This is just outside Paris. It's on the same line where we blew up a German train."'

Charlie made a point of telling Pat afterwards, 'Frenchy's wartime experiences are very interesting. He had plenty of exciting times.' It was only much later that she realised the film showed the location of the robbery. Frenchy and a cameraman friend had been down at least half a dozen times to the spot near Cheddington, Buckinghamshire, where they intended to hold up the train. When anyone asked Frenchy what he was doing he claimed to be a trainspotter. They spent several hours filming every aspect of the crossing area before coming back and showing their footage to the rest of the gang. This research was key to understanding the lighting system and working out how much time it took for the train to gather speed after having slowed for the signal. Further undercover trips to Cheddington were carried out during the day and at night with gang members disguised as anglers. They would sometimes spend an entire weekend on reconnaissance. Charlie helped mark up an Ordnance Survey map of the surrounding countryside for the possible routes they could take when leaving the area.

He, Goody, Wisbey and Hussey were to be the heavies and were briefed to take any measures necessary to combat problems during the job. Charlie armed himself with the same length of copper cable he'd used for the London airport job because he considered it a 'lucky mascot'. They would use balaclavas or stockings as masks.

The precise location of the heist was a railway bridge called Bridego, set in a hollow on rising ground that could not be seen from nearby roads. Charlie and Roy James bought parachute regiment uniforms, badges and berets from army surplus stores. They had decided to wear uniforms because they knew locals would not be suspicious of an apparent army convoy parked under the bridge in the early hours. They had square, coloured stickers that they planned to use to decorate and identify their vehicles as if they were official army issue, and special number plates were made up that followed the real military system of numbers and letters. The team also planned to 'arrest' any nosey policemen who came asking awkward questions.

Three miles away was Leatherslade Farm, an isolated smallholding near Cheddington that was to be the base and flophouse after the robbery. It had been purchased for cash through the gang's legal representative, Brian Field. A horsebox would be used to transport the loot to the farm and Charlie contributed a box of fruit and a sack of potatoes from his father-in-law's grocery shop in Penge to be taken to the farm for the troops.

On the first Saturday in August, 1963, Charlie and four of the team went out for a casual drive in the countryside near Bridego bridge. They rolled up for a pint of beer and a sandwich at a pub close to the village of Brill. The landlord remembered the men because they were all strangers, travelling in a 'posh car' and had said they were all 'bloody starving'. They also enquired about the way to Brill and refused to accept any change when they paid. The team went on to hold a dress rehearsal on a stretch of line near Cheddington. They stopped a train by changing the signals, before allowing it to continue its journey. None of the crew were aware of the role they were playing in the upcoming heist.

On 6 August, alibis carefully established, the gang gathered at Leatherslade Farm for the 'Big One'. All the next day they sat around, trying to stay calm by playing board games and drinking incessant cups of tea. Each team member was referred to by a colour to hide their true identity. At midnight a shortwave radio crackled into life: 'It's tonight.'

The night of 7 August 1963 was warm. As village clocks chimed 1.30 a.m. a convoy consisting of a three-ton lorry and two Land Rovers moved down moonlit B-roads, shrubs and hedgerows flashing past in their headlights. Radios were tuned into the police frequency but there was no activity.

The team eventually pulled up at Bridego bridge just after 2 a.m., following a long route around. They disembarked and huddled in groups by the side of the track and checked their walkie-talkies one last time. Just before 2.30 a.m., they walked up the track to Sears Crossing, where they went over their plans. Typically, Cheeky Charlie even had time for a quip with his old friend Gordon Goody.

'Gordon'll buy a new motor, won't you, Gordon?' he said.

'If I can afford it,' said Goody.

'You can afford a Bentley Continental now,' Charlie grinned.

'I wish I could. I'm fuckin' skint at the moment.' Goody's caution with money was legendary.

Charlie looked at Goody for a beat or two, then, using his friend's codename, said, 'For fuck's sake, Blue, put your mask on. You're so ugly.'

Laughing, Goody pulled his stocking mask down over his face. By 3 a.m. they were in position. It was time to go to work.

8/

Shortly after 3 a.m., two Great Train Robbery gang members rigged their chosen signal to appear red at the isolated Sears Crossing, just before Bridego bridge. They covered the green signal with a glove and shone torches through the red panel of the signal. The train – which was exactly on time – halted precisely where they wanted. So far, so good.

Train driver Jack Mills, fifty-eight, and engineer David Whitby, twenty-six, stepped down to see what was wrong with the signals. They were seized by the bandits, now wearing silk stockings and balaclavas over their heads. At the same time, another group of robbers uncoupled the first two coaches, leaving postal workers in the remaining seven cars unaware of the drama up front.

When Mills hesitated about taking the train down the track to Bridego bridge, where the gang's lorry was waiting, an infuriated Buster Edwards blundgeoned him with his cosh. Charlie eventually stepped between Edwards and Mills and, his bright blue eyes gleaming through the holes in his balaclava, said, 'Don't worry, mate. No one's gonna hurt you now.' Mills, only just able to stand properly, agreed to steer the train down the line.

Another member of the gang shouted, 'Get the guns,' to frighten the Post Office sorters. Charlie was lifted up and smashed the window of the carriage with his cosh. Inside, Charlie ran at the men piling sacks against the door with his cosh raised; they turned and dashed past him down the coach to where another gang member whipped them across the shoulders and told them all to lie face down. One of the robbers then used an axe to smash the padlock to the door containing the mail sacks.

Up front, Bobby Welch was attending to Mills, who'd slumped onto the floor next to his colleague David Whitby. Charlie re-appeared and gave them each a cigarette. Crouching down besides the terrified Mills, Charlie started wiping the blood off his face with a rag. He asked, 'Do you want any money? We'll leave it on the grass verge for you.' Mills shook his head, as the gang formed a human chain to carefully begin sweeping 120 mail sacks containing cash and diamonds into their three-ton lorry.

After three minutes – counted by Reynolds with a stopwatch – Reynolds announced, 'That's it, chaps.'

Charlie chipped in, 'But there's only a few left.'

'Sod 'em,' said Reynolds. 'Time's up. Let's get on the road.' The gang quickly took off, split into their two identical Land Rovers and lorry.

The entire operation had taken just fifteen minutes.

As the robbers drove steadily through the Buckinghamshire countryside in the early hours, Charlie fiddled with the radio to check for police movements. Suddenly over the airwaves came the voice of American crooner Tony Bennett singing 'The Good Life'. It was the perfect comment. The others began laughing and all slapped each other on the back for the umpteenth time that hour. As fellow robber Tommy Wisbey recalled, 'We'd got the big prize. It was a feeling of elation. I think it would have been harder taking sweets off a baby.'

Back at Sears Crossing, one of the Post Office's assistant inspectors and a colleague scrambled out of the smashed-up coach and headed back along the tracks to find the remainder of the train stranded. On the way, they met a guard, told him what had happened, and raised the alarm. A few hours after the raid, Scotland Yard's Detective Superintendent Gerald McArthur and his assistant Sergeant Jack Pritchard – a wartime commando – arrived at Cheddington to assist local chief of police, Detective Superintendent Malcolm Fewtrell, head of Buckinghamshire CID.

Charlie and the rest of the train robbery team pulled up in front of Leatherslade Farm exactly on schedule, at 4.30 a.m. At that moment their short-wave radio crackled into life: 'You won't believe this,' said a policeman, 'but they've just stolen a train.'

The mailbags were quickly unloaded and stacked along the living room walls and in the hallway of the farmhouse. Each bag was carefully checked for any homing devices. The group started ripping open bags and stacking banknotes in small piles. Soon, spread out inside Leatherslade Farm, was £1.2 million in five-pound notes and £1.3 million in one-pound and ten-shilling notes, making a total of around £2.5 million. This would be worth around £40 million today. The average salary at the time was twenty pounds a week and Charlie's own share was £150,000. There was a long pause, as the gang looked at the extraordinary sight of so much money piled high in front of their eyes. Charlie jumped up and punched the air in delight.

Bruce Reynolds wished Ronnie Biggs 'Happy birthday' and went to each man and shook their hands in thanks. Charlie laughed out loud as he pointed to a bag of money, 'Look at that. There's eighty grand in that pile.' He started singing Frank Sinatra's 'Come Fly With Me' as he stared at the piles of cash. Some of the others joined in the singing and changed the tense of the song, grabbing a few old pound notes and using them to light their cigarettes.

The moment didn't last. Radio newsflashes began sending ripples of panic through the gang. Charlie was in danger because he was so well-known to the police. He told Buster Edwards, 'I'll have to go on me toes. Me, who's never been further than Southend.' Charlie knew the moment he saw the newspapers the day after the robbery that the police were going to move mountains to get them and that none of the gang were safe. The initial plan had been to lie low but it was decided to share the money out immediately. Everyone knew they had to go their separate ways but, naturally, each wanted his own cut first. The gang knew how important it was to keep the money successfully hidden from the police and, indeed, no traces would ever turn up at the homes of the various suspects. Charlie believed it was now a matter of each man for himself. It would also be rumoured that Charlie and Buster Edwards held back half a million pounds of a one-million-pound fee that was allegedly to be paid to so-called financiers. It was suggested that they hid this money themselves after dreaming up all sorts of backers who never really existed.

Before anything else, the farm needed to be cleansed of clues that might give away the gang's identity, if and when the police discovered their hideaway. Charlie's old friend the Colonel made no secret of his obsession with this operation. 'Why don't you open a fuckin' office cleaning business, you cunt,' Charlie told him. 'You'd be good at that.' Awkward silence followed the outburst. A broad grin came over Cheeky Charlie's face. 'Just winding you up, old son,' he said to a grim-faced Reynolds.

All the robbers then started laughing, albeit nervously.

9/

It was the morning after the robbery. Charlie was so hungry that he ate two beef sandwiches, over which he also poured a generous covering of Saxa salt, unintentionally leaving a thumb print on the container.

He changed into his working clothes before setting off for London at high speed in a stolen E-type Jaguar. His robbery clothes were left at the farm to be destroyed alongside clothing worn by other members of the gang. Charlie was a fast but safe driver and reached London at around 5 a.m. He left the E-type at a prearranged spot before getting in his Rover, parking at Spitalfields Market to ensure he had an alibi.

Fifty miles away, Frenchy had taken off in a private plane for northern France with two large grip bags containing at least £400,000. Two of the gang were left at the farm to finish wiping everything clean before setting fire to the building. But they left before completing the job and Charlie never forgave them for failing in the clean-up.

Pat hadn't been particularly worried by Charlie's absence the previous night: such occurrences had long since become a regular feature of their marriage. He finally turned up at lunchtime, almost twelve hours after the train had been held up. Pat was listening to a bulletin on the transistor radio she kept on most of the time in the kitchen. Before she could comment on what they were hearing, Charlie said, 'I went straight to work in the market this morning at five o'clock. There are fifty people who can confirm I was there. You understand?'

Pat didn't respond. Her heart was fluttering with fear and disappointment. She asked Charlie on three separate occasions over the following couple of hours if he had been involved in the robbery. Each time he replied, 'Don't ask questions. I've told you I was at work at 5 a.m. So don't ever ask me that question again.' Yet again, Pat thought about the state of her marriage. Could she really survive without Charlie? Would she actually go through with one of her regular threats to leave him? For the moment, she couldn't face it. But if this rollercoaster ride of a marriage continued on its erratic path, she was going to have to think seriously about the future for herself and her daughters.

That evening, Charlie travelled with Roy James in his Mini Cooper to hide his share of the loot in a lock-up garage in the East End, a location also used by two of the other robbers. Charlie and James discussed the heist and how to avoid arrest. James admitted he'd not worn gloves while they were staying at Leatherslade.

Charlie was concerned about the sheer number of people who were involved in the crime, although he believed the weakest link in the chain was the gang's so-called legal representative, Brian Field. He was not a professional criminal and would be more prone to crack under police pressure. Two nights after the heist, Charlie visited a pub in Earlsfield, south London, owned and run by his old friend Nosher Powell, who later said, 'Charlie came in, ordered a drink and sat quietly in the corner, minding his own business as he always did. Charlie only ever talked to people he already knew. But he seemed a bit low that night so I went over and had a chat.'

Charlie said, 'Nosh, I fuckin' told 'em. The lot of them were unreliable. Too many of 'em.' Powell knew immediately what his childhood pal was talking about. Charlie said, 'We had too many on that fuckin' job. I told 'em it was too many. We had fifteen and we could have done it with half that amount.'

The following morning, Charlie rang Field at his office and asked him, 'Has the dustman been?', a reference to Leatherslade Farm being cleaned. Field assured him that everything had been taken care of, but Charlie wasn't happy and arranged a meeting with Reynolds, Edwards and Roy James at Clapham Common underground station. Charlie didn't trust the men who were supposed to have cleaned the farm after their departure. He suggested the group go back and do it themselves but no one else agreed. He didn't pursue the matter. Next morning, they met with Field outside Holland Park underground station, west London. Field was quivering with fear and Charlie was so irritated by his nervousness that he had to be restrained by the others from hitting Field. The lawyer did his best to assure the gang that he hadn't let them down, 'If I get pulled, I swear I'll never say anything. I'll never make a statement. I'll never put any of you in it and all I ask in return is that you look after my wife.'

The others were far from happy. They went to a café after the discussion with Field and Charlie once again brought up the subject of going back to the farm to destroy any evidence. He wanted to wait until dark and then sneak back in and burn it down. 'Mad bastard,' one of the other robbers said years later, 'but that was typical Charlie. He had more bottle than the rest of us put together.' Eventually, the group finally agreed to Charlie's suggestion. They would go back to the farm that night and clear out all the mailbags, the only clue linking the property to the robbery. They decided against burning down the property to avoid attracting attention. But they were already too late.

The gang were halfway through their second cup of tea when Edwards popped out to get the afternoon newspaper. He slapped the paper down on the table without saying a word. HIDEOUT DISCOVERED ran the *London Evening News* headline. The article reported the discovery of two Land Rovers with identical number plates and an empty lorry with an ingenious secret drawer in the middle of the floor big enough to take a large suitcase. The big question no one wanted to ask was whether any of them were already police suspects. Charlie later said he felt the whole robbery was doomed from that moment onwards.

'I'd always known we were gonna get nicked,' he recalled. 'Now, it was just a matter of time.'

But at the time he tried to sound upbeat: 'Let's go down there anyway – we can cop for whoever is there and clear out the place.'

As Bruce Reynolds recalled, 'But it made no sense. There would be more old bill down there than at the passing-out parade at Hendon Police College.'

Roy James interrupted their thoughts, jabbing at the newspaper. 'Look at this! Fuckin' Tommy Butler's now in charge of the London end.' Butler, born in Shepherd's Bush, had joined the Met in 1934. Four years later he'd become a detective and climbed steadily through the ranks. He had three spells on the Flying Squad before becoming a DCS in July 1963 and he got the nickname 'the Grey Fox' thanks to his tenacious efforts at bringing to justice such legendary figures as Jack Spot and Charlie's hero Billy Hill. He was a fifty-year-old bachelor, with receding hair, dark eyebrows and a thin pointed nose like that of Mr Punch. He lived with his mother and adored westerns, but he was a relentless pursuer of villains. An informant in prison had revealed that the gang behind the robbery were all from London, and it was this which had prompted Butler's appointment. Not even Charlie could come up with a quip to counter the shock they all felt about his involvement. As the team shook hands at the end of that gathering in the café, they knew it might be the last time they ever met together in the outside world.

Charlie abandoned all plans to return to the farm to remove any evidence. Later that day, Roy James was driving Charlie home when another report about the police discovery of Leatherslade Farm came on the radio. Afterwards, Roy turned to Charlie and said, 'That's it then, we're nicked.'

In prisons across the country, the Great Train Robbery was the talk of the landings, epitomising every villain's dream of one day getting lucky. The Great Train Robbery gang had the respect of the entire underworld. The stolen cash had weighed one-and-three-quarter tons, yet it had disappeared without trace. How could it have been got rid of without attracting attention? The banks had serial numbers for just fifteen thousand of the five-pound notes.

Tommy Butler ordered a careful re-examination of previous large-scale robberies. In 1952, a mail van in Eastcastle Street, London had been robbed of a quarter of a million pounds. Those bank notes had been unmarked and also vanished into thin air. In 1960, there was the theft of a quarter of a million pounds of bullion in Finsbury, north London, and finally there was the £62,000 payroll snatch at London airport, which had starred Charlie and most of the rest of the gang the previous year. Meanwhile, the farm was painstakingly searched, under the direction of Detective Superintendent Maurice Ray, fifty-four years old and looking like a not particularly prosperous bank clerk. The inch-by-inch examination eventually turned up a number of fingerprints that were sent to a police laboratory for analysis.

On 16 August, Fleet Street claimed a retired army officer had been identified as the brains behind the robbery. The *News of the World* said the man was known as 'the Major'. It was later believed this must have been a reference to Bruce Reynolds – the Colonel – thought by many to be an ex-British army officer. Another popular rumour was that one-time London underworld king Billy Hill had bankrolled the entire robbery from his retirement villa in the South of France. Hill told one reporter who knocked on his door on the Cote D'Azur, 'Look, I know nothing about it. Ring up Scotland Yard yourself. Now, if you like. Book plane tickets for both of us back to London, if you care to do so. I am so flicking mad about all this publicity without the money to go with it.' Behind Hill's irritation was a tinge of jealousy. As he later admitted to another criminal, 'What a masterpiece of a job. If only I could have laid on something like that. Brilliant!'

Charlie and the rest of the train robbers had written their entries in the criminal history books. The Great Train Robbery, as it was now known across the world, would dominate newspapers and TV news bulletins for years to come as the police – under the command of the tenacious Tommy Butler – attempted to unravel the crime.

They were helped when two motorcyclists spotted a couple of suitcases in woodland in the Surrey hills near Dorking. The cases contained more than £140,000 in cash that was traced to the robbery. In one leather case was a hotel bill made out in the name of Brian Field, the solicitor Charlie feared was the gang's weakest link. Hours later, an inch-by-inch examination of a caravan site in Box Hill, also in Surrey, uncovered thirty thousand pounds hidden in the wall of a trailer owned by robber Tommy Wisbey.

The results of the fingerprint tests showed that Charlie Wilson had handled the Saxo salt at the farm and identified two other known criminals – Bruce Reynolds and Jimmy White. Tommy Butler was delighted, although some Scotland Yard officers were already muttering that he was trying to turn the investigation into a one-man show. The bosses didn't care, just so long as he got results. On 22 August – just fourteen days after the crime – Scotland Yard issued descriptions of the three men and top of their list was Charlie. His photo was splashed across every newspaper, the headline in the *London Evening Standard* reading, YARD SEEK THREE MEN. By now writers no longer even had to make a reference to the robbery in the headline, it was already *that* famous.

With two hours of the story first appearing, four Flying Squad cars turned up at Charlie's home in Crescent Lane, Clapham, while he was having lunch with his family. As Charlie was taken away in handcuffs, Pat and his three daughters watched from the front window. A search for Bruce Reynolds and Jimmy White continued, while Charlie arrived at Cannon Row police station in a Ford Zephyr squad car just before 3.30 p.m. to be greeted by Tommy Butler. 'You obviously know a lot,' said Wilson. 'I have made a ricket [mistake] somewhere, but I will have to take my chances.' Charlie was told that he'd be taken to Aylesbury police station and charged, and replied, 'I don't see how you can make it stick without the poppy [money], and you won't find that.'

Butler asked, 'Would you care to tell me where you were on the morning of 8 August?'

'I was in Spitalfields Market. I left home about 5 a.m.' Butler asked him if he had any receipts or any proof of business done there. 'No, they don't give receipts. I saw a few friends, though.'

Roy James heard about Charlie's arrest on a car radio as he was driving back from motor-racing practice at Goodwood, Sussex. James said to his passenger, 'They've nicked Charlie. The cops'll connect me to him now.' They stopped the car and bought a newspaper featuring photos of the three suspects splashed across its front page. James phoned his mother and she said the police had just been to see her.

Back in Clapham, Pat greeted three more teams of detectives at her yellow front door. They searched the property thoroughly and took a pair of Charlie's shoes from the house for forensic examination. Two and a half hours later Charlie was charged with carrying out the biggest robbery the world had ever known. The following day he was escorted from a police van into the court in Linsdale, Buckinghamshire, with a blanket over his head, before making his first appearance in the dock.

In the tiny, crowded courtroom, Pat Wilson heard how her husband was accused of 'being concerned together with other persons as yet unknown, and armed with instruments, in robbing Frank Dewhurst, the GPO official in charge of the train, of £2,631,784, the property of the post-master general, at Mentmore, Bucks, on 8 August.' Charlie denied all the charges, looked over in the direction of Pat and winked. His action summed up the state of their marriage in many ways – he'd shown her she was his one and only true love, and that was still enough for her. As proceedings continued, the legal counsel insisted that Charlie had been at his home during the period covering the robbery and had made no attempt to avoid arrest. Charlie – standing between two burly policemen – was remanded in custody until the following day.

Butler and his train robbery team had rounded up Roger Cordrey, Charlie, Ronnie Biggs, Jimmy Hussey and Tommy Wisbey remarkably quickly. They had calls out for five more alleged robbers – Bruce Reynolds, John Daly, Buster Edwards, Roy James and Jimmy White. Four others were also on their suspect lists.

It was only a matter of time before they'd all be rounded up – or so detectives presumed.

10/

The arrested men admitted to nothing, knowing they might yet be found not guilty at their eventual trial.

A prison officer in Bedford prison said to Biggs, 'We've got one of your mates in here: Charlie Wilson.'

'Charlie who? Never heard of him.'

When Charlie later came across Biggs in the exercise yard they completely ignored each other. Then Charlie said in a loud voice so all the officers would hear: 'Aren't you the bloke who's been charged with the train robbery?'

'Yeah,' said Biggs, 'but I had nothin' to do with it.'

'Incredible,' said Charlie. 'I've been charged with that too. Bloody liberty.'

On 4 September, Gordon Goody became very worried that Charlie might think he was a grass after he was arrested and then released by detectives. He made a visit under the name of Joey Gray to see his old south London friend inside Bedford. Charlie cut such a menacing figure that Goody believed he could be under threat from his associates. Goody arrived with Pat and immediately begged Charlie not to draw any conclusions from his freedom.

'Fuck off out of it,' barked Charlie. 'What you talkin' about?'

'I only wanted to reassure you, mate,' said Gordon, 'because if I was you, the same thoughts would have gone through me head.'

'Don't be fuckin' stupid,' replied Charlie. 'I ain't worried about any of our firm.' He was much more concerned about the gang's elderly railway consultant. 'That old man, Stan, you'd better do somethin' about him, 'cos if he ever falls into Butler's hands, he'll shop us all.' Goody returned to London that night and – during a meeting with Buster Edwards – concluded that Stan should 'get the chop'. But there was one problem: after the robbery, Stan disappeared.

It wasn't until a few weeks later – following their move to Aylesbury prison – that Charlie and Ronnie Biggs talked to each other properly. They spoke secretly in the prison yard and sent messages to one another through trusted intermediaries. Both concluded that if they were found guilty, they'd get very long jail sentences and that escaping from prison might be the better option. Charlie was working in the kitchen of Aylesbury's hospital wing, preparing snacks and hot drinks for prison staff. He told Biggs that the two night guards on their wing could be drugged, providing enough time to get out of the prison before the alarm could be raised. The plan was quickly abandoned after the gang members discovered they could get an extra fourteen years if caught.

As remand prisoners whose guilt was not yet proved, Charlie and the rest of the gang were allowed their own choice of food and drink in prison. Making regular visits, Pat brought some of his favourites, including ham that Charlie – who considered himself a half-decent chef – was allowed to boil in the prison kitchen with vegetable stock and a selection of fresh veg and potatoes. The train robbers' wives began to form a close bond for the most part, although Pat and some of the others were irritated by Ronnie Biggs' wife, Charmian, who they thought was too extravagant with her clothes.

'We didn't want anyone to think we had loads of money because then they'd think it had come from the train robbery,' explained one wife later. The gang were mindful that criminals might think their wives and girlfriends had access to the loot.

The wives frequently discussed their relationships. Some openly derided being married to gangsters, often left in the dark while their other halves lied and cheated on them. A few of them said they'd leave their husbands sooner rather than later because they weren't prepared to wait for them to get out of prison. Pat Wilson kept quiet. Sure, she felt resentment towards Charlie and his criminal lifestyle. She'd even told him this to his face in the past. But she couldn't bring herself to consider a life without him, even if it meant enduring years of loneliness while he served a lengthy sentence.

She was offered an alternative one afternoon in November, when a middle-aged man arrived at her home in Clapham to tell Pat he had something very important to discuss with her. Once inside, he said that if they paid him five thousand pounds, he'd nobble at least one member of the jury at the upcoming trial. Pat was gobsmacked, and asked the man to leave. The following day she told Charlie of the visit. 'That's crossin' the fuckin' line,' he said, 'and I won't have it!'

Charlie immediately sent word to south London friends that he wanted this character 'sorted out.' He instructed Pat to phone the man and tell him she was willing to pay the money. He could come to their house the following day to get it. A couple of Charlie's friends were waiting for him, armed with a mallet and six-inch nails. They grabbed the man and dragged him across the street onto Clapham Common, where they planned to nail him to a tree. The man broke free and ran down the road into a shop, screaming, 'Help me, help me! Charlie Wilson's henchmen are after me.' But Charlie's pals followed him, caught him at the back of the premises and left him bleeding and unconscious in a nearby alleyway.

Wilson had confirmed his reputation as someone not to be messed with. Somehow he had come to Pat's rescue, even from his prison cell. Pat might have entertained thoughts of her marriage being rocky, but her husband had proved that he would always protect her, come what may.

He tried his own approach to avoid prison, attempting to negotiate his way out by offering one senior detective a fifty-thousand-pound bribe in December to 'lose' the evidence. Charlie claimed he had been framed for the robbery by corrupt cops, who had, by his account, taken his fingerprint samples and ensured they were then conveniently 'found' on that container of Saxo salt. The cash was left in a telephone box in Great Dover Street, Southwark and the target of the bribe told his superiors about the attempt. The loot turned out to be money missing from the robbery, the notes so mouldy that they were stuck together.

'Charlie was pretty low after that little caper and he reckoned he was heading for a very long stretch in prison,' one of his oldest friends later explained.

The only reasonable chance of freedom lay with the legal team at the trial. Wilson hoped to be defended by Jeremy Hutchinson, a lawyer with a fine reputation among professional criminals. When he proved unavailable, barrister John Mathew took the job. He had already successfully defended Wilson in previous cases and later went on to represent notorious criminals such as Brink's-Mat gold bullion handler Kenneth Noye.

As the trial date approached, the wife of gang member Brian Field claimed an unnamed man had suggested that six of the jurors should be paid five hundred pounds each to influence the verdict. These sort of allegations did nothing to help the robbers' case as it made them look even more criminally inclined. Naturally, they all insisted that such attempts at jury nobbling were nothing to do with them.

Watching on, the nation was split into those who dubbed the gang evil, violent thugs and those who saw them as modern-day Robin Hoods.

11/

The Great Train Robbery trial began at the Old Bailey on 20 January 1964, the jury were locked away each evening at a secret location to prevent so-called jury nobbling.

Injured train driver Jack Mills delivered his testimony to a hushed courtroom in a quiet, shaky voice, and Charlie Wilson whispered to Bobby Welch that he reckoned Mills was 'a right fuckin' actor'. Yet they knew it looked bad. For the following two months Wilson sat silently in the dock, resigned to being found guilty, and thinking constantly about his next move.

At 10.32 a.m., on 27 March, the all-male jury returned to give their verdict, after deliberating for a record sixty-six hours and fifty-six minutes. The voice of the foreman shattered the silence in the Old Bailey court with one word: 'Guilty.' Over the next ten minutes he repeated the word eighteen times for the various gang members. As the robbers were being taken away, chief investigator Tommy Butler turned to a rookie officer named Ken Rogers: 'You are the youngest officer on the Flying Squad. Take a good look at them, as they will be over the wall soon.'

Wilson was certainly going to try. He and all the other gang members were taken back to the hospital wing at Aylesbury to wait for Ronnie Biggs' separate trial, after which they were to be sentenced by the judge. All of them were resigned to their fate except for Bill Boal and Lennie Field, who insisted they took no part in the actual robbery. The only alleged gang member to be acquitted was south Londoner John Daly.

Wilson and Gordon Goody believed an immediate escape was the only option. The hospital wing was far less secure than any other part of the prison. At night there was just two officers nearby – one on duty in the corridor and another sleeping on the floor below. Wilson organised key copies, but prison staff were able to go straight to the crevices beneath the sinks in the washrooms where Goody hid the keys after someone grassed them up. The escape scheme had failed.

Wilson was further infuriated when newspapers alleged that he and the rest of the gang had offered to tell police where the money was in exchange for reduced sentences. As one of Wilson's oldest friends said many years later, 'No one, least of all Charlie, would give the police the time of day, let alone the key to all that cash. In any case, Charlie had big plans for the future.'

On 15 April, the convicted gang members were brought to the Buckinghamshire assizes court to be sentenced. The building was sombre, with dark panelling and an enormous royal coat of arms above the judge's throne. Mr Justice Edmund-Davies, in wig and robe, was flanked by the county sheriff, also dressed in ceremonial attire.

Judge Edmund-Davies specifically turned towards Wilson as he told the court: 'It would be an affront to the public if any one of you should be at liberty in anything like the near future to enjoy those ill-gotten gains. My duty is clear. If you or any of the other accused still to be dealt with had assisted justice that would have been strongly in your favour.' Charlie was given a thirty-year sentence. There was barely a flicker of emotion in response to the judge's words. This was Charlie Wilson at his most defiant. He certainly wasn't going to give the cozzers and that judge the satisfaction of seeing any shock on his face. And as for the judge's barbed comments about how he had not helped police with their inquiries, Charlie would *never* grass anyone up. *Never* in a million years.

The gang were sentenced to a total of 573 years, all to run concurrently, meaning they would spend 307 years behind bars. Leonard Field's elderly mother shouted, after he was sentenced to 25 years on conspiracy charges, 'He's innocent, sir.' A policemen ushered her out of the court. 'I'm his mother. He's innocent.'

Field shouted back, 'Don't worry, Mum, I'm still young,' as Wilson was being taken down from the dock. He looked up and smiled at the remark. He was followed to the cells by Ronnie Biggs, Tommy Wisbey, Bob Welch, Jim Hussey, Roy James, Gordon Goody, and the rest.

The ever-loyal Pat – dressed head-to-toe in funeral black – managed to get to the exit gates of the court to see the Black Maria carrying her husband off to jail. She caught the eye of Charlie through the tiny van window and the photo that appeared in the following day's newspapers showed her waving a leather-gloved hand towards the police vehicle. Seeing Pat that day almost broke Wilson's heart. As he'd already told friend Nosher Powell, 'The bird [sentence] is easy, but the absence from the wife and kids is sometimes too much to take.' Charlie already knew how much Pat was suffering as the wife of a professional criminal. Despite her own family background, she'd always hoped that she and Charlie could lead a safe, normal life rather than ducking and diving as they had since they first fell in love.

Meanwhile all the train robbers were to be put on Order 44, meaning heavy restrictions on their movements inside prison. Forming part of a specific Home Office policy to separate the gang, the aim was to ensure they didn't team up to organise escapes. The gang saw the move as yet more evidence that the Establishment was marking them out for special punishment.

Wilson knew his sentence was way over the top, but he'd always been a man with a plan and today was no different from any other in that respect. No one would keep him locked up like a caged animal for long. One headline and story following their sentencing summed up the country's mood: THE GOLDEN FLEECE –'They played for high stakes – a cool £2,600,031. And the Great Train Robbers earned the nation's grudging applause. But they lost. Now they must face the censure of the nation's laws.'

Flying Squad chief Tommy Butler admitted privately that he felt great sympathy for the families of the criminals, who were going to have to manage on their own for a very long period of time. He was a strange animal by all accounts: fellow officers complained that, because he was unmarried, he often failed to appreciate the domestic problems of the men he worked long and hard. Butler spent countless hours in his small office on paperwork and created many of the clever traps that helped catch the gang. But he was also old school, prepared to meet underworld informants at any time of the day or night. And it was Butler – the thin-shouldered, bland, school-teacher lookalike – who was there at the final arrest.

As for Charlie Wilson himself, his previous spells inside prison hadn't been so much a punishment as a further education. He'd met a lot of villains, learned a few new tricks, and made important contacts for his future. Now he knew the rules of the game and the thought of rotting away in a prison cell for a third of his life just wasn't acceptable.

It was time to make some 'alternative arrangements'.

12/

Winson Green prison – now HMP Birmingham – stands about 2 miles from Birmingham city centre, in old and crowded streets. It was built in the 1840s for 350 prisoners. When Wilson arrived, it held nearly eight hundred and almost half those inmates slept three to a cell.

From a distance, the prison looked like a little toy fort perched on a hilltop overlooking England's second biggest city. As a maximum-security prisoner, Charlie Wilson had four white patches stitched to his navy-blue inmate's battledress. He was only allowed occasional contact with other prisoners and earned three shillings a week sewing mailbags during his work periods, much to the amusement of inmates and staff, who knew the value of his famous crime.

Initially, he had a reputation for being a quiet prisoner who kept his head down. He followed an obsessive fitness regime, exercising at least three times a week in the small prison gym – the grounds were too small to even hold a football pitch. He was under one of the most secure and restrictive systems that the British prison system could provide. His single cell was always lit, night and day, which was seen as acceptable procedure to follow in the case of any potentially problematical inmates. He was also continually moved about the prison, not only from cell to cell but also from block to block.

Nights were supervised by a warder sitting in a central location while two colleagues patrolled the four landings, checking locks and peeping through the spyhole, or Judas-hole, in each cell door, every twelve to fifteen minutes. Another officer patrolled the block perimeter outside but he did not have the keys to gain entry to the block itself. They were kept with the principal officer on night duty. Wilson's bed was 12 inches away from the wall and he'd have to lie with his head to the door so that the guard who peered through the Judas-hole could see him clearly. His hands had to be visible, on top of the blanket, otherwise the guard would kick his door until he moved.

Within a few weeks, members of the prison staff decided to make Wilson's life even more unpleasant. 'They'd go in his cell two-handed, because Charlie could handle himself, and then the bastards would fuckin' lay into him,' one former Winson Green inmate later claimed. Wilson had to resist the temptation to fight back – that was what the officers wanted. If he was going to beat the system, Wilson needed to remain cool and calm in the face of every adversity.

During the daytime, Charlie was rarely out of sight of a warder. As he moved about the prison, one officer would hand him over to another. And wherever he was, those four white patches on his uniform ensured that he could easily be picked out. But even so, Charlie Wilson still didn't suffer fools gladly. Not long after arriving, he had a confrontation with another inmate on the prison's first floor.

'It kicked off, all of a sudden, as Charlie was talkin' to this fella. The screws left 'em to it and the geezer ended up in a crumpled heap on the ground,' a Winson Green inmate later recalled. Within seconds, Charlie had brushed down his immaculate prison uniform and returned to his cell as if nothing had happened.

Winson Green had no TV sets. Charlie spent most evenings reading either a daily paper or studying Shakespeare and poetry, which he'd first learned to appreciate during an earlier spell in prison. No wonder inmates called prisons like Winson Green 'thinking factories'. Charlie couldn't help scheming because he had little else to do. He was determined to turn his appalling predicament to his own advantage when he came across inmates serving less than ten years for crimes he considered to be much more serious than robbing a train. One man had killed a barmaid by putting cyanide in her beer because she did not serve him quickly enough and was sentenced to just five years. Then there was the night porter who set fire to a Brighton hotel to get rid of some late guests and caused the deaths of seven of them.

He also got just five years. Even the newspapers noticed, with the *Daily Sketch* commenting, 'Thirty years – all Britain argues, is this too harsh?'

Pat and the children had by now moved out of the family home and into her mother's house in the East End. She visited Charlie three times in July and early August. He also had frequent visits from lawyers and associates in connection with his appeal.

All the gang had decided to contest their sentences, even though Wilson was among many others who were pessimistic about their chances of getting their sentences reduced. He even told his lawyers he didn't think there was any point in attending the hearing in London.

Lurking in the back of Wilson's mind all along was an escape plan. Soon after arriving at Winson Green, he'd begun stealing sugar from the prison canteen and he would scatter it outside his cell so at night, when the prison was silent, he would hear a faint scrunch as the screw came to look at him through the Judas-hole and he could time those visits. He also noted that the older officers were replaced at weekends by younger, more vigorous screws who might prove to be a problem during a breakout.

Wilson remained under twenty-four-hour surveillance and other prisoners were even threatened with disciplinary action if they socialised with him. Tiring of the regime, he smuggled some of the black grease used in the workshop to waterproof mailbag straps. He blackened his cell light because the round-the-clock illumination was destroying his ability to sleep properly. Mostly he kept his head down and bided his time, enjoying the loyalty shown to him by the majority of inmates. He had hero status thanks to his role in the crime of the century. He also believed the screws couldn't keep their harsh routine up for ever.

Wilson was eventually allowed to exercise in the prison yard at the same time as other inmates. A few days later, a long-term prisoner slid alongside him and said just five words: 'Frenchy is working on it.' The inmate was gone in a split second, but Wilson's spirits were boosted for the first time since he'd been arrested by Tommy Butler. Pat confirmed later that – apart from Bruce Reynolds and Gordon Goody – Frenchy was the only other man Charlie trusted completely.

Frenchy had already begun assembling a team to help spring Wilson from Winson Green, including a master locksmith, a Belgian light-aircraft pilot, an expert wireless engineer to monitor police broadcasts and two huge bodyguards, experienced mountaineers capable of scaling virtually any wall in the land. They held a dress rehearsal at a derelict monastery in northern France. Frenchy had photographed a small section of an Ordnance Survey map of the area around the prison with a 35mm camera and blew it up to nearly 2 foot square to use during meetings. They perfected their plan before heading to England.

One sunny Tuesday in early August, the escape team discreetly circled the prison to make a note of heights and distances. Charlie's latest cell, on the ground floor of C-block, was pinpointed. They got key moulds via inmates. It was agreed that the breakout should happen just after the appeal court hearing, which Charlie expected to lose. On the day, twenty-five police and prison officers would be due to escort Wilson, Ronnie Biggs and Roy James from Brixton jail to the law courts in the Strand for their appeal court hearing. But Wilson insisted that he couldn't be bothered to leave Winson Green prison. His lawyers warned him it was madness not to appear in person, but Charlie was adamant. 'What's the fuckin' point?' he said.

The appeal began without him and Charlie's counsel said, 'The court has to set its sights on the year 1994 when Wilson's children – one of whom has a hole in the heart – will be in their middle thirties. Many of us in this court will no longer be upon the scene.'

Appeal court judge Mr Justice Lawton summed up the Establishment's attitude towards the train robbers: 'The point is whether some shorter sentence will give some prospect of enjoying the proceeds of the crime. How many men who spend their lives working honestly might think, "Hmm. Fifteen years in jail for £150,000. I don't mind taking the chance. And, even if I am caught, my wife and children can live in Bermuda in comfort. In ten years I will be out and able to join them." These were wholly exceptional sentences for a wholly exceptional crime and in our view they were not wrong in principle or excessive.'

With that, the gang had taken their last glimpse of the outside world for what could be as long as twenty years – taking into account the one-third remission they could expect for good conduct. Back at Winson Green, Wilson greeted the appeal court decision with a shrug of his shoulders.

It was 12 August 1964: Manfred Mann was top of the hit parade, singing 'Do Wah Diddy Diddy', with the Beatles' 'A Hard Day's Night' at No. 2. It was a soggy, cloudy day in Birmingham and the grey stonework of Winson Green prison looked hauntingly gothic. At 5 p.m., Wilson – who spoke to few people – looked mightily pleased with himself as he was escorted back to his cell from the tailor shop where he'd been sewing mailbags. He knew what was about to happen, and he couldn't wait to put two fingers up to the Establishment once again.

13/

It was 5.30 p.m. on 12 August. Charlie was given a supper of bread, cheese and soup in Winson Green.

Two hours later, he drained his nightcap cup of cocoa and whispered to himself, 'Here's to the outside world.' He settled down to read a book on his favourite subject, ancient history, borrowed from the prison library. At 9.30 p.m., it was time for lights out and he climbed into bed. He immediately closed his eyes and, as he later explained, 'For the next few hours my ears became my eyes.' He didn't know exactly what time they'd come for him, just that it was going to be tonight, but he couldn't do anything to help prepare for the escape team in case it was noticed by the warden carrying out the regular twelve-fifteen-minute checks.

The escape team were already in the vicinity. Elsewhere in C-block, other prisoners were also lying awake, including one man who had a tiny transistor radio, modified to transmit rather than receive. Its range was only about 400 yards but this would be enough to reach the fake taxi – fitted with a receiver – that was arriving in the street overlooked by the prison. The driver and passenger soon received a faint message: 'Screws been to Wilson's cell.' The information would be updated each time the guard visited Charlie's cell throughout the night.

A blue Ford Zodiac carrying Frenchy, two other men and one woman, stopped by the corner of the prison overlooking a canal. They parked opposite the home of Rose Gredden, who later said she noticed a blonde woman sitting in the back seat with a wide-brimmed, beige hat pulled down to one side. Three men were talking on the prison side of the canal towpath. 'They were respectably dressed. Two were rather tall,' Mrs Gredden recalled. 'Some prison officers must have seen them. Their social club's only a few yards from where the men were standing and I heard officers leaving the club around that time.' Two more men in a petrol tanker pulled up one block from the prison. At least four of the team, equipped with a set of duplicate prison keys, headed towards the wall.

They ran into some workers, one who spoke to the gang because they were blocking the pavement. He was trying to get home after a late shift at a local factory. The group parted to let the man through and he got a good look at them by the light of a street lamp as they all called out, 'Goodnight.'

At approximately 2.35 a.m. one of the two officers on duty in C-block left to begin cooking breakfast porridge in the kitchen, leaving the prison open to a serious breach of security – the five members of the night staff patrolling the wings were locked in and carried no keys. Just over half an hour later, Frenchy whispered his final instructions to his two mountaineers and, together with the locksmith, they crept off into the dark. Wearing plimsoles and black trousers, they were almost invisible, their oversized, dark raincoats hiding ropes and climbing equipment. The group headed for a favourite spot for escaping – a corner of the wall where the prison met the canal and the grounds of the nearby psychiatric hospital. It was 3.20 a.m. All three pulled black stockings with eyeholes over their faces.

A grappling hook was flung skywards against the outer wall. It caught and held tight after being tested with a quick jerk. The men climbed up and dropped into the exercise yard outside B-block. There were no prison patrols, no dogs barking, and they hugged the shadow of a long, grey prison wall as they headed for C-block. On the way, they forced open an equipment box by lifting the door off its hinge and took a 15-foot-wide plank that could help them get from one roof to another during the escape. The internal wall of the prison was 25 feet high and, using a rope ladder – almost certainly fitted with grappling irons – the gang climbed up and padded softly through to the cell block where they knew Wilson was under virtually constant suveillance.

Less than a minute later, the mountaineers knocked night officer William Nicholls unconscious with a cosh. They tied him up with nylon rope, trusting that by the time he came round, they'd all be long gone. Then they used Nicholls' key to open the outside door. Key two was used to open a steel grille door. Dodging prison staff, they made straight for landing No. 2. The raiders used a key specially cut to open Wilson's cell so quietly that the next-door inmate heard nothing. The door swung open and the three men burst in. 'Let's go,' whispered the first, throwing a bundle of clothes in Charlie's direction.

He pulled on a black roll-neck sweater, dark trousers, plimsoles and a balaclava, and followed the others past the trussed-up warder, toward the centre of the prison. They cut back into A-wing, past the bathhouse and downstairs. The locksmith stayed an extra two minutes to lock the doors. Outside, the full moon meant they had to keep to the shadows of the buildings as they headed for the 20-foot perimeter wall. There were no patrols and they easily scaled the wall with the rope ladder.

The team were out of the prison in under three minutes. Half a minute later they were carrying their equipment along the canal towpath towards a bridge that led to the psychiatric hospital's perimeter wall. That was when Wilson first spotted the petrol tanker parked on the next corner. A flap had been cut in the main tank. He was handed a flashlight and crawled through the opening in the tanker to find three mattresses, pillows and blankets. The two expert climbers clambered in behind him. Frenchy closed the hinged flap and said, 'Next time I see you we'll be drinking champagne, not petrol fumes.' Within seconds the tanker trundled off into the night – heading for a deserted landing strip. Wilson later described the ride as surprisingly comfortable. At the airstrip, he was highly emotional as he was greeted by a welcoming party.

Later, he recounted it all to his wife: 'You know what I'm like Pat – sort of soft inside. I embraced all those tough men in the true French tradition when I thanked them. I was really crying with gratitude.' A small plane then took him to a barren landing strip in northern France.

At 3.20 a.m. in the UK, William Nicholls, the guard who'd been knocked unconscious and then bound and gagged by Charlie's escape team, managed to free himself. He immediately reported the incident to the night orderly officer who spent the next thirty minutes locked in his room in case the intruders attacked him or his staff. As a result of the delay, the police were only notified of what had happened at 3.50 a.m. – and then only by an ordinary phone call, rather than by 999 emergency contact. A group of police and prison officers assembled at the prison gates minutes later but were unable to enter until the chief officer appeared with a set of keys.

The waiting gave Charlie and his escape team valuable extra time. It would be several hours before all the country's police had even been properly alerted and the streets of Birmingham had been sealed off and roadblocks set up. One of the first to be told was Tommy Butler. Three hundred of his men had continued investigating the Great Train Robbery and were still looking for Buster Edwards, his wife June, and Bruce Reynolds. Butler had long thought an escape would be made and was not in the least bit surprised to hear of the prison break. Birmingham's

DCS Gerald Baumber, head of the city's CID, was relieved of all other duties to lead a handpicked team of detectives to hunt for Wilson.

Police initially suspected Charlie might be heading for Ireland, a popular destination for convicts on the run. A special watch was immediately mounted at Dublin, Cork, and Shannon airports. Baumber's squad of thirty officers visited the prison and began interviewing all 120 warders, governor Rundle Harris, civilian staff and some of the eight hundred or so inmates. Detectives also tested the prison's six keys for traces of soap and talked to ex-prisoners. Within twelve hours, the Home Office issued warnings to the eight prisons holding eleven of the other train robbers that more escapes might be planned. The day after the breakout from Winson Green, Wilson's photo and story were splashed all over the front pages, including the *Daily Sketch* delivered to Wilson's cell that morning, despite his absence – much to the amusement of his fellow inmates.

Charlie Wilson's escape was hailed as more daring than the train robbery itself and there were rumours that a syndicate of specialist jail-breakers known as the 'Freedom Fixers' were being paid to free more members of the gang. Winson Green authorities admitted they didn't know the identity of everyone who'd visited Wilson over the previous few months. It was suggested that some of the individuals described as 'legal advisors' had been part of the escape team.

Reporters doorstepping the Wilson's house in Clapham were told by neighbours there had been no sign of Pat and the children since Charlie's sentencing. Journalists initially implied that Pat was missing and probably on her way to meet Charlie at some secret location. In fact she was living at her mother's home in the East End. Pat was so angry about the accusations that she'd disappeared that she asked her solicitors to serve a writ on the *Daily Mail*, alleging libel. She also noticed she was shadowed by two men whenever she left her mother's. For the following two weeks they stuck to her like glue before, just as suddenly, they disappeared. Pat never found out if they were police, journalists or criminals. The notion of bringing up three daughters alone was daunting enough and now she was lying awake for hours each night, worrying about the fate of her fugitive husband.

Charlie hadn't dared contact Pat in case she inadvertently led police to him. He presumed detectives would be watching her mother's home, intercepting all mail and perhaps even monitoring her telephone calls. Pat knew only too well it would be a long time before she would hear from Charlie, but not once did she seriously consider abandoning him and starting a new life. Some of Pat's friends found the loyalty to Charlie almost twisted. She was scared of his lifestyle and everything it represented. Yet she found herself unable to survive without it.

In later life it would prove even harder to handle.

14/

Halfway across the globe in Mexico City, one of the two train robbers who hadn't yet been arrested – Bruce Reynolds – was leaning back on a park bench with his feet in the sun when he opened his three-day-old English newspaper to read, 'Jail busters free train-robber: they knock out guard, open cell, give prisoner new suit.'

As Reynolds recalled, 'I just thought to myself, Nice one, Charlie! His success filled me with pride. We'd finessed the Establishment yet again.'

In prisons across the UK, all the train robbers were under surveillance twenty-four hours a day. Prison authorities soon began moving them around jails to foil any more escape attempts. The Home Office referred to these moves as 'further security measures'. And to all inmates of every kind, Charlie Wilson was a folk hero. Not only had he been part of a team who'd stuck two fingers up at the Establishment, but now he'd broken out of one of England's most secure prisons. One popular yarn doing the rounds was that he was being held captive by other criminals determined to get their hands on the £2.5 million of Great Train Robbery cash. One newspaper even suggested that an inmate involved in this conspiracy in another prison had been stabbed to death, but this was never substantiated. Another, even more sinister, rumour was that Wilson had been freed in order to be killed by the brains behind the Great Train Robbery, who suspected he was a grass. Wilson – by now sipping champagne at his French hideaway – was outraged. For his part, Tommy Butler believed Wilson's associates were planting these stories because they wanted the world to think Charlie Wilson was dead, which would mean the hunt for him would be scaled down.

Pat Wilson later claimed in an interview that the breakout had cost her husband fifty thousand pounds, with the locksmith getting ten thousand pounds. The other team members shared the rest equally, apart from Frenchy, who saw Charlie as an important, long-term investment.

After a couple of weeks, Wilson moved from the French countryside to an apartment in Paris. He decided he needed a disguise when Interpol joined in the hunt, and didn't leave the flat for the following fortnight, while he grew out his prison crop before dying his brown hair jet-black. Later, he grew a beard and a moustache that were also dyed to match his hair. Frenchy suggested that he should also have two prominent front teeth extracted, which formed a distinctive V-shape. But Charlie refused, saying he would never get used to wearing dentures. A few weeks later, Charlie and Frenchy headed south to the French Riviera, where they easily blended in with the wealthy jet set at nightclubs and casinos on the coast.

Wilson adored the life in southern France and asked Frenchy to find him a house and get Pat and the girls over. But Frenchy said he'd have to travel much further afield before he could think about settling. He advised Charlie to visit more potential safe places before making a decision. Wilson amused him by suggesting a multitude of places he'd never even dreamt of visiting, including Mexico City, Rio, Tokyo and San Francisco.

After forty-seven days, Fleet Street said the nation was growing mightily impatient. JUST HOW MUCH LONGER CAN THIS MAN STAY FREE? asked the *Sunday Mirror*. Questions were asked about the quality of the mugshots of Wilson that were supposed to help people recognise him. The paper featured a much more recent shot of the escapee and pointed out few people would recognise him from the official photo that dated back to the 1950s.

The worst aspect of Wilson's escape, as far he as was concerned, was that it shone the spotlight once more on the question of the whereabouts of the Great Train Robbery millions. Scotland Yard believed the money had been dispersed soon after the crime was committed and reckoned the rank-and-file gang members took away £150,000 each. That left at least one million pounds for the so-called principals. Was Wilson one of those? Police were convinced that Wilson would make for the location of his cash.

The Home Office tried to salvage some credibility by announcing they'd foiled another train robbers' escape plot, involving Charlie's old friend Gordon Goody, at Manchester's Strangeways prison. Few details were released about the alleged attempt and Goody himself later dismissed it as rubbish. But he also insisted that Wilson had been murdered since breaking out of jail. DCS Butler was highly unimpressed by the wilder notions and the 'Charlie is dead' stories. He remained quietly poised and extremely focused throughout all the fuss. He believed he'd get his man in the end and his inquiries into Wilson's escape had already led him to a number of countries. He believed it was only a matter of time before Wilson slipped up. Butler was given authorisation for at least four separate phone taps on criminals known to be close to Wilson. He believed the gang member received a salary once a month from a money man in London, sometimes by courier, sometimes by post.

In July 1965, eleven months after Charlie Wilson walked out of Winson Green, Ronnie Biggs pulled off an equally outrageous escape from Wandsworth prison, London. Biggs was not one of the most important members of the GTR team, but he'd been a popular figure. His escape was as dramatic as Charlie's had been smooth: as prisoners exercised in the prison yard, a furniture van drew up alongside the wall of the prison and an armed man leapt on its roof and up the wall. He dropped a tubular ladder into the yard below. Four prisoners ran towards the ladder, scrambled up, and jumped on the van. They entered through a hole in the roof and, half a mile down the road, split up and fled in three waiting cars. Biggs' successful breakout came despite the twenty-four-hour lockdown on all the train robbers following Charlie's escape and only added to the robbers' legendary status. Everyone wanted to know, how could they keep humiliating the Establishment and get away with it?

Biggs' escape was good news for Wilson as the police switched much of their attention away from him. The headlines that followed Biggs for many years turned out to be even bigger and bolder than those that stuck to Wilson. He believed he could gradually disappear from the limelight completely and then he would start planning a reunion with Pat and their daughters.

15/

In November 1965, Charlie Wilson flew into Mexico City to meet GTR friends Bruce Reynolds and Buster Edwards. Reynolds barely recognised Wilson at the airport thanks to a disguise that included small, wire-rimmed glasses.

The pair, pals since schooldays, were delighted to see each other. 'Who would have thought that, thirty years later, we'd be sitting in Mexico City, he an escaped convict and me on the run?' Reynolds later said.

Wilson told the others that he'd chosen Montreal, Canada, as his new home. Mexico itself would never be suitable because he hated not being able to speak Spanish and wasn't too keen on the food. Pat and the girls remained in England for now. But Wilson said he was certain he could smuggle them out to start a new life.

In early January 1966, he flew to Montreal, via Brussels, as a new immigrant, using a fake passport in the name of Ronald Alloway. Three weeks later, he met a visiting Reynolds at the airport, a new girlfriend in tow, an attractive nurse. It seemed to Reynolds that Cheeky Charlie always had at least one 'bit on the side' on the go. Unimpressed, Reynolds returned to Mexico City, telling Wilson, 'Move house, Chas. Lose the girl and, for fuck's sake, be more careful.'

Wilson was officially one of the world's most wanted men, and Pat became a virtual recluse at her mother's home in Whitechapel. The house only had two bedrooms and it wasn't easy for the five residents to share. Pat later said, 'I felt in utter despair.' One morning a telegram arrived. 'Like most people I got a sinking feeling in my stomach every time I opened one of those little buff envelopes.' At every moment she expected to hear that Charlie had died. She went upstairs to the bedroom she shared with the three girls, sat down on the edge of the bed and started slowly tearing it open with her trembling fingers.

The message was short and simple but it made Pat's heart pound: 'I AM OK DO NOT WORRY STOP LOVE TO ALL AND LEANDER MA BELLE MICHELLE STOP RON'. Pat burst into tears and fell back on the bed. 'Ron' meant absolutely nothing to her. But those words 'Ma belle Michelle' meant everything – he was alive. In a split second, all Pat's fears about never seeing her husband again disappeared. He'd proved yet again he was there for her. This was the life she'd chosen. She wanted to be with Charlie, whatever the risks. Pat told no one about the message, not even her mother. Frenchy told her how to change her own name by deed poll – she was to become an 'Alloway'.

Weeks later, Pat was picked up in the street near her mother's house and taken to a London apartment block by a woman driving a Mark 10 Jaguar. Pat entered and Charlie strode across the room, his arms outstretched. Pat felt her knees buckling and had to be held up by her husband as she started sobbing. 'Never mind darlin',' said Charlie. 'Don't worry, love. Everythin' will be all right now.' That first meeting only lasted thirty minutes but Wilson promised her that they'd all soon be together once more as a complete family. As she was driven away, Pat turned to look back at the block and wondered if it really was all going to happen.

A week later, Pat was out walking near her mother's home when a dark blue Ford Zodiac with the same driver from before collected her and took her to see him again. This time he told her to go home and find someone to look after the three girls for two days. She was to return to the flat and stay with him while they discussed their future. Pat was also to bring along every detail relating to her change of name and take twenty-four pictures at a photo booth.

That evening she met with Charlie at the flat, and he cooked her a meal and popped open a bottle of vintage wine. They had their photograph taken. Pat recalled, 'Looking back I suppose it was a risky thing to do – but I was so happy at the time I hardly gave it a thought.'

After two days, Pat headed back to the East End with instructions to visit a café at Paddington station four days later. At the allotted time, Pat was approached by a young woman who said little, but left a large envelope on the table. It contained a passport in the name Barbara Joan Alloway (although Pat's name had been changed to Patricia Ann Alloway). There was also a typewritten note, 'Be at Slough mainline station, 4.15 p.m. Wednesday.'

Pat got up especially early for the meeting and made breakfast for her daughters, and then told her mother she was taking them to the zoo for the day. She crammed some make-up and clothing into a small overnight bag and rushed out with the children. At Slough, Pat and her daughters waited near the station bus stop for ten minutes before the chauffeur who'd previously driven Pat arrived in the black Mark 10 Jaguar.

They were taken to a mansion nestling among beautifully mowed lawns and lavish flowerbeds. The family were greeted at the front door by an elegantly dressed, well-spoken lady. 'Hello, Mrs Alloway,' she said. It was the same woman who'd delivered the passport in that envelope at Paddington station.

Two days later, Pat, her natural blonde hair dyed auburn, found herself at London airport. First the family flew to Amsterdam, where they transferred to a Montreal flight. During the seven-hour flight Pat was a bundle of nerves. When oldest daughter Tracey wrote her real name in a colouring book, Pat leaned across in a panic and whispered, 'Don't do that. Cross it out.' Tracey gave her mum a hurt look and asked, 'Why, Mummy? You must put your name at the top.' Pat pleaded with her daughter to give her the book, but Tracey simply held it further away. Eventually, Pat snatched it off her. Nobody noticed.

Pat and her daughters got through immigration without a hitch, but there didn't seem to be a friendly face to greet them. Outside, Tracey spotted a big car and yelled, 'Look over there!' Standing beside the car was a bearded man with bright, sparkling blue eyes ... It was Charlie. All the doubts melted away. They were all together again. The problems of the past no longer mattered.

Hours later they entered a large detached house Charlie had rented in the suburb of Hudson Heights. As Pat walked into the lounge she found a bouquet of her favourite chrysanthemums and two potted plants. A pink ribbon adorned each with a card, 'Welcome home – all of you. Love, Ron. Now there is no need to worry!'

Wilson thought he had secured the means to be financially independent in Canada. His share of the robbery money was back in London with an old friend whom he'd known since the 1950s. They'd invested in some legitimate businesses such as betting shops, restaurants and, it was later rumoured, a part-share in a chain of provincial newspapers. But he soon discovered that his partner had been investing so erratically that Wilson's own share was now just thirty thousand pounds. He'd even had to pay a 10 per cent fee to his associate in London to ensure all the money got to him.

With money worries looming, Wilson decided to go back to what he knew best. When Bruce Reynolds and his wife came to stay with them in Canada, he told his old friend how he hoped to pull off a couple of jobs in Canada to make ends meet. A contact had told him about the movements of several large consignments of Canadian dollars returning from New York. Wilson established that two security men each picked up half a dozen sacks of the money every month. He and Bruce Reynolds staked out the shipment company where the money arrived from the USA, watching as the mailbags were unloaded into an estate car before being driven into central Montreal. They talked up what they thought was a decent plan until Wilson decided it was too risky. Some of his friends later claimed that he'd ditched the job because he didn't want to risk losing Pat and the girls again. Times had changed and this new Charlie realised he needed to tread very carefully on all fronts.

16/

Starting a new life in Canada might have seemed a dream come true but there was one overwhelming problem for Charlie and Pat Wilson – their three young daughters. Wilson knew they could accidently give them all away in a split second.

He got the girls sitting on separate cushions in the lounge at home and began asking them over and over again, 'What's my name?'

Eventually, they were all able to answer, 'Ronald Alloway.' But it wasn't going to be easy.

As Pat later recalled, 'We played this game incessantly for days until the children were perfect nearly every time. Even sudden trick questions over lunch or at bedtime couldn't catch them out, although occasionally one of the girls would slip up. In that case the other two would receive a "prize" of a bar of chocolate.'

Wilson initially worked in Canada in a silver and glassware business. Then he switched to selling cars. Occasionally, he'd have a bundle of cash from London and the family would go on a shopping spree. A new house was built ahead of schedule and the 'Alloway family' quickly became close friends with neighbours, including local police chief Charles Pooley. The house was guarded by an Alsatian and a Dobermann – dog-lover Wilson could never get out of the habit of watching his back. He also liked to know that Pat and the girls had good protection whenever he was away from home.

They lived in an idyllic countryside location, but Wilson had always loved the hustle and bustle of the city and the raucous, exciting crush of a racetrack crowd. Sometimes he'd slip away to Montreal's Blue Bonnets and Richelieu racetracks – 35 miles from the US border. But his addiction to gambling was nothing compared to his desire to stay free.

In mid-1966, the UK police issued fresh wanted posters for all the missing train robbers, appealing to people going on holiday to be on the lookout. Rewards totalling £225,000 were offered, and Jimmy White was the first of the gang to be captured when police got a tip he was staying at a block of flats in Grand Parade, Littlestone-on-Sea. On 19 September, Buster Edwards surrendered to police after carefully negotiating a lower sentence with Tommy Butler. His gamble paid off and he got fifteen years. The police – particularly Butler – had proved they were still as determined as ever to capture the rest of the gang. Wilson, Bruce Reynolds and Ronnie Biggs were now the only ones still on the run.

Nineteen sixty-seven was probably the quietest year of Charlie Wilson's adult life. The publicity surrounding the wanted men seemed to quieten down. The key to his survival was to ensure that all his money from the UK always travelled a very devious route to avoid the police, who still monitored his London associates. Wilson's hideaway in Canada could only become known to police if the money suppliers gave him away.

Late in the year, tenacious Tommy Butler – still on the case – launched Operation Perpendicular to recapture Wilson. Butler's impending retirement was suspended by Met police commissioner Sir Joseph Simpson on his fifty-fifth birthday that year so that he could continue the hunt. Only two other officers – Assistant Commissioner Peter Brodie and Commander Ernest Millen – knew about the latest plan to track the train robber. Strict instructions were given that any messages coming into the Yard with the code signal Operation Perpendicular should be given only to those two officers.

Butler was already aware that Pat and the children had disappeared from London and were most likely reunited with Wilson. Just after Christmas, Charlie and Pat started to get a strange, ominous feeling that the net was closing in on them, although they didn't know why. Pat hated this feeling as it was a constant reminder of the perilous state of her marriage, causing her countless sleepless nights and leaving her with deep psychological scars.

17/

It was a discussion in the South of France that first alerted Tommy Butler to the possibility Charlie might be in Canada. Detectives had been shadowing two of Charlie's London associates and overhead a conversation that clearly indicated Wilson's location.

Butler sought his most reliable south London informants and tried to find out if they'd heard anything on the grapevine. When Wilson's brother-in-law and one-time business partner Georgie

Osborne was found to be planning a trip to Canada, Butler knew immediately that he must be on his way to see Wilson.

Osborne arrived in Montreal on a flight from Europe, with his movements plotted by the Royal Canadian Mounted Police who reported back to the Flying Squad that Osborne was staying with a character who resembled Wilson called 'Alloway'. Butler requested that the Mounties keep close watch, but not go near Wilson for the moment. Butler was hoping that if he monitored the criminal for long enough, Bruce Reynolds might also pop up and he could nab two runaway robbers at the same time. For more than three weeks Butler sat back and waited, while his superiors were less sanguine. They panicked that Charlie might slip the net and put immense pressure on Butler to arrest Wilson as quickly as possible. They were furious that he was risking the big arrest on a hunch that he might nab Reynolds at the same time.

In mid-January 1968, while Wilson and Pat entertained Georgie Osborne, blissfully unaware that a team of Mounties was watching their every move, Tommy Butler planted an article in British national newspapers to put Wilson off his guard. The story suggested that he had been spotted in Tangier, Morocco, where he had enjoyed a casual drink and a chat with an unnamed traveller. The day after publication, Butler flew to Montreal with colleague DS Eddie Fuller and began surveillance. They watched Pat stand outside in the snow waving the girls off as they were driven down the hill to the school bus by Wilson in his Cadillac. Pat later spotted four men trying to fix a snowmobile which seemed to have broken down nearby.

As she explained, 'A little shiver of fear ran through me, because it was so rare to see anyone out in such cold weather.' She didn't bother mentioning it to Charlie because, 'We still didn't really ever discuss that side of things.'

Two days later, the family Alsatian, Cadillac Rocky, who had a kennel in front of the house, began barking uncontrollably and continued most of the day, only falling silent after darkness fell. A few days later, Pat spotted the men whose snowmobile had broken down. This time they were in a Dormobile campervan, at the end of the Wilsons' quiet lane. Again, Pat didn't tell Charlie about the strangers.

Tommy Butler finally made his move on the twenty-fifth – day 1,261 of Wilson's freedom. In temperatures of -19C (-2.2F), wearing snowshoes, he tramped through the 2-foot-deep drifts in the forest behind Charlie's house and paused. He watched Wilson walk out to his Cadillac. Wilson's piercing blue eyes sparkled in the strong winter sunlight, and he turned around, and walked back into the house. Butler had Mounties stationed in key positions around the house, the police operation a closely guarded secret. Not even Charlie's neighbour, the local provincial police chief, knew about it.

A few minutes later, Wilson left the house to take Cheryl and Tracey to meet the school bus. He drove down the hill, and spotted a blue van that had half run off the road and was stuck in deep snow. Three men were trying to push it out. As Charlie later recalled, 'I thought, poor devils, I'll give 'em a hand on the way back.' He dropped Cheryl and Tracey at the school bus, then went back up the hill and stopped his car by the men.

'Want some help?'

'Yes, please, we can't shift it at all.'

Wilson heaved and helped push the van, and a voice behind him said, 'Good morning, Charlie. Want some help?' At first, Wilson hadn't a clue who was talking to him. As Butler later said, 'I looked more like an Eskimo than a Yard man.'

Wilson recalled, 'I didn't recognise the voice, but the word "Charlie" made me freeze. Then, as I straightened up and half-turned, I looked straight into the face of Tommy Butler from Scotland Yard.' Wilson staggered and gasped with surprise, then, typically, he straightened himself up. 'Morning, Tom,' he said. 'Fancy seeing you out in all this cold snow. You'll catch your death!'

Wilson was grabbed from behind by Eddie Fuller and made to stand facing his car with his hands on the roof while he was searched. A couple of minutes later, Wilson, Butler, Fuller and at least half-a-dozen Canadian detectives walked up to the front door of his house. Wilson was handcuffed to Fuller.

'Sorry, darling,' Wilson said as Pat opened the door. 'Don't worry. Everything will be OK. Tell the girls I'm goin' back to England for a while and they should look after their mum and be good.'

Less than an hour after the arrest, a message arrived at Scotland Yard for Assistant Commander Peter Brodie. Decoded, it simply read, 'Wilson has been recaptured.'

As Butler hoped, Canadian authorities swiftly granted Scotland Yard a deportation order and Wilson returned to the UK the following day. Pat and the girls were also ordered to be deported. They were moved to a city hotel and kept under close scrutiny by immigration officials. It was expected they would leave Canada within three or four days. Police told reporters they'd recovered a cache of more than C$35,000 (£15,000) from Wilson's house. About C$20,000 (£8,000) of it was in Bahamas currency and about C$14,000 (£7,000) in US dollars, plus a much smaller amount of local currency.

A young British journalist discovered a cupboard in the main bedroom filled with picture albums that provided a fascinating insight into Charlie's activities on the run. Photos clearly showed Charlie with Bruce Reynolds. One shot pictured Reynolds and his wife at the Stardust hotel in Las Vegas. At that time there had been virtually no trace of Bruce Reynolds since the Great Train Robbery five years earlier.

Wilson's extradition hearing was held in the harbour master's office at Sutherland Pier, deep in Montreal's dockland. He was quickly declared an illegal immigrant and Butler moved swiftly to get him booked on the following day's London flight.

That evening, Charlie and Pat had a tearful reunion in his cell in the basement of Montreal police headquarters. They talked about selling their house: Pat was determined to get home to London as soon as possible. She'd even accepted the deportation order, meaning she'd have to pay her own way home.

Butler showed great sympathy towards Pat and the children, saying, 'It's the kids who are going to suffer. And I hope the authorities will do all they can to make things easy for them.' But he also insisted there was no room on the plane for Pat and the children when he took Wilson back. He did not want the media to snap the couple together in London.

Wilson and his two Scotland Yard escorts travelled economy, at the rear of a British Airways Boeing 707. Wilson was neatly dressed in a fawn suit with white shirt and tie and had shaved off his beard. He looked tanned, fit, and surprisingly cheerful. Butler unlocked his handcuffs for the duration of the flight and the former fugitive tucked into a supper of smoked salmon and fillet steak, washed down with white wine as other passengers watched curiously. One asked if the robbery had been worth it and he chirpily said, "'Course it wasn't worth it. Look at me now. I know it wasn't worth it; believe me, I know.' Reporters on board asked why he'd chosen Canada: 'We liked it and there are a lot of Englishmen there – at least of English stock. I liked some of the French Canadians too.' How had he escaped? He smiled and, with a sidelong glance at the inscrutable Butler, said, 'I don't know, do I? I was asleep at the time. That's right: one minute I was fast asleep in my bed and the next I was standing outside the wall.'

Wilson and Butler both burst out laughing.

A few moments later, Cheeky Charlie offered two journalists his wife's story of their three-and-a-half years on the run for thirty thousand pounds. 'I don't want the money myself – where I'm going it won't be any good to me. I want it for the wife and children.' Wilson evaded other questions. On the subject of the whereabouts of his old friend Bruce Reynolds, he said: 'I haven't a clue where he is, honest.' *Daily Express* photographer Terry Fincher managed to get a brilliant picture of Wilson sitting alongside Tommy Butler on the Boeing 707 which ran the following day with the front-page headline: BACK TO JAIL WITH A GRIN!

Wilson's cocky routine hid his annoyance at himself for having been caught. He felt bad about Pat and the children. He knew how much Pat suffered, how worried she was about their life together, and he wondered if she would be there for him after everything he had done. When Butler insisted on locking his handcuffs as the plane touched down in Prestwick, Scotland, for refuelling, Wilson ensured his handcuffed wrist was low between himself and Butler and asked the detective to drape a carrier bag across the chain before passengers disembarked.

The final destination was Heathrow, where three of Wilson's favourite brand of car – Land Rover – slid forward onto the tarmac. Two police vanloads of officers unloaded and with dogs they ringed the aircraft. From rooftops, plain-clothes detectives watched the Sunday crowds. Other police radio cars took up strategic posts around the aircraft. The mobile steps rolled to the door, and six detectives ran up into the plane as other passengers filed off. Inside, Wilson was moving along the gangway towards the front of the plane. He even had time to pat a three-year-old boy playfully on the head, winking at the child. Wilson hid his head under an overcoat to foil press photographers as he was led out, handcuffed. Butler handed his prisoner over to a Flying Squad team led by DS Ronald Hardy, who immediately directed Charlie into one of the waiting Land Rovers.

Butler watched as the police convoy pulled across the tarmac and headed to the Isle of Wight and Parkhurst prison. He now had even more important fish to fry, which he summed up in five words: 'Ronnie Biggs and Bruce Reynolds.' He was heading off for the South of France to check out a tip concerning Reynolds.

Meanwhile, Charlie's dad, Bill Wilson, was telling journalists he was glad his rascal of a son was home. 'At least he can't get in any more trouble.' But Bill Wilson's comments were tinged with sadness because Charlie hadn't seen his father for more than ten years and he himself had no plans to see his son in Parkhurst.

Pat was told she could stay in Canada until the following summer, but she remained convinced that she needed to get back to London. She felt the urge to be as close to Charlie as possible.

The tabloids calculated that, of the £2,595,997 stolen during the Great Train Robbery, only £648,948 had ever been recovered. In today's terms that meant the master blaggers had still got away with in excess of £30 million. But all the money in the world couldn't help Charlie Wilson now.

18/

At just after 2 p.m. on 26 January 1968, in bright sunshine, the Flying Squad car carrying Charlie Wilson passed police patrolling the perimeter wall of Parkhurst prison. After three and a half years it was all over for Wilson. Stretching bleakly ahead was a thirty-year stretch. Twenty warders – one of them with an Alsatian – lined up inside the prison reception centre as Wilson strolled in. He ignored the screws and leaned towards the dog and said, 'Hello, Rin Tin Tin. I must get to know you. We're going to be great friends.'

He swapped his smart suit for a grey flannel prison uniform and a crowd of staff watched, open-mouthed, as if they were in the presence of a Hollywood star. Less than a hundred yards away, building work on the new high-security wing at Parkhurst – known as 'the cage' – had just been completed and it now housed many of Wilson's train robber pals. There had been a ripple of excitement amongst the seventeen high-risk inmates in the cage ever since news of Wilson's capture had filtered through the prison grapevine, among them train robbers Gordon Goody, Roy James, Jimmy Hussey, Roger Cordrey and Tommy Wisbey. The last time Wilson had seen any of his old friends was at their trial back in 1964.

An almighty cheer went up as Wilson was escorted by two burly prison officers into the cage during the mid-morning break. This was followed by the rattling of cups on the metal fencing around the gangways. Charlie looked up and smiled, a tad embarrassed but also grateful that so many of the chaps were on his side. Inmates greeted him with shouts of, 'Hard luck, Charlie,' and, 'Let's 'ave another go, Chas,' as he walked around the cage, shaking their hands. Soon, they were all discussing his exploits. Later on that first day, Wilson chose his prison job – making toys for sick children in the local hospitals.

Wilson tried to settle down to prison life once again. Escape was virtually impossible and while he might have constantly thought about it, the reality was that he was now inside for keeps. The gym would be the most important room as far as keep-fit fanatic Wilson was concerned. As he languished in a cold British prison cell on the Isle of Wight, the only heartening bit of news was a letter from Pat saying how good his old neighbours and friends back in Canada had been to her and the girls.

Wilson was soon being treated for serious psychological problems that doctors put down to delayed shock following his return. All those years of bottling up his feelings to protect his family had come to a head and sent him spiralling into a deep depression. His condition wasn't helped when Butler interrogated him about the missing millions. Butler and other senior Scotland Yard officers believed they could crack the 'Silent One' with the right approach. They also wanted him to help them find Bruce Reynolds and reveal the secrets of his escape from Winson Green. But despite Wilson's psychological problems during his early days and weeks in Parkhurst, he was not for turning. His inbuilt hatred of grasses had left him as defiant of the police as ever. He felt that he and the other robbers were being treated like animals, and this hardened his resolve not to let *them* – the Establishment – beat him.

Many of the screws once again administered their own form of 'punishment' on star inmate Charlie. He was often served cold or half-prepared food. The train robbers were only allowed to exercise in a small, inner yard where they couldn't see any grass or even hear the trees rustling in the wind. Eventually, Wilson refused to go out in the exercise yard at all in protest against the restrictions. His skin soon became tinged with grey from the lack of sunlight. He told one long-standing friend that prison was like being 'pickled in fuckin' vinegar'. Stuck indoors, the breathing difficulties of his younger years returned. The prison doctor diagnosed a worsening of his earlier problems with emphysema. It had likely flared up again because of Pat's incessant smoking and 80 per cent of his fellow prisoners were also heavy smokers. He was warned that the condition would gradually deteriorate, and he requested not to sleep in cells next to smokers. Such was the volume of smokers that it was impossible to accommodate his request. Wilson undoubtedly suffered like the other robbers, but was such a resilient character he rarely showed his emotions to those he considered to be his enemies.

The train robbery gang became even closer friends inside the cage at Parkhurst, their infamy setting them apart from other inmates. Wilson was immensely proud that not one of them had grassed to the police and this helped bond them, much to the irritation of the staff. Home Secretary Jim Callaghan still hadn't made up his mind if Charlie was going to be further punished for his breakout from Winson Green and, as those first few months inside passed, Charlie's laidback, jokey temperament gradually returned. He tried to give the impression he'd accepted the prison regime while continuing to plot all sorts of criminal enterprises.

Pat, meanwhile, had been left with just a handful of friends and family prepared to help her and the children survive. As the years passed, many other train robbers' wives also found maintaining relationships hard. Pat spent much of her time either alone or with just her own children for company and her life centred around visits to Charlie in Parkhurst. The journey involved taking a train from Waterloo to Portsmouth, a ferry over to the Isle of Wight and then a bus or taxi. She loathed it. Sometimes she'd get to Waterloo with her three daughters feeling so distraught that she wondered if she could go through with yet another visit. She also lived in dread of getting to the prison to find something awful had happened to Wilson. Between each trip lay weeks of anticipation, and all for just thirty minutes with her husband, meeting either through glass or under supervision by a team of hefty prison warders. It took an emotional toll. Pat became increasingly worried about how thin Wilson was getting, even though he always had a smile and joke for her.

The couple's three children, Cheryl, Tracey, and Leander, were openly derided at school because their father was a runaway train robber. All three daughters would grow up to be vital and attractive women determined not to marry criminals who'd end up in prison half their lives. They saw their mother virtually never going out socially unless she was chaperoned by the wives or girlfriends of other robbers. Pat primarily saw her role as mother and housewife, not star-struck criminal's moll. She became quite reclusive, fearing that danger lurked everywhere in the outside world. It was better to stay indoors and watch TV as much as possible. Then her inbuilt fear would subside.

Over in France, the only train robber who hadn't yet faced a criminal trial – Bruce Reynolds – was making his own plans to return to the UK. His wife had already moved to a mews flat off Gloucester Road, in South Kensington. Reynolds joined her several weeks later, entering the country via Shannon in Ireland. He was eventually picked up by Tommy Butler while staying in a rented house in Torquay, Devon. Reynolds was sentenced to twenty-five years at his trial in January 1969, five years less than Charlie and the original trial defendants had received. This raised questions about sentencing anomalies.

On 24 October, Charlie Wilson, Jimmy Hussey and Roy James got caught up in a riot that erupted in the cage at Parkhurst after other inmates began protesting about conditions. For forty terrifying minutes that evening, seven members of staff at Parkhurst were held captive by furious inmates. One prisoner came within a whisker of slitting the throat of a prison officer. The three train robbers barricaded themselves in their cells as part of their protest against conditions. Eyewitnesses later claimed inmates were screaming abuse as the staff began dismantling doors. Fists flew, as did beds, mattresses and chairs. Wilson and other protesting inmates were seized, one by one, and locked in unused cells. Two officers ended up with suspected hand fractures and another had a badly cut face. None of the prisoners were seriously hurt.

Wilson was placed in solitary confinement, but he was more worried that he might not get parole on his thirty-year sentence. He asked his solicitor to write to the Home Secretary asking for consideration and, having been interviewed by two visiting justices, it was decided he should lose only six months of remission on his sentence, because of his earlier escape. As with any escapee, Wilson's sentence had been suspended when he went on the run. It only started up again on the day he was rearrested, three and a half years later. When the six months was added to this 'extra' time, the result was in practice that Wilson would be inside for another four years. But he was, at least, assured that he would qualify for parole within ten years.

Wilson returned to his regular cell in the cage and, despite the early stages of emphysema, continued to exercise furiously, boosting his already muscular physique with a punishing regime that he intended to keep up for the rest of his life. Wilson saw each press-up as a mark of defiance against the system. In his mind, they'd never beat him. Ever. He also got to meet the younger generation of professional robbers and they intrigued him. He got to know people like Mickey Green, who'd been part of the so-called Wembley Mob, a bunch of blaggers who were London's most successful bank robbers until one of their team turned grass.

Green was another schemer like Charlie, always looking for the main chance. He was happy to bide his time in Parkhurst safe in the knowledge that once he got out there was money to steal and girls to bed. He was the original gold-medallion-man, with his penchant for flash cars and sparkling jewellery. He gave Wilson hope – there was a life to look forward to after he finally got released.

Two other characters Charlie came across in Parkhurst were young robbers Roy 'the Lump' Adkins, from Notting Hill, London, and 'Mad Mickey' Blackmore, from Camberwell. They and many others inside the cage looked up to Wilson as a hero. In turn, Wilson said he would invest some of the little remaining train robbery cash in the pair, should they come up with targets for robberies after their release.

Bruce Reynolds arrived at Parkhurst shortly after the riot and was kept apart from the other robbers. It was only after some time that the prison governor agreed to allow him to meet Wilson, and then only well away from the prying eyes of the cage. They got together in the so-called 'nonce' wing, where child molesters and other special category inmates were kept. Wilson bought a plentiful supply of chocolate bars, luxuries that Reynolds had not been allowed since his arrest since when, to his friend's surprise, he had become a dedicated smoker. The men discussed their families and Wilson reiterated how much he'd relied on Pat and missed her now he was banged up again. They got on to the subject of business and Wilson's face turned to stone as he told Reynolds he was convinced someone had grassed him up to Tommy Butler and helped to ensure he had been tracked down to Canada.

As time passed inside, Wilson's power and influence within the prison walls grew immensely. He focused on the weak, impressionable members of staff, those prepared to turn a blind eye to certain things. It was similar to the world outside, where bank robbers had become the new criminal aristocracy, admired by up-and-coming villains, fancied by the prettiest girls in the most expensive West End clubs and bars. These new, cocky young villains played The Doors and T-Rex on their flashy eight-track car stereos as they marched across the nation's pavements brandishing sawn-off shotguns. For Wilson, even away from the action, the reputation meant a plentiful supply of everything from porn magazines to chocolate. He even managed to get baby oil brought in because he didn't like using soap, believing it would age his skin more quickly. Whenever Wilson needed to talk about any sensitive subjects with a visitor, he'd promise certain warders 'a drink' to stand well back, so they couldn't hear what he was talking about.

In the summer of 1970, Wilson and the rest of the train robbery boys in Parkhurst gave a loud cheer when news filtered through that Ronnie Biggs had once again evaded capture, this time in Melbourne, Australia, where he'd moved his wife and children and then disappeared as the authorities were closing in. Biggs may have been considered to be a junior member of the gang but knowing his antics were infuriating the Establishment was a real tonic for the other robbers.

Other, more serious aspects of the robbery grabbed the headlines. Just after Biggs slipped out of Australia, train driver Jack Mills died. The media claimed his death had been caused, in part, by the beating he got at the hands of the train robbers that night in Cheddington seven years earlier. The question of who injured Mills and whether he suffered later illnesses as a result would remain highly contentious. Mills had been plagued by suggestions he'd dramatised his injuries and consequent physical disabilities when giving evidence at the trial in 1964. The robbers were adamant that his injuries had been very slight and believed that he was put under pressure by police to exaggerate what happened to ensure they all got heavy sentences.

That same year Tommy Butler also died, aged just fifty-seven. This sparked a completely different reaction from friends and foes alike. Even so-called enemies like Wilson sent their respects. Criminals felt no anger towards Butler because of his absolute fairness. When Bruce Reynolds was jailed, his solicitor even thanked Butler in open court for the kindness and courtesy he'd shown Reynolds' wife and son.

Meanwhile, Charlie Wilson remained inside and took full advantage of his confinement to carefully think through his plans for when he was eventually released into the so-called real world. He knew he needed to reinvent himself if he was going to join the modern underworld.

PART 2 – NARCO CHARLIE

I come to lead you to the other shore; into eternal darkness; into fire and into ice.
Dante, *The Inferno*

19/

In 1972, Charlie Wilson met a Colombian called Carlos in Parkhurst prison. Carlos had been convicted of cocaine-trafficking in London and, at first, Wilson was unfriendly towards the South American because he was a 'druggy'. So-called 'real' criminals robbed banks and trains. They definitely didn't deal in drugs. Wilson then believed that narcotics were never to be touched, either personally or professionally.

But charming Carlos – a tall, handsome, dark-haired man who talked with an educated, upper-class Spanish accent – had a friendly, relaxed manner that eventually put Wilson at ease. Carlos was intrigued by the Great Train Robbery, so Wilson told him all about it and how he'd ended up with one of the longest prison sentences in British criminal history. Carlos in turn explained some of the basic economic reasons for cocaine dealing making good criminal sense.

'What's the point in risking your life to rob a bank or hold up a train when you can make ten times that money and never even have to touch the product?' Carlos told Wilson that cocaine was emerging as a dominant industry in Colombia: a handful of small-time thieves and hustlers in the country's second and third cities, Medellín and Cali, were already handling millions of pounds worth of coke. It was flowing out of South America every year. He predicted that, within ten years, cocaine would be one of the biggest-selling products in the world. The Brits had to get a piece of the narcotics trade or else foreigners like Carlos were going to hoover up all the big money. 'Mad Mickey' Blackmore, Mickey Green and Roy Adkins had told Wilson they would most likely take the drugs route on their release from prison. But Charlie remained far from convinced.

Five thousand miles away, Colombia was imploding, thanks to the production of cocaine. The drug was well on its way to becoming the country's number one export, despite being an entirely illegal product. Entire communities were reliant on it providing them with economic security. Successive governments were failing to tackle the problem. The drug was exported to the USA in quantities that stretched into tons, having a serious effect on crime in general. Murders rates in US cities skyrocketed and drug smugglers and dealers grew immensely rich from other people's misery.

In 1974, Ronnie Biggs was arrested in Brazil and it looked as if the last of the Great Train Robbers would soon find himself inside a British jail. But in the end, Scotland Yard's dogged DCS Jack Slipper had to fly back to London empty-handed because the Home Office had not prepared the right paperwork. Biggs announced his Brazilian girlfriend was pregnant with his child, and that meant he could not be legally extradited under Brazilian law. His fellow robbers were delighted that Biggs had avoided being brought back to Britain because it meant he'd beaten their age-old enemy, the Establishment.

The warmth didn't last as Biggs' big mouth soon got him into trouble. One well-known British criminal's identity was revealed in a book by Biggs and he swore to tear him into little pieces if he ever saw him again. A lot of the growing animosity towards him was the result of Biggs having been, after all, a relatively unimportant member of the gang who had become the most infamous, thanks to his escape and subsequent life in Brazil. Wilson certainly didn't appreciate being fed a non-stop diet of Ronnie Biggs stories every time he picked up a newspaper in Parkhurst. On the other hand, Biggs' antics did help Wilson maintain a low profile. He was rarely mentioned in the media by this time and he believed that had to be a good thing, especially since he was carefully planning for when he was finally released.

That same year, Buster Edwards and Jimmy White were released from prison, after serving nine years of their sentences. The other train robbers inside Parkhurst thought it was a bit out of order since both men had been amongst the last robbers to be caught, but Wilson continued to keep his head down. He was a frequent visitor to the library and when staff asked why, he'd simply reply: 'I want to learn about things. I missed out on school, so now I'm making up for it.' Other inmates started calling Charlie 'Mister Brains' because of his ferocious appetite for reading and researching. Wilson knew that it was important to keep focused on being released, or the sentence would once again drag him into the depths of despair.

He had access to US newspapers such as the *International Herald Tribune*, which regularly carried stories about the cocaine epidemic that was sweeping the USA at the time. It was giving him ideas. If cocaine was that popular, then it was high time it got sold in other parts of the world, surely? Wilson talked to other inmates about their knowledge of drugs. Many of the younger prisoners were smoking cannabis regularly in prison at a time when drug tests were few and far between. Wilson began putting out feelers to some cannabis dealers he contacted through other inmates.

The following year, Wilson part-financed a large shipment of cannabis into the UK from his prison cell. There were later rumours that he had made a sizeable investment in the Bank of America robbery in Mayfair in April 1976, when eight smartly dressed men got away with eight million pounds. At a time when all the train robbers except Wilson and Reynolds had been released, Charlie continued to keep himself informed inside, learning from recently released inmates that cocaine was starting to appear in the clubs and pubs of his beloved London, on a relatively small scale.

Cocaine in the UK had been perceived as a rich man's drug, at a price of around sixty pounds a gram. Cannabis, on the other hand, was everywhere – but that meant the pot market was already overcrowded. More importantly, cannabis was much bulkier to handle so it was harder to smuggle. Hundreds of thousands of pounds worth of cocaine could be hidden inside the lining of a suitcase. In Wilson's world, that was a no-brainer.

Wilson was informed that his release would come within two years and was transferred to Long Lartin top security prison, near Evesham, Gloucestershire. Long Lartin was a much smaller and more restrictive prison than Parkhurst, but he didn't care. He had big plans. In Charlie Wilson's world, you said little and concentrated on the future. In Rio de Janeiro, meanwhile, Ronnie Biggs continued to manage very nicely, cashing in on his notoriety with books, recording contracts, and even advertisements for British Leyland cars. Wilson was of the opinion that you didn't go around blabbering about your past exploits. When the released GTR gang members were offered ten thousand pounds each to help respected author Piers Paul Read write a book about the much-heralded 'crime of the century', Wilson was far from impressed. The others promised him a share of the proceeds and he reluctantly agreed to let them form themselves into a limited company. He was a sleeping partner because jail regulations did not allow inmates to conduct business from their cells.

Wilson agreed to help with the Read book on condition the author did not include too much detail about him. It was a typical back-scratching deal. Roy James, Jimmy White, Jim Hussey, Tommy Wisbey, Gordon Goody, Roger Cordrey and Buster Edwards all believed the book would be the first of many projects in which they'd make money by offering technical advice to anybody wishing to write or film any aspect of the robbery. An agent was appointed who would negotiate deals for newspaper stories, features, photos and possibly another book, which the robbers wanted to write themselves. But when an MP described the Piers Paul Read book deal as 'monstrous', Wilson accused his old mates of making things even worse for him and for Reynolds.

'Charlie reckoned every time there was a story in the papers about the robbery it meant their chances of parole took another knock,' said one old friend. Many of the stories published about the Great Train Robbery still mentioned that driver Jack Mills had been battered with an iron bar during the raid and that he had never properly recovered from his injuries. Mills' widow was frequently featured in newspapers and by television reporters whenever there was a suggestion the robbers were about to cash in on their crime. Wilson seethed because he'd personally taken the time to try and make sure Mills was all right after he'd been injured.

Aside from being involved with media coverage of the robbery, Wilson used his time to develop skills as a talented artist. He had a penchant for startlingly life-like portraits of celebrities such as Tom Jones and Barbra Streisand. He also proved a dab hand at copying some of the old masters, and was so good at duplicating northern artist L. S. Lowry's matchstick figures that one inmate told him to try and flog them as fakes. Wilson didn't want to give the authorities an excuse not to release him at the earliest possible date.

Wilson also met an Indian drug smuggler, Surya 'Chris' Krishnarma, who was making a point of getting to know some of the heavier British criminals inside the prison. Charlie had already had a 'good tickle' out of his earlier cannabis deal and was interested in possibly investing in more drug deals in the future. Krishnarma claimed he had the connections to line up top-quality cannabis shipments. He was also an expert tester of the produce. Wilson reckoned he could be a very useful character to employ in the future.

Wilson now had his sights firmly set on cocaine but, for the moment, cannabis connections would suffice because he knew full well that he'd be punished much more severely if he was busted for dealing in a Class A drug such as cocaine, especially from his prison cell. He set up some more cannabis deals and sat back to earn what were very reasonable returns from his investments.

Wilson was eventually moved to Coldingley prison in the village of Bisley, Surrey, to further prepare him for his release. Coldingley was relatively new and was the first prison in the UK to give prisoners specific training for life after release. He joined a course in jewellery-making, and studied French. He was soon boasting that he could read and understand entire French novels.

He wanted the authorities to believe he was deadly serious about going straight on his release from prison and told the prison governor that he intended to work in a market while trying to get a jewellery business off the ground.

Charlie Wilson wasn't afraid of anything or anybody. He'd proved it over and over again during the Great Train Robbery period and now he was going to prove it all over again. Unlike many of his contemporaries, Wilson didn't hate foreigners, which was why he'd got on so well with Colombian cellmate Carlos. All Wilson's adventures on the run from prison in Mexico and then Canada had turned him into a man of the world. He accepted people for what they were, whatever their skin colour or accent and told many of his friends that he looked forward to enjoying the company of people from other countries when he was eventually released. He even admitted that he preferred many foreigners to his fellow Englishmen.

One acquaintance later said, 'Charlie was determined not to be a typical Englishman. He'd already learned fluent French in prison but was also determined to pick up other languages, so he could blend in better when he got out.' He continued carefully mapping out his future career. He could see, more clearly than ever, the attraction of cocaine as a criminal enterprise. He even worked out that in order to orchestrate the sale of the drug across Europe and the UK he needed to have a base well away from London. He settled on Spain as his final destination and for now he needed to keep his head down and hope that his release from prison would come sooner rather than later. This feeling was compounded when he heard that he'd become a grandfather for the first time. He was yet more desperate to be released back into the real world. This represented the 'other' side of his life. The side where he was a normal family man, keen to provide for his loved ones like everyone else.

Typically, the 'other' Charlie always had an ulterior motive. Learning about jewellery enabled him to study the gold market while he was still inside prison. There were no guarantees about the cocaine business as yet, so he needed some back-up ideas when it came to other money-making enterprises. He thought that gold could provide him with a quick hit of income to support his family. He could also build up cash to invest in cocaine from South America.

Gold had recently become a favourite commodity for swindling the UK government out of VAT, then at 15 per cent and levied on a variety of goods, including gold. The VAT was paid by the buyer to the person selling the gold, and should then have been returned to HMRC. But Wilson had discovered there were a variety of scams that could easily be operated to deprive the taxman of his share. One was to smuggle the gold into the country, then sell it to a reputable dealer. The 15 per cent VAT would be pocketed by the smugglers. Another scam was to draw up documents showing that the gold had been exported immediately after its arrival in Britain, and was not liable for VAT. The honest trader, meanwhile, would still have to pay the 15 per cent VAT to the 'company' selling him the metal. That company, usually based in short-let office accommodation, would fold within a matter of months without making any VAT returns.

Gold was particularly suitable to such schemes, with its high value resulting in large returns with a minimum of delay. It also had an official price, fixed twice daily by the London gold market: the smugglers did not have to worry about commercial competitors undercutting their prices, and that was without mentioning that it was compact and relatively easy to transport. The other major attraction was the maximum penalty if you were caught: just two years' imprisonment. Small wonder, then, that VAT fraud involving gold was becoming very popular among well-organised, professional criminals like Charlie Wilson, even if he was still in prison at this time.

To pull off any scam involving gold, the identifying marks had to be removed and the purity of the gold needed to be disguised. Failure to do so would create a risk that legitimate traders would quickly become suspicious that the quantities they were being asked to buy were either smuggled gold or stolen bullion. Wilson told his criminal associates outside prison they'd need specialised smelting equipment, the sort used by only a handful of people in the UK. Most of them were in the Hatton Garden area of central London, internationally renowned as a centre for the jewellery trade. Such shops were on their guard against suspicious customers ordering smelters, so Charlie's team would have to tread carefully.

In August 1977, Charlie was transferred to Pentonville prison, London, to prepare for his release on parole. He was amazed that, having been warned he might spend at least half his full sentence in prison, he was actually in line for an early release. The tide had truly turned.

He knew it wasn't going to be easy for the first few months because he'd be under strict parole conditions. He had lined up a job carrying fruit and vegetables at a stall owned by south London pal Paddy – they had known one another since the 1950s, when they had been in prison together. In 1964 Wilson lent forty thousand pounds to Paddy, used to set up a successful road haulage business that was partly responsible for Paddy becoming a millionaire, living in a comfortable, detached house in the Kent countryside. Wilson got him to repay the original loan by allowing him to use some of those lorries to run smuggled goods into the UK from Europe and Paddy had also made smuggling a profitable sideline.

Now Charlie Wilson was on his way out of prison. He couldn't wait to get back into the real world once again.

20/

Charlie Wilson had hit middle age and had three daughters who'd grown up without him. But the strange thing was, as he later admitted, he didn't really feel that old. One inmate he'd shared a cell with at Pentonville told him life in the slammer kept you young and healthy. He had a point.

'The outside world moves at a hell of a pace,' said that wise old lag. 'Meanwhile, we're all stuck in here, frozen in time. No reason to get old if you ain't got the problems they 'ave out there, son.'

But now Wilson was getting out. After the thick flannel of his prison uniform, his old windcheater felt cold as he stepped out of Pentonville at 5.30 a.m. on 15 September 1978. He paused for a few seconds outside the building and looked back at the gates. Then he shivered. Not from the cold but as his old man used to say, 'because someone just walked over your grave, son'.

That was the only encouragement Wilson needed to get the hell out of that place before they changed their minds and dragged him back inside again. All he had, as far as the cozzers were concerned, was the suit he was standing in and a holdall containing a razor, a clean shirt and some clean underwear – all care of Her Majesty's Prison Service. He also had a hundred pounds cash from his workshop duties – other money he'd sent to Pat and the girls.

On the streets of London, it was still too early for the rush hour, although commuters and lorries were already starting to jam up the city streets. And then there were the black cabs. They looked almost the same, except some of them were no longer black. Luckily, they still made that same familiar clunking diesel noise … peace and quiet, London style.

At Waterloo, Wilson got a no. 49 bus to the Central After-Care Association – if he hadn't, he would have been banged up again within twenty-four hours for violation of his parole licence. He was soon sitting in the drab waiting room opposite a couple of old lags puffing away on roll-ups. It was just like being back in the joint. He hated smoking so much and he already knew from prison doctors that his own respiratory problems had been caused by passive smoking. Eventually, he saw his parole officer and informed him that he was working for a 'businessman' called Paddy. He didn't bother saying that Paddy was one of his oldest criminal associates.

A few nights later, Charlie enjoyed a special homecoming party hosted by his old friend Joey Pyle at Nosher Powell's pub, the Prince of Wales, in Tooting. A lot of the old faces were there but Pat took centre stage. Charlie genuinely wondered how he'd managed to hold on to such a gem of a woman. He knew there must have been moments when Pat considered leaving him but she'd stood by him throughout everything. No one will ever know if Charlie took Pat for granted but they seemed joined at the hip, despite all the dramas that had dominated their adult lives.

Powell said later that his old friend behaved that night 'as if he hadn't even been away', explaining, 'I came out from behind the bar and gave him a hug. He'd been to the dogs earlier and was flush. He kept sayin' "You all right, Nosh, any problems? Need some dosh?"'

"Nah, Charlie. Just good to see yer back, mate."'

Wilson noticed that some of the 'lads' were a bit hyper and kept disappearing to the gents at regular intervals. When he asked one old associate what they were up to, the man put his fingertip to his nostril and said, 'Fuckin' idiots are on the gear.' Wilson shook his head slowly and smiled. This was yet more evidence that cocaine was here to stay, and he needed to get his skates on if he was going to cash in on it.

English life had changed drastically for the better since Wilson's incarceration in 1968. The rigid distinctions in dress and manner between one class and another had given way to an informality that he would take some time adjusting to. Some of his fellow robbers, who'd got out before him, still seemed unsettled, but he quickly slipped back into domestic life with ease. He was soft and indulgent with all his daughters, one having married and had children. There were the usual clashes with one who remained at home about clothes and lifestyle. But the Wilson family managed to pick up the pieces very well, all things considered.

Wilson did notice that Pat had changed to a certain degree – she was far more streetwise and savvy than before his recapture in Canada. Pat was also not quite so prepared to give her husband complete, unquestionable support. She wanted to know more about what he was up to because she didn't want him to be put away, never again. Not that he took much notice. He was soon popping out until all hours and it became clear to Pat that in reality there was little she could do to alter his criminal habits. Her tendency to stay in seemed to grow almost as fast as Wilson's insistence that he would not stop his criminal activities and womanising.

21/

By the time Charlie Wilson had been released from prison in 1978, the level of corruption in Scotland Yard's Flying Squad had reached such an epidemic that rumours began circulating in police and underworld circles that officers had been indirectly involved in at least three actual robberies. It was far from the days of Tommy Butler – the image of the Flying Squad as courageous men dedicated to upholding the law had taken a battering. Detectives were often viewed with as much suspicion as the criminals they dealt with.

Wilson heard that some of London's finest had cocaine habits, fed by the drugs they confiscated while pursuing some of the most notorious bank robbers in British criminal history. But he still looked at the police and, in particular, the Flying Squad as the enemy, no matter what they got up to. He would only ever help them to divert attention from his own activities and ensure a degree of protection from prosecution. Many detectives would either turn a blind eye in return for a cut of the action or –

if information led to the recovery of stolen property – reward money that detectives would claim on the informant's behalf, as well as a proportion of whatever was recovered. There were even said to be strategically placed officers who could, for a fee, ensure bail was granted, and hold back evidence and details about past convictions from a court. They would pass details of a case to those under investigation, and warn of police operations.

By the end of the 1970s, Scotland Yard finally decided the Flying Squad should be completely overhauled. Instead of dealing with serious crimes in general, they'd tackle armed robberies only, with the squad's officers forming a central robbery squad based within a coordinating unit inside Scotland Yard, and four smaller groups strategically placed around London. Their corruption problems were further evidence for Wilson that the old enemy occupied the same moral ground as the very people they were supposed to be bringing to justice. And he was far from convinced that the Flying Squad would suddenly become honourable and honest overnight.

Meanwhile, waiting in the wings was the nation's security service, MI5, on the lookout for new areas to add to its empire. MI5 had already informed the Home Office that it considered itself ably equipped to tackle major organised crime, but was unwilling to share its secrets with the police, who they didn't trust.

Charlie Wilson was himself now participating in the occasional gold scam and some reasonably profitable cannabis deals. They lined his pockets with cash but didn't provide the big money he lusted after. His efforts to enter the lucrative cocaine market had come to nothing. He'd discovered that South Americans were even more suspicious of so-called gringos than the British were of foreigners. He was going to have to prove himself as a serious player before he could enter the cocaine underworld. For the moment, he had to bide his time. He needed to find a direct route to the cocaine barons in Colombia. He believed that once he got to them directly then he'd easily convince them to allow him to become a player.

In March 1980, Wilson was ordered to pay tax on a thirty-thousand-pound fee that Pat had received from the *News of the World* for articles published twelve years earlier. Pat and the children had still officially been residents in Canada at the time, and the couple had assumed they were exempt. Wilson was infuriated that this decision came from judicial supremo Lord Denning, Master of the Rolls, who'd earlier turned down Charlie's appeal against his original sentence before his escape from Winson Green prison. Denning sat with Lord Justice Walker and Lord Justice Dunn, and said people 'regretted the practice of some newspapers in paying money to criminals or their wives so as to get a sensational story to publish'. But the overriding message to Charlie was, 'It's legal and the payments are taxable.' Wilson saw it as yet more evidence that the Establishment was still after him, even twenty years on. Meanwhile, the London he now frequented was starting to be filled with stinking rich bankers and Tory toffs all having a much better time than they deserved. Many of these filthy rich characters seemed almost as amoral as the criminals from his own heyday. They were getting away with things he'd never have even dared back in the day, while he was being 'fucked' by the system. Many of these 'arrogant bastards' were splashing their money on bags of cocaine to feed their decadent lifestyles.

Instead of rolling over and conceding defeat, Charlie gritted his teeth and said to himself, 'Fuck 'em all. I'm gonna take these bastards for every penny they've got.' He started to put more feelers out. He wanted to meet the real cocaine cartel chiefs of Colombia.

22/

Charlie and Pat Wilson lived in a small first-floor flat in a quiet street in suburban Twickenham, just west of London. He was still obsessed with keeping a low profile, and he wouldn't have splashed out on a big mansion, even if he could have afforded it.

Wilson assured his parole officer his move was further proof that he was still going straight. But the truth was that Wilson had a lot of schemes up his sleeve and didn't want loud-mouthed regulars in his old haunts knowing what he was up to. He did hook up with one old friend, fellow Great Train Robber Roy James, still known to many as 'the Weasel', thanks to his short stature and propensity for wearing the most ludicrous fur coats. James had proved to have good contacts when it came to their gold VAT scam.

Over the following few months, Charlie and Roy James personally imported more than 76,000 Maple Leaf gold coins, issued by the government of Canada, and Krugerrands – South African gold coins. These were VAT-exempt and melted down to swindle HMRC of 15 per cent tax, exactly the way Wilson's people had done while he was inside. The haul was worth a total of sixteen million pounds, and was bought legitimately. As one detective said at the time, 'It was a brilliantly simple operation.'

Wilson had no idea that customs' officers were probing the racket, and had been doing so ever since he'd bought his first shipment of gold from inside prison. Scotland Yard detectives, assisting customs men, stopped one taxi in Hatton Garden carrying a passenger and gold bars. Another cab was stopped under similar circumstances the following night and more gold bullion seized. The police knew the former train robbers were up to their old tricks again. On 4 April 1983, Wilson himself was arrested after a couple of junior members of his gang confirmed his role to police. He immediately swore revenge on whoever had grassed him up and, as usual, refused to say a word to police investigators.

He and six other men, including Roy James, were eventually charged with conspiracy to defraud the Customs and Excise department over VAT claims on gold bullion. They were all remanded in custody at Clerkenwell magistrates' court. Wilson was upset, believing he'd been arrested on trumped-up charges linked to the police's hatred of him because of his role in the GTR. But being banged up in Wormwood Scrubs, awaiting trial, didn't stop him offering fellow inmate Tommy Mason five thousand pounds to smuggle a consignment of cocaine from Spain to the UK. Mason later backed out of the deal, but it was a further sign that Wilson was still planning to go through with his plan to become a cocaine baron.

On 7 April 1983, Pat visited with the news that his dad, Bill, had died, never having reconciled with his son. Wilson was lost for words. This was the man who'd single-handedly ensured his son had an inbuilt hatred and mistrust of most men. But at the same time he had desperately wanted to clear the air with his dad and now that would never happen. An application to attend his father's funeral in south London was refused, further fuelling his hatred of the Establishment.

In the middle of Wilson's gold coin-induced 'problems', a historic robbery was carried out in London that threatened to overshadow the exploits of the Great Train Robbery. A week before Wilson heard about his father's death, armed robbers struck at the supposedly impregnable Security Express depot in Shoreditch. Charlie later told associates that he'd had a chance to help finance the job, but had to pull away in the early stages because he was under so much heat from the police. Almost six million pounds was stolen but only a small amount of the money was ever found, despite the company offering a £500,000 reward.

Shortly afterwards, Wilson attended his Old Bailey trial, denying conspiring to defraud HMRC of tax on sixteen million pounds' of gold coins between 1981 and 1982. Two months into proceedings a retrial was ordered by the judge, after new evidence emerged that put the prosecution in some doubt. Wilson had by now spent almost a year in prison on remand and had even begun thinking seriously about escaping again.

Inside, he came across an armed robber pal from Parkhurst, 'Mad Mickey' Blackmore. Blackmore was a bit of a loose cannon but the two men from south London became friendly. Blackmore said that he'd already lined up a massive cocaine deal for his release. 'Drugs, Charlie. That's where all the money is,' he said.

Wilson already knew this only too well. And his problems with the gold scam convinced him that it was time for him to focus entirely on the drugs trade.

A new hearing on the VAT scam began at the Old Bailey in October that year. Meanwhile, towards the end of the following month, a gang of south-east London robbers, well-known to Wilson, raided a Brink's-Mat security warehouse near Heathrow airport. They neutralised alarms and headed for the vault where they found a carpet of drab grey containers, no bigger than shoeboxes, bound with metal straps and labelled with handwritten identification codes. There were sixty boxes in all, containing 2670 kilos of gold bars worth £26,369,778. There were also hundreds of thousands of pounds in used banknotes locked in three safes. One pouch contained traveller's cheques worth $250,000. In the other was a stash of polished and rough diamonds worth at least £100,000. The gang had expected riches but nothing like this. The Brink's-Mat robbery – ruthless in its conception and brilliant in its execution – had just landed them the biggest haul in British criminal history.

In January 1984, Roy James was cleared of involvement in the VAT fraud. Wilson had spent months glaring at the public gallery and the press corps assembled to watch his downfall and remained convinced he was heading for yet another custodial sentence. However, the jury failed to reach a verdict and Wilson was released on bail. The public prosecutor then decided to abandon proceedings because of the not-insignificant matter of public expense, although the charges against Charlie Wilson were to be left on file.

He also secretly agreed with Customs officials that he'd settle a vast outstanding VAT tax bill connected to the scam. The prosecution said HMRC were satisfied with the offer and would no longer prosecute Wilson for the outstanding offence.

He tried to maintain a dignified response outside court. 'I am very relieved,' he told waiting reporters, 'but there will be no champagne celebration – more likely lemonade.'

And newspaper headlines such as SECRET DEAL FREES TRAIN ROBBER ON £2.4 MILLION CHARGE did nothing to cheer him up since they clearly inferred that he had been up to no good. Still, even if his pocket was about to take a real hammering, at least he wasn't on his way back to prison.

23/

Charlie Wilson had just escaped prison by the skin of his teeth, but he was facing a VAT bill of at least £400,000 that destroyed his dreams of a quiet retirement with Pat. Police and customs' officers had deliberately pushed for Wilson to be hit where it hurt most – in his pocket. He would have to hand over the full amount or the gold coin case could go to a third trial.

Wilson was gutted. He'd always considered VAT nothing more than tax, which he'd avoided paying all of his life. His old friend Joey Pyle later recalled, 'I remember bumping into Charlie one day just after the gold coin trial … he had a big fine to pay and he said it was a fuckin' lot of money. He seemed a bit shocked by it.'

Pat was even forced to give evidence regarding her own finances at a bankruptcy hearing in London because HMRC were determined to prove Charlie could afford to pay the settlement he'd reached after the trial. The court heard Pat had £180,000 in her bank account, which was immediately frozen. Charlie sat outside in the corridor throughout the thirty-minute hearing while Pat, shaking and with tears in her eyes, was interrogated by the registrar. Pat later told a friend that her court appearance was one of the most harrowing experiences of her life. She hated being in the spotlight and she was fearful that she might in some way let Charlie down. Fear was the constant theme in her married life, yet Pat refused to let go of Charlie.

Those two trials utterly convinced Wilson yet again that the Establishment was still after him and he became even more defiant. He firmly believed that the long arm of the law would keep chasing him for the rest of his life. He remembered those earlier plans he'd had to move to Spain. It made sense, especially if he could get a hook into the cocaine business. In any case, the recent imprisonment of his fellow train robber Bruce Reynolds on a drugs charge proved to Wilson that it was a matter of now or never.

'Charlie knew others were entering the frame when it came to cocaine and he needed to step up a gear and get himself a piece of the action before it was too late,' one of his oldest friends later said. But Wilson's old enemies the police had other plans for him.

On 4 October 1984, Wilson and his former Parkhurst jail-mate Colin King were arrested for plotting a robbery and being in possession of two sawn-off shotguns. A Flying Squad surveillance team alleged they'd seen Charlie passing a bag containing the two sawn-off shotguns to King in a south London café. According to police, the bag was later seen in a green van parked near King's home in Sidcup, Kent. Detectives also said they found a scrap of paper with three index numbers on it in Wilson's car. The third number, which had a line through it, was the registration of a Group Four money van. Confronted with this evidence, both men were alleged by police to have made full confessions. Wilson was refused bail and found himself back in the slammer yet again. The London underworld was in shock. Why would Charlie Wilson go back to the blagging game? It didn't make any sense.

During the trial three months later it was revealed that the green van was not lockable. The question was, why on earth would anyone leave a bag of guns in an unlocked vehicle? Wilson's defence team reconstructed the police's alleged surveillance of the van and showed they could not have seen what was going on inside it, unless they'd been standing right next to the vehicle. Alan Rawley – QC for Charlie's co-defendant Colin King – told the Old Bailey there'd clearly been 'a fit-up, and a deliberate one'.

Charlie's counsel, Stephen Solley, said 'the real horror in the case' was the piece of paper, bearing vehicle registration numbers, allegedly discovered in Charlie's car. 'That piece of paper was never found,' Solley told the court. 'It is a piece of paper written by an officer knowing, as he did and must have done, that the index number was not only of a Group Four van but another wholly innocent vehicle.' The two other number plates read out in court related to innocent vehicles in Cheltenham. If the line running through the third number was removed it became another Cheltenham-registered vehicle. There were also no fingerprints linking Charlie to the guns or the van.

On 5 June 1985, Charlie and King were cleared of plotting a robbery and having sawn-off shotguns after the prosecution agreed there were 'disquieting features' about the case. A detective sergeant and detective constable involved in Wilson's arrest were later suspended and charged with serious offences. Wilson summed the case up to reporters, 'It was a fuckin' joke. They thought they could fit me up but, thank gawd … they didn't get away with it.'

The attempt to frame Wilson further convinced him that he needed to push through with his cocaine plans and get away from London. He was going to show them that he was cleverer than all of them. Wilson was about to enter the stratosphere when it came to criminality. Going across pavements for a few grand was child's play. He planned to become the richest criminal Britain had ever seen and he'd never again have to get his hands dirty to do it.

For the first time in almost two years, Wilson didn't have to report to the local police station. He planned to take Pat on a special holiday to Spain where he'd just bought an apartment in Nueva Andalucia, near Marbella, on the Costa del Sol. He wanted them to make a full-time move to the sunshine. Pat's heart sunk at the suggestion that she would have to leave her beloved daughters behind in London. Wilson's criminal pedigree was undeniable but would this old-fashioned English gangster really be able to thrive in a chilling new drug-dominated underworld where villains usually shot first and asked questions later? Wilson put it around that he was sick of all the police harassment he'd suffered in London and now planned a quiet life in the sunshine.

Bruce Reynolds later explained, 'Charlie didn't want any aggro. He knew they'd never leave him alone – so off he went to Spain.'

Joey Pyle was even less surprised when Wilson packed his bags. 'He'd had enough. The way the police treated him was a disgrace. He had to get away from London. I never saw him again after he moved. But I knew it was the right move for him.'

The weather was another draw. On the Costa del Sol you could usually expect sun, sun, and yet more sun. The days were long, and nights hot and windy for most of the months of the year. Wilson adored the 40-mile stretch of golden beaches and bars. It was also safer. In the summer of 1978, Spain finally decided the UK was making it too difficult for them to retrieve their fugitives and the extradition agreement between the two countries collapsed. This was good news for many old-school London criminals on the lam from British justice and the Costa del Sol became synonymous with fugitives from the British justice system, but Wilson wasn't overly keen on rubbing shoulders with the most-wanted because he liked to keep a low profile. But at least he himself wasn't actually wanted for any crimes. The 'Costa del Crime' was already a well-used cliché, and the activities of many British criminals were threatening to blow a hole in the idea of a villains' nirvana, but for now the chaps could still enjoy all the pleasures of home – Carling Black Label, bacon butties and the *Sun*. Spain had become a safe haven for runaway English gangsters; close enough for the family to come out and visit yet far enough away to avoid the attentions of the police. Scotland Yard reckoned that within a couple of years there were at least a hundred wanted men on the Costa del Sol.

By the time Charlie and Pat Wilson arrived in the Marbella area, the Costa del Sol had already become spoiled, decadent and dangerous. Some right sleazeballs had popped up alongside the old faces, which was something that was only to be expected in a place where fish and chips were as popular as paella. Wilson immediately adored the country and having the necessary distance from all the old problems of London. Now he could safely sit down and start mapping out his future.

Just across the narrow Strait of Gibraltar from Spain was Morocco, from where vast quantities of cannabis could be smuggled into Britain for a huge profit. Much further away, across the Atlantic Ocean, were plentiful supplies of cocaine, the evil 'marching powder' of South America that was taking over the world. Cocoa plants themselves grew virtually everywhere in the moist tropical climate of the Andes – Peru, Ecuador, Chile, Bolivia and Colombia – but the really good quality produce tended to come from areas not too high above sea level. The growing was never a problem; the biggest challenge for cocaine production was transportation. The drug had been quickening the spirits and brains of some on the continent for at least four thousand years by the time Colombia's deadly drug cartels emerged, in the second half of the twentieth century.

From the leaf, cocaine was turned into paste in laboratories – located close to the fields, meaning the drug could then be shipped far more easily. The paste evolved into a form of cocaine called 'base', 100 per cent pure cocaine alkaloid and very potent. This was too sticky to snort or inject. 'Street' cocaine was what you got when you dissolved base in ether and combined it with acetone and hydrochloric acid. It dried into a white, crystalline substance. The cartels found that pack animals and aircraft were the best ways to move the drugs from their place of origin.

Charlie Wilson had gone out of his way to educate himself about cocaine in prison libraries. Now he needed to pull off something to make the Colombians realise he really was a serious player. He didn't care that the Colombians had a reputation as 'psycho bunnies' prepared to kill their own grannies if they got in the way of profit. His focus was entirely on earning money. He'd never forgotten how, ten years earlier, his Parkhurst cellmate Carlos had explained the economic end of the cocaine business. The combined costs in Colombia added up to less than a thousand dollars per kilo of 100 per cent pure cocaine. This was then sold on for six thousand dollars. Cocaine would go on the wholesale market for $50-60,000 a kilo. It was cut a number of times by dealers down the line to boost the weight and maintain the profit margin. Often, the end product contained no more than 15-20 per cent actual cocaine. Wilson calculated he could sell coke for sixty pounds a gram, meaning a kilo bought for six thousand pounds from Colombia would generate street sales in the UK of £200-300,000.

The cocaine business was already on its way to becoming the sixth largest private enterprise in the American Top 500. Companies like Boeing, Proctor & Gamble, and Chrysler Motors were behind the drug on the rich list of industries. There was so much profit and so many shipments available for US customers that the Colombian cartels had calculated they could afford to lose one third of their product and still make hundreds of millions of pounds in profit each year.

'Money, money, money. It's what makes the world go round, son,' Wilson told one of his oldest friends. And he meant it.

24/

Charlie Wilson was already a shrewd, artful crook when the perfectly timed seismic shift in criminal opportunity presented itself when he and Pat had arrived in Spain. Just as his cellmate Carlos had predicted, the whole of Europe was discovering cocaine. Coke was evolving into the fashionable drug of choice for all backgrounds, rather than just being the exclusive drug for the rich and infamous.

With the US cracking down heavily on the cocaine flooding across its borders, Spain was becoming a new gateway for the world's supply. Wilson had bold plans to be one of the big boys in Europe, controlling the flow into the UK. Approaching middle-age, Charlie Wilson was clearly not one for settling down. He was determined to get a piece of the multimillion-pound industry in his new backyard. He had already had success with softer drugs.

Wilson had been happy to 'buy into loads' of cannabis, frequently part-financing other people's deals and avoiding direct contact with the actual drugs. He would take a 20 per cent stake in large consignments of hash from nearby Morocco. It cost £250 a kilo in North Africa and could be sold in the UK for upwards of four thousand pounds. Once he got a call regarding 15 tons of Lebanese cannabis resin, hidden in a cave on the Costa Brava by a bunch of young wannabes from Kent. He organised a search party to drive up the coast and locate the drugs, stole them and then sold them through to the UK.

Wilson roped in associates, including his old mate Paddy, whose team of smugglers were already so successful they were known inside criminal circles as the 'Organisation'. Paddy and Wilson went back to the fifties when they'd been banged up together in prison. The Organisation were renowned for transporting virtually anything across continents without any problems.

Wilson also met with the Haynes family, notorious drug smugglers. Michael Haynes, from Egham, Surrey, was part of an international family-run drugs ring. Haynes was later arrested on the French border after being tailed from the Costa del Sol. Police found 36 kilos of cannabis hidden in secret compartments beneath his car.

These gangs were extremely adept at persuading innocent, one-off couriers – known as mules – to smuggle drugs by plane, the gangsters often including other smugglers on board with much more valuable consignments of drugs. The mules could be sacrificed to customs inspectors, giving the big-time operators more chance of getting through. Another trick was to get a driver to pick up a seemingly innocent cargo and then tip off the local police. They would arrest the person at the wheel of the lorry who had no idea the concrete blocks – or whatever he was carrying – contained a relatively small amount of cannabis.

'That way the police thought they were winning the battle against drugs while all the big consignments were still getting through,' explained one veteran smuggler.

Having arrived in Spain, Wilson quickly became a banker to one of the large hash-trafficking firms operating between North Africa and Spain. In Marbella slang, small groups dispatching 20 kilos of cannabis a week to Britain were known as 'hash gangs', while those that moved 30 or more kilos were known as 'firms'. There was a huge amount of money at stake and, as one smuggler explained, 'If you fell foul of the people running it, they'd kill you no matter who you were.'

Wilson realised that his cannabis smuggling operations were being watched closely by the world's richest cocaine producers, Colombia's Medellín cartel. He knew they had to be convinced that he had a fully efficient smuggling operation before they'd even consider inviting him to buy their cocaine. The Colombians were impressed that Wilson had such a low profile on the Costa del Sol that the local police had no idea the former great train robber was even living in Spain, but the cartel still told him to keep dealing in hash until they came calling. Then, and only then, would he be invited to join the big boys.

It was frustrating, not least because the physical size of cannabis produce made smuggling more risky. The profits were nowhere near as large as they could be for moving cocaine. But Wilson soldiered on, convinced that he'd soon pass the cartel's test. He made regular, discreet visits to Tangiers in Morocco, avoiding the touristy kasbah and the museum of antiquities to head up into the Atlas Mountains, where 70 per cent of the world's best marijuana was produced.

Back on the Costa del Sol, one of Wilson's neighbours was bank-robber-turned-drug-baron Tony White. South Londoner White, mid-forties and nicknamed the 'King of Catford', had been cleared of involvement in the historic 1983 Brink's-Mat gold bullion robbery. The same Old Bailey jury dubbed him a 'dishonest man with an appalling criminal record' who had come into substantial wealth after the raid. White was suspected of involvement with a number of other notorious blaggings in London. But following Brink's-Mat, White had been sued by insurers Lloyd's in the high court, who named him as one of the gang. He was ordered to pay them millions of pounds in compensation, although no one knew if he ever came up with any of the cash.

White moved to Spain soon after Brink's-Mat. His house on the Costa del Crime, appropriately called the Little White House, was massive and he sent his children to an expensive local British school. White was eventually arrested by Costa del Sol police on money-laundering charges and detectives who raided his mansion found a secret Scotland Yard surveillance report, clearly implying that he had a number of senior British police officers in his pocket.

He had close links to Brian Doran, a Scottish-born criminal who'd once run a travel agency in Glasgow. He was known as 'the Professor' because of his university education and degree in Latin American studies, plus his ability to speak four languages. Doran would be jailed for twenty-five years over cocaine deals worth in excess of thirty million pounds. At the time he was in Marbella he set up a bar where he began to nurture contacts amongst the Colombian cartels. A ton of drugs was found in a house connected to his name, and he fled to Colombia before he could be arrested. It was the Professor's connections to the

Medellín cartel that made him such an important player for criminals like Charlie Wilson. Doran was the first British gringo to be accepted inside the cartel. He cleared the way for other UK and European gangsters to make inroads into the cocaine trade.

Another old mate Wilson linked up with in Spain was one-time Parkhurst resident Mickey Green, former Wembley bank robber turned drug baron. By this time he was already worth many millions, owning eleven yachts, a Rolls-Royce and half a dozen other luxury motors. Green described himself as a car dealer but lived lavishly in a huge villa near Marbella. He also part-owned a nightclub overlooking the marina at Puerto Banus, and spent much of his time cruising the port in his white Rolls-Royce or red Porsche looking for blonde dolly birds. Green was later described by Ireland's Criminal Assets Bureau as one of the world's biggest cocaine traffickers. He became so adept at escaping justice in his days as a notorious London armed robber that he'd been nicknamed 'the Pimpernel' by authorities. He was now also in his mid-forties and had, over the years, been shadowed by UK, Dutch and French law enforcement agencies. There was even a rumour he kept a million pounds in French francs hidden in a box in the flowerbed of his villa.

Back in England, barely a month went by without new seizures and lengthy jail sentences for drugs offences. Amongst the faces getting caught up in the new drugs game were Wilson's train robbery pals Tommy Wisbey and Jimmy Hussey. Wisbey later explained, 'We were against drugs all our lives, but as the years went on, towards the end of the seventies, it became more and more the "in" thing. Being involved in the Great Train Robbery, our name was good. They knew we never grassed anyone, we had done our time without putting anyone in the frame.'

Another old-time robber, Jack Browne, said, 'In the sixties, if you were a drug-taker, you could never be a proper thief. It just wasn't acceptable. But that had all changed by the time Charlie arrived in Spain. The big money was no longer in going across the pavement or holding up a security van – drugs were a far steadier, low-risk option.'

One criminal associate told Wilson, 'Don't worry, my friend. You can get you all the cocaine you want, if you have the money. But you need to get to the head of the cartel if you want the really big shipments.'

25/

Pablo 'El Doctor' Escobar was head of the Medellín cartel, the most powerful group of cocaine gangsters in the world.

They'd been formed in early 1982 after the Colombian guerilla movement M-19 kidnapped a cocaine gangster's sister. In response, the gangsters set up their own group to counter them. Pablo Escobar was one, then a notorious cigarette smuggler and his business partners were Carlos Lehder, José Gonzalo Gacha, Jorge Ochoa and his brothers Juan David and Fabio. Their alliance ensured the Medellín cartel quickly gained an international stranglehold on the cannabis and cocaine marketplaces. Like all cartels, it agreed on things as if they were regular commodity prices. 'It's a bit like General Motors, everything's connected,' explained one old hand from South America.

Lehder had been a pilot flying cocaine in and out of Miami for years when he joined forces with Escobar. He had even bought a deserted island near the Bahamas to use as a transit point for cocaine headed for Florida. Power-hungry Escobar eventually split from his original partners as he became the dominant force in the cartel, trading on the fear and loathing sparked by his ability to order a killing with the flick of a finger.

By the mid-1980s, the Colombian authorities were under US pressure to rid the country of the lawless cocaine gangsters. Pragmatist Pablo Escobar recognised there would be long-term business problems with the lucrative US marketplace. He started seriously thinking about Europe, where a ripe, young market of wealthy, upwardly mobile yuppies were prime potential customers for his product. Eurotrash and cocaine went together as naturally as strawberries and cream.

Enter Charlie Wilson. He believed he could offer more security and more profit for the Colombians than the predominantly Spanish drug lords, who'd been handling European cocaine for the trigger-happy Escobar and his cartel since the early days. Wilson's trump cards were his reputation and his contacts in the UK underworld. He could position himself as the perfect conduit to spearhead the exploitation of the drug in his home market. UK sales of cocaine were still comparatively low and the drug was sold through many different gangs with no clear sales strategy. Wilson knew from his own sources that the Colombians did not want to supply the UK market directly because they believed that, as foreigners, they'd stand out and that would be asking for trouble. The cartel needed a British partner they could trust – a facilitator who knew how to get the drugs into the country safely and in much larger amounts than had been done in the past.

Wilson told the Medellín cartel's main man on the Costa del Sol that he knew who to bribe and who to avoid in the UK. These were the sort of connections the Colombians needed. He had dipped his toe in the water with all those cannabis deals. But now he was in a much stronger position to hammer out a deal with Escobar and his Medellín cartel.

As one old associate later explained, 'Charlie had bided his time like a true professional. He had a plan and he was sticking like glue to it. If he played his cards right, he'd get fuckin' rich beyond his wildest dreams.'

Wilson didn't really care what he had to go through in order to achieve his goal. None of it mattered anymore. Here he was, a slum kid from south London, about to become a powerful world player in one of the most profitable industries in history.

As Charlie Wilson himself would say, 'Can't be bad, can it?'

26/

Many of Charlie Wilson's oldest London associates, now on the Costa del Sol, warned him against joining forces with Pablo Escobar and his Medellín cartel.

One smuggler whom Charlie had known for more than thirty years since they were tearaways together said, 'Don't mess with 'em, Chas. I know what them fuckers are like. I wouldn't piss in their mouths if their throats were on fire. Keep away from them, for fuck's sake.'

But Charlie and a handful of others from the British underworld ignored the warnings and were out to make their fortunes from drugs. Meanwhile, their old, burned-out contemporaries were left happily wallowing in the sun with a pint of lager in one hand and a rolled-up note in the other.

At the same time, Wilson began to be close with shadowy Irish drugs baron Brian Wright. Wright was born and bred in London's Irish community in Kilburn, and started work as a bookies' runner. He had first met Wilson when he'd worked as a teenager at the Charterhouse club, owned by London crime king Billy Hill in the early sixties. In just twenty years, Wright had become a phenomenally successful gambler, well-known at virtually every racetrack in the UK. Wright had a house near Wilson in Spain and frequently invited his friend to fly back to the UK from Marbella to use his private boxes at various racecourses across southern England.

A court would later hear that Wright's criminal network was responsible for importing up to 2 tons of cocaine a year. Yachts were bought and subcontracted back to smugglers and Wright was said to be 'swimming in money'. He handled the cocaine for Pablo Escobar's rival, the Cali cartel, after the two groups reached an agreement to carve up the big cities in the US between them to avoid a war. Wright didn't mind advising Wilson because his deal with the Cali cartel was rock-solid. But he did warn Wilson that the characters who ran the Medellín cartel needed to be watched like hawks, especially Escobar.

Wright told Wilson that cartel members used light aircraft to parachute cocaine drops of up to 600 kilos a time to waiting boats. Smaller speedboats would then take the produce to shore. Ocean-going yachts and other larger vessels in the Caribbean, off Venezuela and South Africa were also used for long-haul journeys. As well as advising on life in Spain and who the emerging players were, Wright also introduced Wilson to Ronald Soares, a middle-aged Brazilian who had a direct line of communication to the Medellín and Pablo Escobar.

Unknown to Wilson, there were problems brewing on the Costa del Sol. The King of Catford had been flashing his cash around and UK Customs and Excise investigators now had Tony White and his associates in their sights as part of the ongoing investigation into the whereabouts of the proceeds of the twenty-six-million-pound Brink's-Mat robbery. The customs operation had started as a fairly routine monitoring job of at least a dozen names, until it became clear that there were some huge drug deals going down which were being financed by the missing gold.

Law enforcement had flagged up the involvement of Wilson and White's new Colombian-based friend the Professor, who was now working as a consultant for the Medellín cartel. He had become a big fish whose name was also known to the US Drug Enforcement Administration (DEA). And then there was Medellín chief Pablo Escobar, already a prime target for at least half a dozen law enforcement agencies from across the globe. But Escobar was a wily operator and ruled Medellín with an iron fist. The cartel even had local and national politicians, as well as the police, in their pockets. Escobar was not in any way a washed-up, stoned hippy, even though his own personal drug of choice was hash and he usually had a joint in his hand most times of the day and night. On the contrary he was a cold, calculating corporation chief who liked to control every aspect of his business.

One Medellín expert explained, 'Escobar was already actively looking for new partners in Spain whom he could trust. He also knew that the UK was potentially a massive marketplace for cocaine.' Escobar knew about Charlie through Soares and Doran, as well as the cartel's people in southern Spain, who were still watching to see if Wilson was the real deal.

One cartel member later explained, 'No one can just walk in and expect to buy large amounts of cocaine from a Colombian cartel. You have to earn their respect and their trust.'

At length a Medellín cartel agent stopped Wilson in a busy shopping mall near Malaga. He was informed he had passed all their initial tests. 'Then Charlie did something very clever,' one of his closest associates later explained. 'Instead of pushing to immediately purchase a shipment through the Medellín people in Spain, he insisted on flying to Colombia to meet Escobar and his associates personally.'

At first the cartel's people on the Costa del Sol refused the request. But then Wilson got hold of Brian Doran and promised him a sizeable fee if he put his request in directly to the richest and most powerful drug dealer in the world. Doran had no hesitation in recommending Charlie to Pablo Escobar. Charlie Wilson's legendary reputation preceded him.

27/

In late 1984, US law enforcement agents were watching the cocaine cartels in Colombia. They matched Charlie Wilson's description to a man who flew into Bogota from Europe and then travelled to Pablo Escobar's estate Hacienda Nápoles.

The estate included a private zoo and was located between the Colombian capital and Medellín. But Wilson and Escobar were said to have clashed so badly during their first meeting that Charlie stormed out of the drug baron's vast ranch. He later admitted that he'd taken a 'fuckin' big risk' losing his temper with Escobar, who was suspicious that their deal might have been orchestrated by the rival Cali cartel, through their gringo, Brian Wright. Wilson was outraged that the Colombians would think he was being set up by his friend and also annoyed that they'd been spying on all his movements for months.

Escobar's own resident gringo, Brian Doran – the Professor – was sent to persuade Wilson to return to the meeting. 'In fact, Pablo was impressed by Wilson's toughness,' one source later recalled. Escobar was proud of the way he had worked his way up from the bottom. He had earned money by digging up grave memorials, grinding off the inscriptions, and selling the gravestones to people in the market for cheap funerals. 'Pablo later said he recognised in Charlie much of the same characteristics as he had himself. They were both fearless and strong and from poor backgrounds. But they also had soft centres, or so Escobar liked to think at that time.'

Wilson had thought this would be the case. He was the ultimate gambler and he had calculated that the Colombian drug lord would trust him more if he challenged his authority during that first meeting. He also wanted to demonstrate loyalty to Brian Wright, who was innocent of any double-dealing. Escobar was always impressed when business partners showed loyalty to their friends.

Back in the room together with Escobar, Wilson secured a two-year initial agreement to purchase and distribute cocaine on a vast scale throughout the UK. He would also handle some big shipments destined for other parts of western Europe. This was part of Escobar's plan to diffuse the threat from Reagan's administration by showing the Colombians didn't even need the USA to make their billions.

Wilson later told a friend that Escobar ordered him to get himself a team of 'ambassadors' in the UK, Spain and Holland to represent his interests from the moment shipments of Medellín cocaine began arriving in Galicia, northern Spain. As one old-time villain in Spain explained, 'You needed these type of people because they helped you distance yourself from any problems with the police, customs and suppliers. They were the front men, in a way.'

No one knows if Wilson fully appreciated the enormity of his achievement in pulling off the deal by going into the wolf's lair. 'Many had turned up in Colombia and never been seen again,' said one former cartel member. 'Yet here was this old gringo, and he'd just been given carte blanche to handle more Medellín cocaine than anyone else in the world.'

Wilson stayed in a hotel on the outskirts of Medellín, a place where kids were hired to do any and all jobs for the drug lords. Their briefs included working as *sicarios* (assassins). These cold-blooded youths used motorcycles and worked in pairs: the driver would pull up alongside the car of their intended victim, and the *sicario*, riding pillion, would empty his machine pistol into the vehicle before the pair took off in the chaos of the city traffic.

Even for a hard-case such as Charlie, the level of danger in Medellín must have been a bit disturbing. The number of violent deaths in the city during the mid-eighties was more than five thousand a year – twenty times the murder rate of London, that then had a population seven times the size. Medellín was teeming with hustlers, smugglers, con-men and wheeler-dealers, ranging from one-legged beggars who flagged down tourists in taxis to pickpockets and sharpsters pushing stolen TV sets along the street. And at the centre of it all was cartel kingpin Pablo Escobar, allegedly so wealthy that he'd been said to have offered to personally pay off Colombia's national debt of thirteen billion dollars if the government would leave him alone. It was said that the Medellín cartel was earning seven million dollars a day from cocaine.

What Charlie Wilson perhaps didn't fully appreciate was that he was now personally dealing with a character many had already dubbed the devil. The same man who ordered an employee to smuggle a briefcase onto a crowded airliner without telling him it contained dynamite set to explode in midair. The same boss whose employees were caught trying to buy 120 Stinger anti-aircraft missiles in Florida.

During Wilson's short trip, Escobar assigned him a personal bodyguard, 'Popeye', later thought to have been responsible for killing dozens of Escobar's enemies. Wilson assumed Popeye primarily kept an eye on him, but he also knew no one would take a pot-shot as long as he was alongside him. On their second night, Popeye drove him to a restaurant on the outskirts of Medellín where Escobar hosted a special dinner in Wilson's honour. It was said that it was on this occasion that Escobar and Popeye first began calling their new gringo partner 'Narco Charlie'. Escobar thought it was highly amusing for the association of 'Charlie' with the slang for cocaine.

As Wilson returned to southern Spain, law enforcement agents in the UK, US and Spain began to take a much closer look at this man who seemed to have the ear of the world's most dangerous criminal. The US's DEA had been watching the Professor for more than a year in Colombia and had already confirmed Wilson's identity following his visit. Wilson had known he'd be flagged after going to Colombia, but it was worth the risk and, in any case, he was going to take Escobar's advice and distance himself from direct involvement with the cocaine itself.

Wilson was now on a mission to make tens of millions of pounds. Escobar agreed. He told one associate in Medellín that he believed Wilson would become the godfather of European cocaine-trafficking.

But there was still much work to be done.

28/

Charlie Wilson's first move after his return from Colombia was to meet the all-important Dutch connections that Escobar had made a point of mentioning.

Wilson contacted Netherlands-based former armed robber Roy 'the Lump' Adkins, who he'd known when they were both in Parkhurst prison. Adkins introduced Wilson to his boss, Klaas 'the Preacher' Bruinsma, in Amsterdam. The city had been chosen as the base for a complex network of violent, international drug traffickers because of its close proximity to Rotterdam, Europe's biggest and busiest port. The Netherlands had evolved into a key hub for drugs coming from Pakistan, South America and North Africa – and just about any location throughout the world. Most of the drugs did not stay long in the Netherlands before being distributed around Europe to be sold on the streets for vast profits.

The Preacher was alleged by law enforcement to be one of the six most powerful drug barons in the world. He'd also personally killed a number of those involved in the industry and was suspected of ordering hits on at least half a dozen more.

In the late 1970s, Bruinsma had joined forces with Adkins, who had a wide circle of contacts in the British underworld. Adkins always kept one step ahead of the UK police and had been deeply involved in narcotics trafficking for years. 'Roy was known as the Lump because that's what he was. He wasn't a subtle sort of fella. He just charged in, all guns blazing,' explained one of Charlie's oldest associates.

Adkins had operated first from Spain before moving to Holland, when he and Bruinsma set up phoney businesses in such countries as Morocco and Pakistan as cover to ship narcotics through Holland. The two men were careful not to pack entire lorries with drugs, preferring instead to divide the produce amongst a number of smaller vehicles.

Adkins was a much more abrasive character than he had been when Wilson first met him in prison more than ten years earlier. Paranoia was fuelled by his own vast intake of cocaine. He'd also had a few problems with one Colombian cocaine-smuggling gang, who'd accused him of ripping them off. Despite the smiles when they met again, Adkins was irritated that Wison thought he could just waltz in and get into bed with Escobar and the Medellín cartel and make millions when he had been risking life and limb for years in the game. There was also the matter of a shipment of Adkins' hash – this was the same delivery that Wilson's boys were rumoured to have stolen from a cave on the Costa Brava a few months earlier. Adkins didn't have concrete evidence Wilson was behind the raid but his young hoods insisted he was involved. For now, he was content to play along with Wilson.

Adkins was in league with another London criminal, 'Mad Mickey' Blackmore. Wilson had also met him while in Parkhurst, as well as Brixton and Hull prisons. Adkins and Blackmore had direct links to Wilson's Costa del Crime associate Tony White and there were rumours that some of the gold from the Brink's-Mat heist was being offered in payment for shipments of cocaine from Colombia. Wilson's alleged connections to other UK criminals had put him even more firmly in the sights of customs' investigators and members of the National Drugs Intelligence Unit, as well as drug investigation authorities overseas. The Spanish government were not enthusiastic about having any foreign law enforcement units on their territory, but they were even more irritated by the presence of so many British criminals.

The US's DEA were capable of putting entire gangs of criminals under constant surveillance. This involved staking out their secret meeting places, eavesdropping on their conversations in the street, photographing diary entries and uncovering secretive money transfers across the world. They could even trace bank accounts under false names to places as far afield as Geneva and the Caymen Islands. The operation to watch people like Wilson, White, Green and Doran would require the most sophisticated surveillance techniques and the UK's Customs and Excise officers called upon the DEA's expertise to help them shadow their targets. Wilson and others on the Costa del Sol knew the UK police were in Spain watching their movements. But they had no idea about the other agencies at this time.

The weak link in the chain proved to be the Spanish police. Whenever Charlie Wilson needed to know about Scotland Yard's movements, he just picked up the phone and spoke to a man who in turn spoke to one of three Spanish police officers based on the Costa del Sol in exchange 'for a beer'. Wilson had heard many times how badly the British police and their Spanish counterparts got on. The local police were considered slow, dogmatic and ill-equipped to deal with the wealthy drug barons who had relocated to the area. The new police station in Marbella embodied everything their foreign counterparts disliked. It remained unfinished and its completion was five years behind schedule. The old cop shop at the back of town was 'like something out of a spaghetti western', according to one British police officer who visited in the mid-1980s. 'The boss used to come into the station at about 10 o'clock in the morning. It was a struggle for him to get up the stairs. He used to sit at his desk, light a "lah-di-dah" [marijuana cigarette] and examine the solitary piece of paper in his in-tray for a while. Then he'd walk back down the stairs, go into the café next door and get a large brandy and a coffee, and stand there playing the fruit machines. After that he would go home for his siesta. Sometimes he would reappear at teatime and do another two minutes' work.'

Spanish police equipment at this time was also notoriously antiquated, as were the wages the officers received. Many in the police in Marbella also genuinely believed that the British criminals were bringing much-needed money into the region and that meant jobs for the locals, so why not leave them alone? Police officers from the UK had the overall impression that the Spanish were resentful and many officers believe to this day that there should have been a British police station in southern Spain. Simple tasks such as checking a British-registered vehicle were an administrative nightmare for the Spanish that took up to four weeks, when UK law enforcement officers managed to complete the same job in a few minutes.

British police were also restricted because a suspect in a police station in Spain would have to be interviewed by a Spanish officer while their British counterparts waited in another room. But it was the leaking of the movements of British officers in Spain to Wilson and other criminal faces on the Costa del Sol that really made the UK police's blood boil and it was in this atmosphere that Wilson's old enemies in the Flying Squad tried to keep tabs on numerous familiar criminal faces. No wonder Charlie Wilson and others believed they could remain one step ahead of the boys in blue.

The first team of London detectives to start gathering evidence about the activities of Charlie and his associates returned home in 1985 with numerous pages of reports. But they could do little without actually catching these high-powered criminals in the act of committing a crime.

Wilson was able to meet up once again with Indian drug smuggler Surya Krishnarma. They'd first got to know one another in Long Lartin prison almost ten years earlier. Krishnarma had since been getting to know a lot of the British criminals on the Costa del Sol. Wilson had always been impressed by Krishnarma's knowledge of drugs, as well as his high-powered criminal connections in the narcotics trade. Krishnarma soon became a regular breakfast-time caller at the Wilsons' apartment in Marbella.

Another visitor was old south London friend and master-smuggler, Paddy and his wife Julie, who regularly flew over from their home in Kent. Paddy later admitted he was quite envious of Wilson. 'It was a good lifestyle and he didn't seem to have none of those problems with the law like you got back home. Charlie in his suntan seemed to have the perfect setup to me.' Wilson and Paddy usually had a bit of business to discuss, and would first have dinner with their respective wives before slipping off to Puerto Banus where many of the bars were filled with familiar faces.

Pablo Escobar and his associates back in Medellín hadn't realised that Wilson was by this time under round-the-clock international law enforcement surveillance. Many believe that had they known, the long-term cocaine deal they'd agreed in South America would have been dropped like a stone. But the cartel had other things on their minds between 1985 and 1986. Escobar was commissioning multiple contract killings of politicians, police officers and other public figures in Colombia. He'd become in effect the de facto ruler of the city of Medellín. But in order to maintain his power, his men were constantly asserting themselves within the community. They thrived on a climate of fear, which meant that few residents in Medellín would ever stand up to Escobar's rule of terror. His plan to flood Europe and the UK with cocaine seemed like a masterstroke.

The Americans had, as expected, cut off much of the Colombian cocaine supply routes through the Caribbean. This had forced shipments of cocaine to go through Mexico to reach the US. Escobar knew this would eat away at his profit margins because the cartel would have to pay huge shipping costs to the new Mexican cartels, who controlled all the supply routes into the US. But Escobar and his cronies weren't worried because criminals like Charlie Wilson were buying big loads of cocaine for Europe and the UK. Soon the USA would no longer be the largest marketplace.

Escobar still hoped that by cutting back on supplying so much cocaine to the US, the DEA might relax their campaign to bring him to justice. And the DEA did start to seem more interested in characters such as Panama's despot dictator General Noriega, who was alleged to be a cocaine middleman between the Colombian cartels and US gangsters distributing cocaine. Yet the US priority remained cutting off the snake's head in Colombia. They did want Escobar to believe they were easing off on him. But in reality there was no way they would ever cease hunting the world's most powerful and dangerous cocaine producer.

'El Doctor' was still firmly in their sights.

29/

In the summer of 1986, Charlie Wilson held a meeting with a Medellín cartel accountant at the Atalaya Park hotel, just off the main N340 coast road, west of Puerto Banus, Costa del Crime.

Neither of them realised a DEA agent was sitting across from them in the lobby, watching and monitoring every word. But the DEA had no idea who Wilson was at the time; photos of the former great train robber in Colombia had not arrived at the agency's Malaga office.

Wilson's meeting was with a man who had all the usual Colombian features; pale white skin, lots of dark wavy hair and a small moustache. He was immaculately dressed, wore a gold chain around his neck and a chunky Rolex on his right wrist. Wilson was asked back to a cartel-owned house in the hills behind Puerto Banus, near Marbella's bullring. It was a large, two-storey, stucco-fronted hacienda with a red-tiled roof. The cartel had taken over the property from a Spanish cocaine dealer who owed them money. In the gated driveway sat an assortment of Ferraris, Lamborghinis and Rolls-Royces, while the back garden sported an Olympic-sized swimming pool. Around it were at least a dozen women in various stages of undress. They were all dripping with gold, emeralds and diamonds. Nearby, a group of men were sitting nearby at a card table playing poker.

Soon after arriving at the house, Wilson met in an upstairs office with the cartel accountant, who suggested that he re-invest some of his earnings in a series of legitimate businesses recently set up by the Colombians in Spain. Wilson tactfully declined their kind offer, knowing only too well that the next time they came back to him it might be with an offer he couldn't refuse. He later told a friend that he'd really wanted to tell the Colombians to 'fuck off', but realised that would probably be a stupid thing to do in their own backyard.

Also in attendance that day was Pablo Escobar's new European chief, a thirty-five-year-old known as 'the Mexican'. He organised numerous shipments from Colombia and lived in a beautiful former monastery, 20 miles south of Valencia, with his wife and their two young children. The Mexican also owned numerous other residential and commercial properties in Spain and regularly made vast money transfers to offshore bank accounts. He'd been personally ordered by Escobar to keep an eye on 'Narco Charlie' because the boss still suspected that Wilson was in contact with the Cali cartel. They sold cheaper cocaine than the Medellín clan. These rumours were never substantiated and Wilson later claimed they had been started by British gangsters who were jealous of his deal with Escobar and hated Brian Wright, who worked for Cali.

This was the dicey state of life for Narco Charlie in Spain. He was in foreign territory, and not just in a geographical sense. In many ways, he was on his own. It made him feel more vulnerable in one sense, but also much freer in another. He didn't have access to any number of old-school criminals for protection and he was outnumbered by the established South American operators.

Some sixty thousand Colombians entered Spain each year, perfectly legally, the country being the only one in Europe that did not require a visa from Colombia. Madrid had become a haven for South American drug bosses who were regularly involved in bloody gun battles. They had a carefully planned strategy for everything: after any arrest, the networks simply regrouped and business went on as usual. Everything was arranged by telephone in carefully worded code. The cocaine supply chain from Colombia to the Caribbean was now closed, thanks to the DEA, and the Colombians instead delivered their drugs to Spanish fishing boats, which met cartel vessels in the middle of the Atlantic.

The boats would head to the jagged, lawless coastline of Galicia, in north-west Spain, where these so-called motherships would be greeted by fast launches or smaller fishing boats waiting just offshore to pick up the merchandise. It was this place that ancient mariners had once believed was the end of the Earth itself; the rocky Galician inlets, swept by incessant drenching winds. Now the smuggling vessels relied on narrow landing spots along the mostly deserted 700 kilometres of coastline.

Such activity was nothing new – many of the pueblos on the western coast had suffered in the sixteenth and seventeenth century from attacks by English and Turkish pirates, and the presence now of a few drug smugglers drew little or no attention. In any case, police chiefs and mayors in the Galicia region were in the pockets of the Colombians. Laureano Oubina, a vineyard owner, frequently hired boats to collect cocaine from Costa Rica, Panama and Venezuela. He would later be imprisoned for his role in smuggling. One Colombian alleged to be the boss of bosses, José Ramón Prado Bugallo, was also later arrested in Galicia when 5 tons of cocaine was seized on a mothership off the coast.

After arrival on the Spanish mainland, the drugs were often stashed in caves or seaside pueblos that had aerated storage buildings raised on stilts. These were designed to prevent rats getting into precious grain, vegetables and fruit preserved for the severe winters and were ideal hiding places for narcotics. Associates from Madrid would arrive to collect the produce in a car, take their cut, sell the drugs on and remit the profits in US dollars to their bosses back in Colombia. The rest of the money would be shared among the sailors and the distributors. The cocaine would be transported throughout Europe, often disguised in cans of hake and shellfish.

Charlie Wilson knew all about Galicia through his associates on the Costa del Sol. They'd regularly send scruffy-looking soldiers up in campervans to take delivery of drugs that were then taken through France and across the Channel. Demand for cocaine and cannabis had skyrocketed, resulting in even higher prices than in the US. Cocaine bought for £1,000 per kilo in Colombia was sold for £20,000 per kilo in Galicia.

In late 1986, Wilson journeyed to Spain's northernmost coastline in Galicia to hammer out a deal that would cut out the middlemen that Escobar and his cartel had insisted he deal with. The first big surprise was the weather; temperatures in Galicia were more akin to the most remote parts of Wales than the Costa del Sol. More concerning was the purpose of his trip, which could have been very dangerous for him – some would say to a foolhardy extent – if Escobar and his Medellín men interpreted it as an attempt to cut out one of the cartel's main partners.

There was another potential hazard in Wilson's move. Only a few weeks earlier, Spanish customs officials had boarded a rusty old trawler some 60 miles off the coast near Vigo and seized a ton of cocaine. It was a rare victory for law enforcement and seemed to show that not even Galicia was completely beyond the law, although it was nothing more than a drop in the ocean compared to the amount of drugs travelling through this inhospitable corner of Spain.

Wilson was well aware of the risks he was taking. But he'd grown increasingly frustrated by the way the middlemen took a huge chunk of every deal while simply overseeing the transfer of cocaine once it arrived on Spanish soil. He wanted Escobar to agree to cut out these middlemen and allow his gangsters to collect the cocaine as it reached shore in northern Spain. He got a message along those lines to Escobar and had been advised to head to Galicia to deal direct with the men in question.

'It just shows how confident Charlie was becoming at this stage,' one associate later explained. 'Most villains would never dare take on someone like Escobar but Charlie didn't give a fuck.'

Wilson was increasingly confident moving in the local underworld. Some Spaniards and Colombians didn't even know he was British. He dressed more like a local, casual brown jackets, jeans and flowery shirts. He also spoke Spanish reasonably well.

'Charlie had turned into a right fuckin' chameleon,' said one old-school Costa del Crime criminal. 'He didn't look anything like a British villain no more. He was smooth, tanned and looked as fit as a fiddle, even though he did often have to pause for breath because of his emphysema.'

Wilson's first stop was, bizarrely, an ice-cream parlour in the village of Cambados, near Vilagarcia. This community was one of those that had got fat and rich thanks to drugs. Its roads were lined with mansions of staggering luxury, sprouting fat radio antennae behind spiked granite walls inset with electronically controlled gates. There were also brand-new restaurants and nightclubs, most of which had undoubtedly been built with drug money. Wilson was driven to another village, Vilanova de Arousa, past its tiny harbour and on to a neighbouring coastal area. This was where he was to meet the cartel's local contact.

DEA sources say Wilson met Carlos Goyannes, a high-society playboy and the link between the Colombians, Galician smugglers and Spain's 'coca jet set', the middlemen who handled the shipments of cocaine. It was this last group of men who had become such bugbears for Wilson. But Goyannes surprised Wilson, almost immediately agreeing in principle to a special deal that meant he could pick up his cocaine from the Galician coastline as it came ashore without using those very same middlemen. This meant that Escobar and his Medellín cartel had decided to grant Wilson his wish, knowing in doing so that they could also save money.

However, there was one big obstacle for them all to deal with.

30/

'Narco' Charlie Wilson was working towards taking out a whole layer of cocaine smuggling management. He had a successful meeting in Galicia but was told that if he really wanted to pick up the cocaine himself in the area, he would have to shake hands with ETA, the Basque separatist organisation. Their brutal campaign to establish an independent region made Ireland's IRA look like a bunch of schoolkids.

ETA's people were notoriously cold, dedicated killers who'd slaughtered upwards of five hundred people in a fifteen-year war against the Spanish government. They had been using the drugs trade in much the same way as the IRA had done in Northern Ireland, to help finance their terror cells. One group of Wilson's old associates on the Costa del Sol had formed an uneasy alliance with ETA in the early 1980s to smuggle contraband through northern Spain. That agreement had ended when ETA killed two British gangsters because they believed they'd been cut out of a drugs deal.

A British smuggler later recalled, 'ETA muscled in on the drugs business to raise funds for their campaign. They'd turn up at meetings and say, "You're workin' with us". There was no "please" or "thank you".'

One retired smuggler explained, 'We all thought ETA would just be a bunch of college kids. But they're colder and tougher than most criminals because they have a cause. It's not just about money with them ... ETA's motivation was always to buy enough weapons to kill as many Spanish government officials and politicians as possible.'

On one occasion, a beautiful brunette called Maria – known as 'the Tigress' in the Basque country – pulled a gun on two British gangsters during a heated meeting about drug shipments in a Marbella hotel room. The ETA member was later alleged to have been involved in twenty-four murders, including the deaths of seventeen members of Spain's Guardia Civil police.

Wilson had to cut a deal with this uncompromising group to get his drugs safely through northern Spain, otherwise the Colombians would never go through with their part of the agreement to drop the layer of local handlers. He recruited a North-African woman with connections to two senior members of ETA, who were responsible for fundraising. She also became one of Wilson's lovers and helped him hammer out a cash-per-shipment agreement with ETA. In private, Wilson admitted he had severe reservations about dealing with terrorists but, for the moment, he had no choice. He believed that he'd set up a supply route that would earn him three times the money he'd made through the previous system.

Back in Medellín, Escobar begrudgingly acknowledged Wilson's *cojones* and later explained that his sole intention had been to double the amount of cocaine being smuggled into the UK. This simply meant keeping everyone – including Narco Charlie – happy. At the same time, he unsubtly reminded Brian 'the Professor' Doran that it was he who had first set up the deals with Narco Charlie, and it was the Professor who would be responsible if anything went wrong. Doran contacted Charlie and told him to 'keep it clean', or Escobar would come after both of them.

Everything was now in place to ensure Charlie Wilson could become an extremely rich man.

Wilson's status as an up-and-coming drugs baron was soon much talked about in the clubs and bars that criminals frequented in southern Spain. Wilson would have hated to know that his business was now common knowledge but, in a place like the Costa del Crime, it was impossible to keep such things quiet. The DEA and British and Spanish law enforcement agencies were also aware of events. They were not only watching all this from a distance but also being given regular updates by informants inside the Spanish underworld. There were rumours that the DEA had secretly and unofficially opened a 'branch office' inside a newly created US bank office in Marbella. Some also alleged that DEA agents thought themselves above the law and had taken part in the torture/interrogation of prisoners alongside Spanish drug police.

One of the DEA's most energetic European agents operated out of an office in Madrid. He was authorised to tap Wilson's home phone because it was known by this time that he provided a vital link to the cartel. The agent's wife was also a DEA employee and in the USA she was assisting Scotland Yard in the Brink's-Mat robbery inquiries that had first alerted them to Wilson's Spanish activities. The DEA operation was unofficial at the time and did not even have a code name. Eventually, it drew in law enforcement agents from Holland, Canada, Pakistan, Philippines, Hong Kong, Thailand, Portugal and Australia.

The DEA believed that they could gather enough evidence against characters like Wilson to 'turn' them – forcing them to choose between becoming an informant or facing a heavy prison sentence. What the DEA completely failed to appreciate was that Charlie Wilson's entire criminal ethos was based on never grassing up another villain.

In early 1987, DEA and UK customs' officers in Spain monitored a meeting between Wilson and Doran in a bar in Fuengirola. Doran had slipped into Spain from his base in Colombia. Wilson might have been putting himself more into the spotlight but he wasn't being entirely careless, as one senior customs officer involved in the surveillance operation later explained. 'Charlie was using Doran to smooth things out with Escobar. But he was talking in Cockney rhyming slang a lot of the time, so it was impossible to be certain of anything he was saying. He was clearly being incredibly careful not to say anything incriminating.' The DEA and UK customs were left with no actual concrete evidence when or if a specific cocaine deal was actually going to go ahead.

'Charlie was clever like that. He smelt a rat and covered his back,' explained one of Wilson's oldest associates. 'He told me afterwards he didn't know for sure the feds were listening in but he had this uncanny nose for trouble, which was usually always right.'

For the moment, then, no one had any concrete evidence, as Charlie Wilson continued marching towards his ultimate goal of accumulating untold riches.

31/

Flushed with new funds from a number of recent, highly lucrative drug deals, Charlie Wilson decided to splash out on a villa. His old-school gangster friend Freddie Foreman had heard about a property in a very sought-after area, just behind Marbella, which he mentioned to Wilson when they bumped into each other in a bar.

The Wilsons went to look at the detached house on the Urbanización Montana, directly beneath the mountains that overshadow the Costa del Sol. To the east was Marbella old town and to the west lay the British criminals' favourite haunt, Puerto Banus. The estate was filled with rutted roads and lined with expensive properties hidden behind high walls and security gates. They were protected by surveillance cameras and burglar alarms. It was definitely not the kind of area where you'd ask your neighbour what he did for a living.

The house in question was a rather small, nondescript bungalow but it had a superb quarter acre plot of land and was just far enough back from the road to ensure complete privacy. On the side furthest from the road, the property backed onto a small woodland area that separated the property from a new development of flats being constructed in an adjoining street.

The Wilsons liked the property and Charlie bought it for a bargain twelve million pesetas (£48,000) cash. He planned to spend at least three times that amount to create their dream home, so there was no chance of an early retirement quite yet. Wilson told Foreman the property had 'bags of scope for improvement'. Intriguingly, the house was number thirteen in the street and the previous owner had refused to use the number because it was unlucky. Charlie immediately named the property 'Chequers', after the British prime minister's country residence because, as he later explained, 'The fuckin' government have got all me money.'

Pat gave the impression she was blissfully unaware of her husband's career in crime. She saw the property as the perfect place for Charlie to retire and hoped that, once they settled into the house, Charlie would finally change his ways. She later explained, 'Charlie came here to find peace. We weren't a couple who entertained or joined the so-called Costa del Crime party set. But if we saw any of the English people, it was usually just to say, "Hello", while we were passing in the street. Very rarely did we go to their homes. We lived like a retired couple. Our love for the children, dogs and each other was enough.'

Pat preferred to stay at home and watch all her favourite TV soap operas beamed in from the UK through their huge satellite dish, a permanent eyesore in the garden that also carried her husband's only sporting interest, horse racing. The dish sat next to their newly built swimming pool in a garden that was lovingly cared for by Charlie. He grew a vast assortment of kitchen herbs, including parsley, sage, thyme, rosemary, coriander, basil and mint. He nurtured plants and flowers from classic English roses to chrysanthemums. But neighbours noticed that he was nearly always alone in the garden while Pat remained inside. Perhaps it was no surprise, then, that Charlie was also regularly spotted out and about in Puerto Banus, drinking in the Navy Bar, a block back from the harbour and frequented by a lot of British criminals and opportunistic women.

Wilson hired a beautiful Argentinian architect, Marti Franca, to help rebuild Chequers, transforming it from a small, single-storey home into a mansion. Would-be artist Wilson even provided Franca with drawings of how he wanted the house to look, right down to a sitting room area filled with furniture and an expensive Chinese-style rug. Franca later recalled, 'It took more than a year to rebuild the house and we completely changed the shape of it. Charlie paid cash for everything direct to the builder and my fee at the end.'

Wilson and Franca formed a close bond. He even admitted to her that he'd been a criminal. She later recalled, 'At the beginning

I did not know who Charlie was. Then as we became friends, he said to me, "Marti, I must tell you something before you hear it from someone else and get upset." So he told me he robbed a train and was put in jail for many years. Little by little I got to know the whole story and when I saw Charlie working on his house every day, working, working, working, I started to feel pity for Charlie. Poor man. Years and years of his life in prison. I felt so sorry for him. I even asked where is the money and he said it had all gone. I'm sure he was telling the truth. He said he gave a lot of the money to friends and they took it. But he made a lot of jokes about it. I'd always thought criminals were supposed to be terrible people but he wasn't like that.'

Wilson was always very polite to Franca and it was clear to her that he was a workaholic, always thinking one step ahead. He told Marti he'd paid his dues in jail and had left England because he was being blamed for so many different things. 'He loved that house,' recalled Franca, 'and made it clear he'd never sell it. In many ways it was his life.'

The architect met Wilson's three daughters when they stayed at Chequers in the late summer of 1987. 'They all came over to my house for dinner. He was a good father and they clearly loved him.' Franca was another who was struck by how rarely Pat went out. 'She was always at home and didn't even go out to buy a newspaper. I thought that was a bit strange.'

Wilson employed half a dozen builders full time for many months, spending considerable sums of money in renovating and rebuilding Chequers, transforming it from a pokey little bungalow into a garish hacienda, including bathrooms complete with gold-plated taps and pink marble imported from Portugal. Hand-painted, bone china ornaments and expensive imported Chinese rugs were everywhere. A second storey was added to the property, including two balconies and a turret featuring windows inlaid with coloured glass.

Pat was away in London during a lot of the reconstruction work, which suited her husband perfectly because he wanted to add some very special extras to the house. At one end of the sitting room area he had installed a floor-length mirror with a shelf running across it. Underneath the shelf was a small button that released a secret door that led down to a specially built underground area. This was a small room about 8 foot by 6 foot and not dissimilar from many prison cells that Wilson had called home over the years. A 5-foot-high safe was set into the wall of this secret room, which also had a tiny window large enough to give him a view of anyone approaching the house.

'He never said why he needed it,' recalled Marti Franca of the space. 'The secret door seemed kinda strange, but people have a right to do what they want in their own house and I never questioned it because I sort of knew it was his business and not mine.'

To many of Wilson's neighbours, he was obviously a criminal who was still actively pursuing what he knew best. They noticed many late-night comings and goings at Chequers. Some had even heard about the secret basement he'd had built in the house where he no doubt stored all his ill-gotten gains. Those who visited said there were other strange features in the house. One of his guests recalled, 'Charlie had the main bathroom floor raised above the level of the bedroom, as if he kept something underneath it. The fireplace was also much deeper than the actual fire area but that might just have been down to the design.' In fact, Charlie had secretly built a safe room below the bathroom floor where he could hide if any unwelcome visitors ever showed up. No one knows to this day if Pat knew about this secret room.

'Charlie had thought of everything,' explained one old school associate. 'He told me one day that he believed having that safe room might mean the difference between life and death if the wrong sort of people decided to break his door down. Charlie was constantly thinking about this kind of stuff.'

Charlie Wilson might have been keen to keep a low profile on the Costa del Crime, but some of his underworld contemporaries seemed unable to keep out of the headlines. In 1987, his good friend Mickey Green was named by Spanish police as the criminal mastermind behind an extensive drugs network known as the Octopus. In a series of raids on Green and his associates in Spain, cannabis worth two million pounds, eleven yachts and powerboats, a Rolls-Royce, a Porsche and five other cars were seized, and six of Green's British 'associates' were arrested. Green himself had been tipped off and managed to flee from the Costa del Sol before he could be arrested. He was also wanted for questioning about another VAT gold fraud, similar to the one for which Wilson had almost been imprisoned in 1983.

When Wilson heard about the police raid, he got in touch with Green's 'people' and offered to take all Green's boats and cars off his hands. He was always thinking about how to make a bob or two, whatever the circumstances.

Mickey Green eventually turned up in Paris a few months after his disappearance from the Costa del Crime. Interpol were alerted and French police swooped on Green's tastefully decorated Left Bank apartment – where they found gold bullion and cocaine … but no Mickey Green. His next stop was California, USA, where he rented Rod Stewart's mansion under an alias. A few months later FBI agents knocked down his front door and this time he was to be found on the premises, lounging by the pool, where he was arrested.

Green was put on a flight for France and that jail sentence, but exited when the plane made a stopover at Ireland's Shannon airport. Using an Irish passport, he slipped past customs men and headed for Dublin where he had many contacts. He took full advantage of the weak extradition laws between Ireland and France at the time and settled in Dublin. He was certainly living up to his nickname of the Pimpernel.

Pablo Escobar watched the developments from Colombia with mixed feelings. On the one hand he was amused by the Mickey Green shenanigans, but was also irritated at the amount of publicity surrounding British gangsters. This was definitely not good for business. However, he chose not, for the moment, to change Narco Charlie's deal because Wilson had always paid everything on time and there had been no problems since he persuaded Escobar to cut out those middlemen.

But a different kind of problem was lurking just around the corner.

32/

Dawn might be streaking the Mediterranean with crimson by the time Charlie Wilson's white Toyota with Gibraltar plates nosed its way homewards, through the back streets of Puerto Banus. His working nights were heavy and it could be any time when he would finally get back to Pat and the dogs.

Wilson now rarely went to any business meeting on the Costa del Sol without being armed. His favourite stunt, to make sure those present knew he was packing a weapon, was to greet other criminals with a hug, letting them feel the hard metal of his gun pressing into them. More often than not it had the desired effect. At home in his secret basement room he stored at least three handguns plus a sawn-off shotgun that he'd been looking after for a criminal associate who was doing a five-year stretch back in London. But increasingly, the armoury wasn't there to protect himself from fallouts with major drug cartels – somewhat ironically, given Wilson's career, petty crime was beginning to be a huge irritation for him.

It might seem strange for someone like Charlie Wilson to complain of being on the wrong end of the underworld, yet he was beginning to see a huge change in Spanish society. He said to one friend that he wished the country was still in the grip of dictator Franco, a time when the police had more authority and bad pennies never had a chance to develop into deadly criminals. Charlie Wilson, like thousands of British expatriates, was feeling the impact of living in a free, more liberal Spain. OK, he hadn't come to southern Spain to retire and bask in the 320 days of sunshine a year, or to enjoy a peaceful life. But the problems with other criminals he was starting to encounter did make him wonder if it was all really worthwhile.

He was, in a sense, caught up in the growing pains of an infant democracy. Sure, the living was easy in the whitewashed villas overlooking a rippling blue sea, and the wine and food remained cheap. But the twentieth century was moving on at such a startling pace that the entire area was threatening to turn itself into a seedy, crime-riddled Spanish version of Los Angeles. It was developing appalling traffic problems and a bunch of psycho-bunny criminals could be found on virtually every street corner.

Naturally, Charlie Wilson didn't see himself as one of those types of gangsters. As far as he was concerned, he was a businessman doing what he did best. He didn't want to step on other people's toes. He just wanted to invest his money in his shipments, then reap his reward for taking such big risks. The property sharks, small-time drug dealers and bank-busters showing up on his doorstep in paradise were a constant source of irritation. The old boys from back home were fine, but some of the newer faces really got on his nerves. He even sympathised with local government officials who hated the label 'Costa del Crime'. Wilson wanted to maintain a low profile and any mention of a crimewave in the area was certainly not good for his own business. He was particularly outraged by the way petty crime was creeping into local society on the coast. Muggings were now commonplace in Marbella. Burglary was so rife that anyone in a detached property was advised to keep dogs and a decent burglar alarm with connections to the local police station (Charlie naturally chose just to have dogs).

Add to this potent mix the fact that some of the scumbags Wilson was having to deal with would rob their own granny as soon as look at her and it was no wonder he started to become a little paranoid about life in Spain. 'It's gettin' bad out here. The police need to sort out all this street crime,' Wilson told one old pal, without a hint of irony.

Wilson continued to maintain a lower profile than any other underworld figure, while the Spanish and UK press branded ex-pat criminals Freddie Foreman, Ronnie Knight, John Mason, Ronnie Everett and Clifford Saxe the 'famous five' because of their alleged links to the Security Express heist of 1983. But Wilson had tasted 'fame' after the Great Train Robbery and knew that was both short-lived and also annoyed the police so much that they had made an even greater effort to catch him.

There were still plenty of occasions when Wilson enjoyed life, even if he had to be discreet about it. One of his favourite off-the-beaten-track restaurants was Ventos de Paco, just down the hill from Chequers on the N340 main coast road. The restaurant was always packed, with loud conversation and plentiful bottles of wine. While his Spanish was good enough to communicate with waiting staff and he enjoyed the cuisine, Pat wasn't keen on 'foreign food'. She preferred Charlie to cook a slab of red meat on the barbeque and rustle up one of his finest mixed salads, together with a few baked potatoes.

Out on his own, nightlife was a different matter altogether for Wilson. One of the most popular watering holes was Silks, a restaurant in Puerto Banus run by a boxer, the former British, European and Commonwealth light heavyweight champion Eddie Avoth. When one young London criminal dared to barge his way into Silks without a booking, the old school criminal associates sorted it out by having a 'friendly chat' with the young gangster outside. The hoodlum ended up in hospital. As usual, Wilson sidestepped any direct involvement in the incident.

Many of the British criminals had also discovered a fondness for cocaine and Wilson did follow their lead in this respect. Pablo Escobar had personally warned Charlie not to get hooked on his own supply because it would lead to problems. The cartel boss himself stuck to a few cannabis joints a day and believed this kept him calm enough to make effective, unemotional decisions. Charlie Wilson broke Escobar's golden rule and was regularly using his own produce. But he was unlike a young person discovering drugs for the first time. Wilson – like many of the other, middle-aged, British gangsters in Spain at that time – was so flush with cash and had such easy access to drugs, that he didn't just sample the produce, but consumed it by the bucketload.

Wilson could soon be found pulling out bags of cocaine while chairing meetings to discuss deals. He would invite everyone in the room to take a snort. 'Charlie wouldn't touch the stuff when he first came to Spain, and that had made some of the chaps a bit nervous,' explained one old friend. 'Then one day, this mouthy villain says to Charlie, "How do I know you ain't rippin' us off. You won't even try it yerself." So Charlie chops out a line and off he goes. Trouble was he got a bit hooked on the stuff.'

Meetings called to discuss new shipments of drugs could be reduced to hyped-up bartering matches where nothing much got achieved, except a massive hoovering of marching powder by greedy, cokehead gangsters. Consuming such large quantities of cocaine didn't help Wilson's respiratory problems, initially caused by his worsening emphysema.

By the mid-eighties the use of cocaine had become so flagrant in the nightclubs of Marbella and Puerto Banus that it was taken for granted most people were on it. Some characters were so blatant they'd openly take the white powder and then get abusive if the management complained. And the sight of three or four hefty faces disappearing into the toilets for a snort was commonplace. Now Narco Charlie – once completely anti-drugs – was regularly starry-eyed and dry-mouthed just like everyone else. He even laughed at his own expense when one wise-cracking crook offered him some cocaine with the question, 'Want some charlie, Charlie?' He frequently stayed up all night drinking and snorting cocaine, rolling home in the early hours and telling Pat he'd been involved in some 'heavy business meetings'. She must have wondered what that meant, but chose not to confront him. Wilson never once discussed drugs with his wife but he did assure her he intended to retire sooner rather than later. For Wilson and his circle, the only time when cocaine wasn't on the menu was when old-school gangsters like Wilson took their wives to Freddie Foreman's Eagles Country Club, near Puerto Banus, for a roast beef Sunday lunch.

It's impossible to know if Pat really believed her husband's empty promises about giving up crime but she was clearly responding to what was happening by retreating into herself and rarely venturing out of the house. Watching her new favourite soap, *EastEnders*, which began in 1985, must have avidly reminded her so much of the life she'd left behind in London. It was almost as if the TV drama gave her a free ride back to the world she still wanted to be part of. Long trips back to London to see her daughters were the only occasions for which when Pat left the house. She felt much safer in the UK but, ultimately, she always returned to Charlie because he was her life.

Wilson's highly lucrative operation was leading to increasing amounts of time on aeroplanes, or waiting to board them. He remained in the firing line, buying shipments from Escobar's Medellín cartel and arranging to have them smuggled out of northern Spain along the co-called European pipeline via Holland to the UK and other parts of Europe. He always travelled on a false passport, going through the documents at the rate of one every three months, each costing five thousand pounds. At one stage, Wilson later told one friend, things got so hectic that he was finding himself waking up in a plane, after a brief shut-eye, having forgotten where he was heading. In Amsterdam, his personal attention was required on a virtually weekly basis. He would send one of his guys as a bagman with cash to pay Roy 'the Lump' Adkins and his gang to ensure all the shipments could get through without hassle. Wilson's ever-increasing consumption of cocaine wasn't helping his business acumen. Some of his associates believed that his cocaine habit made him more short-tempered and affected his judgement. One night, Wilson accused his smuggling team of disloyalty, when they were together in a clip joint in Puerto Banus.

'It's all going fuckin' bad on us,' Charlie ranted at his crew. 'There's no fuckin' loyalty. You lot think I'm just a stupid old man.'

But there was another, softer side to Charlie Wilson, that was on display when he was back home with Pat at Chequers. He'd go out of his way to play the role of gracious host to regular visitors from London, although even here there was a sleazy edge. His old friend Paddy returned on numerous occasions to Spain, as did other familiar faces from south London, including his great train robber pal, Buster Edwards. Their arrival often meant that beautiful women had to be made available as entertainment. This was when Charlie used a secret and notorious club specially set up by British criminals on the Costa del Sol to supply reliable prostitutes. Even undercover UK police detectives working on the Costa del Sol had been known to pay for sex at the club.

The venue was nicknamed the Wooden Horse Club, as some of the girls involved also acted as couriers for drugs and dirty money. One villain, a regular at the Wooden Horse, later explained: 'It was a bit like joining the Freemasons – only we had a lot more money to spend.' Popular girls were circulated amongst members and orgies were alleged to have been held in specially rented houses up in the hills behind Marbella.

Escorts also advertised in the biggest-selling English-language newspaper, *Sur In English*. And as soon as some villains had snorted their first line of the day, they'd be on the phone ordering girls to meet in hotel rooms or spare apartments. The London crowd usually preferred English girls, who'd charge between forty and eighty pounds an hour, for a list of sex acts that would test most people's physical endurance.

Call girls arriving to meet Wilson and his pals would feast their eyes on the cocaine piled high on a glass coffee table. They'd usually phone their agency bosses and tell them they were going off-duty, before staying as long as their client wanted.

Some villains even took the girls out on dinner dates, usually to Puerto Banus, where dozens of expensive restaurants lined the waterfront and overlooked multi-million-pound yachts and luxury sports cars. Many of the sex workers were trying to earn extra money to support their young children or their university careers. Others were genuine hustlers, open to the main chance and keen to snare a big-time villain with a bulging waistline and wallet to match. Some British criminals had marriage-breaking affairs with sex workers who went on to become their wives.

Wilson was already involved with the North African woman he'd met who had good contacts inside the ETA terror group. The two formed a close friendship for more than a year and Charlie even allowed her to stay at an apartment he owned in Puerto Banus. But it was a very fiery relationship, punctuated with huge rows in public places and threats from the woman to tell the police about her boyfriend's activities.

This was the complex world in which Charlie Wilson now lived, a grandfather in his mid-fifties. He was dealing with vast shipments of cocaine, consuming huge amounts of drugs himself, enjoying a lively sex life and spending his vast income with creditable panache. The Medellín cartel and Pablo Escobar still seemed happy enough to continue dealing with Narco Charlie, who somehow maintained a reputation as a smart, reliable, yet tough operator.

All was not as it seemed. Escobar and his associates were beginning to hear that Wilson might not be using his money very wisely, and the Colombians believed that the weakest link in the cocaine trade was always money.

33/

Charlie Wilson encountered a nightclub entertainer called Mel Williams who'd lived on the Costa del Sol for more than ten years. They were introduced by ex-Krays hardman Freddie Foreman.

Williams wanted a quote for a book he was writing about his showbusiness adventures in Spain. Wilson's reply summed up the way he felt about the so-called 'crime of the century', the robbery that had gained him so much notoriety for almost thirty years: 'I wish the fuckin' train hadn't stopped,' he muttered.

When fellow train robber Gordon Goody was asked the question, he told Williams, 'Well, the mail bag hanging up in this bar probably brings in more money.'

Charlie Wilson had been, in many ways, severely damaged by his train robbery experiences, which had made him suspicious of everyone. He constantly found himself wondering why people wanted to be his friend. He'd paid such a high price for comparatively little money and it certainly hadn't improved the quality of his life. Now he was risking life and limb, handling lethal amounts of drugs supplied to him by the world's deadliest cocaine merchant, Pablo Escobar.

Mel Williams explained, 'Charlie only socialised with people he already knew. He didn't say much unless someone went up and specifically talked to him at parties. I didn't know if he was "retired" or not because when you're in a group like that you don't talk about criminal activity. It's just not mentioned.'

By this time, Wilson had multiple financial commitments and continued smuggling hash as well as cocaine because he wanted to keep his hand in, just in case the Colombians pulled the plug. A typical villa for stashing cannabis would be rented by a family on their holiday as a front, complete with kids playing in the pool. This would usually be in coastal resorts between Marbella and Fuengirola. The property would have a garage, front gates and a driveway. Between 1 and 5 tons of hash could be stored and, having prepared the house as a temporary drug warehouse, the smugglers would go to the nearby beach and await a boat crewed by specialist Spanish powerboat drivers to deliver the hash from Morocco. Within twenty-four hours, at least half a dozen cars would be packed with the drugs and were ready to depart for the rest of Europe, including the UK.

Not surprisingly, many police officers in the local Guardia Civil on the Costa del Sol were on Wilson's payroll by this time. As one of his former smugglers explained, 'I remember one time we even took photos of the police helping carry bales of hash from a boat on the beach into the back of a four-wheel drive. They didn't even mind posing.'

One of the biggest headaches for Wilson was laundering the vast amount of dirty money he was earning, although there were far fewer checks in place than today. One source said, 'There were banks in Gibraltar where no questions were ever asked. I know one time Charlie turned up with half a million at a bank on the Rock and no one cared.' Sometimes Wilson resorted to old-fashioned methods of handling money, stashing it in carefully dug holes in isolated spots in the mountains behind his home, so that it could easily be retrieved if and when he had a need for it.

Another highly effective way to launder a limited amount of money was selling second-hand cars from Germany. Classic Mercedes, Audi and BMWs were traditionally much cheaper than in Spain. Wilson would cough up some cash for his boys to go to Germany to buy three or four cars. It was all perfectly legal. 'Then they'd drive them back here and flog them for a healthy profit,' said one of Charlie's associates. 'Charlie and some of the other London villains out here also bought houses and flats just on plan, then sold them on before they were even built.' Wilson was extremely proud of his organisational skills. His associate said, 'Transport was separate from everything else and Paddy was the main man for that. Then you'd have the packer who'd fit the stuff in the vehicle. Charlie used one particular firm who had a canning machine in a garage and they'd put kilos of cocaine in tins labelled "canned tomatoes" and other produce. We all knew Charlie was dealing direct with the Colombians. We thought he was fuckin' mad because they was right evil bastards. But Charlie didn't scare easy and he was after the big money.'

Narco Charlie was trying to squeeze at least a 50 per cent profit out of every deal for himself after buying cocaine direct from Escobar. He kept an empty apartment locally in Marbella that contained a false passport and a ready-packed bag in case he had to do a quick runner. But he avoided bodyguards because he reckoned all they did was attract more attention.

One of his smuggling team explained why the centre of the operation was in the Marbella area. 'At the end of the day, Marbella was the upmarket crime centre while places like Fuengirola and Torremolinos further down the coast were full of lowlife scum. It's like the difference between the Old Kent Road and Knightsbridge. All the big deals happen in Marbella. The Colombians, Russians, Irish, they're all here. These guys are like managing directors of companies. They walk around in suits, drive classy cars. They're not the sort of people who often do business in bars. Never.' The terminal at Malaga airport was a popular place to meet, or one of the hotels near the airport – the Méridien or the Hilton. There were business centres that could be hired by the hour.

If he was in London, Wilson sometimes held meetings at the swish, old-fashioned Institute of Directors, Pall Mall. He and his associates saw themselves as hard-working, rich businessmen, no different from the chairman of ICI or any other major corporation. One of his closest friends later claimed the IRA were also active in Spain during the late 1980s and they had a similar attitude. 'They were often completely open about who they were. They stayed in hotels. They'd come here on holiday with their wife and kids and then pop down for a meeting with Charlie.'

It seemed that Wilson was having to dirty his hands with just about every rat who'd ever worked on the Costa del Crime. For the moment, he was outfoxing them all.

34/

In the late spring of 1987, law enforcement agents intercepted telephone calls to Florida and London from Charlie Wilson's home. This led officers to believe he was financing a huge cocaine shipment from South America, although he wasn't giving everything away.

Wilson once again deliberately slipped into Cockney rhyming slang to confuse anyone who might be listening, although his phone calls did reveal he was attending meetings in various parts of the world. 'But you can't nick someone for getting on an aeroplane,' explained one senior UK customs source.

One agent – who heard this and many other surveillance tapes – later recalled that Charlie sounded like a pushy businessman working on his investments, or a company chairman keeping an eye on his empire. People phoned Wilson to get decisions and he usually responded calmly and swiftly. The authorities listened in and it was increasingly clear that he was the head of a substantial drugs empire. Occasionally, his respectability slipped and his love of women took over, like on the occasion he discussed another criminal's wife with one associate on the phone, 'She's fuckin' tasty. I'd love to give her one.' Most of the time his conversation was more mundane, although the surveillance team later alleged that beatings and sometimes killings were authorised in carefully worded codes.

Wilson, for his part, constantly monitored what was happening in Medellín, reading as many newspapers as he could lay his hands on. Pablo Escobar was the most feared drug baron in the world and his antics in Colombia were being reported in the global media, virtually on a daily basis. When his one-time Medellín cartel partner Carlos Lehder was arrested in Colombia and extradited to the US in the middle of 1987, Wilson immediately tried to make contact to find out if this would affect their business relationship. Escobar avoided talking directly and got his favourite gringo, Brian Doran – the Professor – to speak to him instead.

Charlie told Doran he wanted another face-to-face meeting with Escobar in Medellín. Doran warned that Escobar had become much more volatile since his last visit to Medellín, but

Wilson wasn't put off. In the late spring of 1987, he flew into Medellín and was escorted, blindfolded, by Escobar's trusted hitman Popeye to meet in a secret location outside the city.

The DEA confirmed the meeting through their agents on the ground after picking up a reference using airborne surveillance eavesdropping equipment in Colombia. They were regularly using specially adapted Beechcraft light aircraft that closely resembled standard two-prop commercial planes. These spy planes were crammed with state-of-the-art electronic listening and direction-finding equipment. The plane's wingspan was 6 inches longer than standard models because of the built-in antennae. Operators worked at computers set up for listening once the aircraft reached an altitude of between 20 and 25,000 feet.

Shortly after Wilson's meeting with Escobar, he spoke by phone to Doran. The conversation was recorded by the DEA and included the following:

Charlie:	If you get this deal firmed up, I can find a home for it all.
Doran:	Look, Chas, I can get you any amount you want. That's not the problem.
Charlie:	What d'you mean?
Doran:	The people out here don't like the idea of you changing the system.
Charlie (quietly):	Fuck the system.

Listening law enforcement agents were astonished by Charlie's bravado. 'I remember thinking, he must be crazy,' recalled one UK customs officer, who heard the excerpts from the surveillance tapes. 'I really thought to myself, this guy's got a death wish.'

Law enforcement agents also focused on Wilson's financial transactions. They turned up bank accounts everywhere from Gibraltar to the Caymen Islands, but where did all the cash come from? 'At first, we wondered if maybe he was fronting all this up for another, even richer criminal,' explained a UK customs source. 'But as we started to track Charlie Wilson's finances we realised he was heavily reinvesting his own profits.'

Soon after arriving back from Colombia, Wilson got a call through a translator from Pablo Escobar on his untraceable satellite phone with the boss's favourite phrase and standard greeting, '¿Qué más, caballero?', or 'What's happening, man?'

'Not a lot,' answered the man Escobar called 'Narco Charlie'.

Wilson later told a friend that Escobar warned him that DEA agents might be on his tail. But Charlie didn't believe he was a big enough fish to warrant such intense round-the-clock surveillance. He had no idea he'd actually already had one close shave with a woman drugs courier he'd used a few months earlier. She'd offered information about Wilson to British customs after being 'fired' by him, following an incident in a bar when he came on to her. But law enforcement agencies considered her information to be so tainted that it was not even written up in Wilson's file.

However, Wilson knew only too well he needed to watch his back even more closely. He'd even begun using a special scanner to uncover listening devices in phones or rooms he was in. Regular cocaine and alcohol binges didn't help, fuelling huge bouts of paranoia. Such cocktails, combined with adrenaline, might end up impacting on his already poor health.

35/

Charlie Wilson was usually so exhausted when he arrived home in Marbella following yet more globetrotting that he was happy not to go out on the town for a bit.

As one neighbour later explained, 'Pat didn't mind. The longer they stayed in Spain the less she seemed to go out. Charlie even did the shopping when he was at home and he certainly did most of the cooking.' Pat seemed to have cocooned herself inside Chequers to block out what her husband was really up to. She had long since given up asking him any awkward questions about his criminal activities. No doubt it was having an impact on their relationship.

One of the few occasions that Charlie and Pat did go out as a couple at this time was to Security Express robber Ronnie Knight's wedding reception, held on a baking hot Saturday in June 1987 at a Marbella beachside restaurant called El Oceano. Knight's bride, Sue, wore an ivory-coloured, silk and satin wedding dress costing three thousand pounds, carried a bouquet of orchids and salmon-coloured roses and sported a large, diamond-encrusted wedding ring. Knight – previously married to *Carry On* star Barbara Windsor – had even given his bride a top-of-the-range black BMW 325i sports car.

That evening they had a firework display with the words 'Ron' and 'Sue', surrounded by sparkling pink Catherine-wheel hearts, shot into the moonlit sky. Everyone who was anyone on the Costa del Sol was there, including Freddie Foreman and his family plus villains Ronnie Everett, John Mason and Clifford Saxe, as well as great train robber Jimmy Hussey. Many of the guests drew the line at posing for wedding day snaps since at least four of them were on the Spanish police's list of more than thirty Brits wanted in the UK. Across the street in unmarked cars, members of Scotland Yard's Flying Squad indiscreetly watched and photographed all the guests coming in and out of El Oceano. The British media was also out in full force, photographers spying with long-range telephoto lenses from motor launches and an overhead helicopter whirring away as it circled the reception area.

Charlie and Pat didn't stay long. Pat hated every moment and, as usual, felt vulnerable. However, Wilson did manage to stop and have a chat with drug baron Brian Wright. Wright advised him to be careful when dealing with Roy 'the Lump' Adkins and 'Mad Mickey' Blackmore, the Brits now working with Klaas 'the Preacher' Bruinsma in Amsterdam. 'Keep an eye on them, Charlie. They're a right pair o' nutters,' said Wright in his friendly, London-Irish brogue.

One of UK customs' most senior drugs investigators later told this author, 'We were working hard on Brian Wright at that time and Charlie Wilson kept popping up with him in Spain and sometimes even the UK. We could see what was happening with Charlie but until we had some concrete evidence it was difficult to even contemplate an arrest.' The same agent also read extensive US and UK law enforcement surveillance reports on Wilson and his associates. He said, 'We mapped Charlie's movements across the world. He only went to Spain in the first place because he thought there would be less heat on him from the law ... I was on four different drugs seizures in Pakistan at the time and during one of them we nicked two Brits – a minder and a drugs courier – well known to Charlie and many of the UK criminals on the Costa del Sol. Neither of them said much, but when I traced back their movements to a hotel in Rawalpindi, Pakistan, I found that a man whom I believe now to have been Charlie Wilson was also staying in Rawalpindi at the same time. The funny thing is that I wasn't even after Charlie myself. I just knew his details through another customs investigation and then up he pops like a bad penny.'

So, Wilson's 'world tour' had also taken in the heroin killing fields of Pakistan and Afghanistan. Explained the customs' source, 'This had to be heroin rather than cannabis because Rawalpindi is the jumping-off point for all heroin in the region. Charlie's appearance in Pakistan fitted in perfectly with his movements and activities at that time. He'd definitely stepped up a gear in Spain and was trying to be one of the big boys.'

But Charlie Wilson was playing with fire. Was he trying to expand his drugs empire to take in other narcotics besides cocaine? One of his oldest associates later explained: 'This was typical Charlie. He knew that Escobar and his Colombians could pull the plug on their deal at any time and he wanted to have other fish to fry. Dealing in heroin and other drugs was a backup plan, as far as he was concerned. Charlie wasn't necessarily going to start dealing in those other drugs yet. He just wanted to know he had an alternative if the cocaine suddenly dried up.'

Over in Medellín, Pablo Escobar soon got to hear about Narco Charlie's activities with regard to heroin. At first he did nothing, knowing full well that characters like Wilson would always be on the lookout for new 'business opportunities'. But Escobar also knew that by turning up in places like Pakistan, Wilson was flagging himself to law enforcement across the world. That was something to be avoided at all costs. For the moment, Escobar and his Medellín cartel would still continue to deal with Wilson because he was earning them big money, always paid on time and was very adept at avoiding any problems with the long arm of the law. Meanwhile, Wilson continued his criminal activities as if he didn't have a care in the world. He even knew that law enforcement agencies had failed to pin anything on him to date thanks to a new source he had inside the ultra-secret and hugely important National Criminal Intelligence Service (NCIS), a UK police organisation recently set up with a staff of five hundred and an annual budget of twenty-five million pounds.

NCIS's job was to gather intelligence on serious, organised UK criminals like Wilson and to also coordinate work between customs and police agencies. Those working at NCIS had access to reports from Interpol and, sometimes, even MI5 and other security services. Wilson said to one criminal associate in Spain that his tame NCIS detective told him about all inquiries that targeted him. Unfortunately for Wilson, though, the DEA and UK customs were deliberately not revealing the full extent of their surveillance operation to either the British or Spanish police. Wilson never realised how closely others were watching him.

There was another complication. One of Pablo Escobar's senior associates in Medellín had become a secret informant to the DEA and was feeding them information about the cartel, further convincing the Americans that Escobar needed to be taken out. Escobar himself gave the impression he was blissfully unaware of all this. He was still seen by many as the most powerful man in Colombia, thanks to the billions of dollars he'd earned from cocaine. But when the deluded Escobar got himself elected as a Medellín congressman and then began hinting at running for president of Colombia many inside the country and in the United States decided enough was enough. He'd evaded capture so far – but for how much longer would he do so?

'Escobar was the most powerful drug baron in the world,' explained one former DEA agent. 'He prided himself on the systems he'd helped set up. Criminals like Charlie Wilson were nothing more than pawns in Escobar's worldwide cocaine empire. Remember, Escobar saw himself as something of a Robin Hood type figure. People in Medellín still loved him, especially the poor whom he gave money to. He even built schools and sponsored football teams. The guy was untouchable on his home turf but he'd been taking liberties elsewhere in Colombia.'

One of Wilson's oldest criminal associates later explained, 'I'm not sure Charlie took Pablo Escobar seriously enough. He used to tell us that Escobar was some kind of nutter, always puffing on a joint and talking nonsense half the time. I said to Charlie one time, "You need to be careful of him, 'cos you're not that important to him and he'll drop you right in it if you cross him in any way." Charlie looked at me and smiled, "He hasn't got the bottle."'

Narco Charlie looked on southern Spain as his territory and he believed that no one – not even Pablo 'fuckin'' Escobar – would dare come after him there. Others weren't so sure.

36/

For the moment, Charlie Wilson and other old school criminals like Brian Wright and Tony White, continued to thrive in Spain.

The government in Madrid was still under pressure to clean up the so-called British 'Costa del Crime' fraternity, whose presence gave the impression Spain provided a no-questions-asked safe haven for wealthy crooks on the run. But Spanish laws were complicated and open to abuse. In theory a foreigner could be expelled if he'd served more than a year's imprisonment in another country or if his presence was an embarrassment to a nation considered friendly. In reality, the Spanish had only really required foreigners living in their country to have a genuine up-to-date passport. Yet there were incidents on the Costa del Sol which should have served as a warning to Charlie that Spain was no longer such an easy-going place. The authorities were becoming fed up with the area's image and they didn't like the way many British gangsters were openly laundering their money in nearby Gibraltar.

A new Spanish police crackdown in late 1987 led to two busts of million-pound British drug-smuggling operations in less than one week. This coincided with the arrival of twenty senior detectives from other forces to boost the Spanish crime squad on the south coast of the country. But these raids were small fry compared to what Wilson and his associates were up to. Then he heard from his tame Spanish police friends that local officers had been ordered to step up their monitoring of various British criminals. They'd been told to follow up the slightest infringement of regulations. Wilson also knew full well that two-man teams of British policemen continued to turn up with specific targets that undoubtedly included Wilson himself.

One member of Wilson's smuggling gang told this author, 'Then we started to hear that the fuckin' CIA had turned up on the Costa del Crime watching the IRA and ETA. There were a lot of Libyans around as well. There were rumours that the CIA and British spooks from MI6 had witnessed killings and stuff, which they did nothing about because it suited them that way. The spooks seemed to be more evil than any criminals or normal coppers. We were just vermin to them and Charlie was getting himself sucked into something much bigger than he realised.'

With Pablo Escobar's people closely monitoring Wilson and their other partners in Spain, it was inevitable that others would soon hear how well he was doing in the coke trade. Towards the end of 1987, a gang of British criminals proposed investing in Wilson's operation. One of his oldest criminal associates later explained, 'Charlie was gobsmacked. He didn't want a partnership with anyone but he also knew he needed to keep this lot away from his marketplace because he didn't want them setting up an independent operation. So he took their money and gave them a fat return on their investment within two or three weeks. Then he prayed they wouldn't come back for a while. I dunno what happened after that.'

On the social front, Krays associate and runaway armed-robbery suspect Freddie Foreman was delighted when he persuaded his friend Wilson to attend a full-fledged world boxing title fight in Marbella that he had organised on behalf of his Marbella boxing club, despite being on Britain's most-wanted list.

Every important face on the Costa del Crime looked set to make an appearance at the Lloyd Honeyghan vs Gene Hatcher world-welterweight bout to be held at the bullring in old Marbella, on 29 August 1987. Also on the bill was the UK's finest heavyweight, Frank Bruno, against a relatively unknown American called Reggie Gross and another contest featuring lesser-known British heavyweight Gary Mason. Others due at the ringside included Security Express robbery suspects Ronnie Knight and Clifford Saxe, Jimmy Hussey and Ronnie Everett and John Mason. Everett had been acquitted of murdering British underworld figure Ginger Marks while Mason was cleared of a role in the eight-million-pound Bank of America raid in the late seventies.

The big night out turned into a disaster when the coast was hit by torrential rain and the main fight had to be postponed until the following evening. It ended up being fought in front of a half-full stadium and Honeyghan knocked Hatcher out in the first round. Bruno won his fight with embarrassing ease and Wilson, Foreman and all the rest of the chaps retired to ex-boxer Eddie Avoth's Silks, Puerto Banus, to drown their sorrows.

Wilson's only real refuge from the big, bad world of international crime remained Chequers, his now fully modernised hacienda, overshadowed by those vast mountains behind Marbella. It was rumoured that many drug dealers' bodies had been dumped there over the years and the rugged terrain also now contained stash holes filled with Wilson's cash. Pat was always relieved to see Wilson home in one piece when he returned from his business trips. She begged him to slow down and start enjoying a simple life with her and their dogs. Their daughters were settled back in the UK with their own families.

Pat reminded Wilson he was a grandfather, in his mid-fifties, and not a young hood out on the streets of south London. Pat knew that Wilson still constantly worried about money, but surely they didn't need that much to live on now it was just the two of them? However, her husband remained a driven man. Before, it was a big family he felt obliged to provide for. For him it was all now about pride and greed. He loved the freedom that money gave him and he didn't want to give up the lifestyle – the women, the booze, even the drugs. He thrived on buying and selling shipments of drugs and landing a big property deal. All of it gave him a slight buzz that he'd always needed. It would never match that feeling of grabbing sacks of money from inside the train during his biggest moment, but this was the nearest Charlie could get.

Yet his health problems with emphysema were worsening. By early 1988, Wilson's breathing difficulties had become so acute he'd sometimes lose his breath just climbing the stairs to the bedroom at Chequers. Pat was so concerned she persuaded him to see a specialist in London on his next trip back to the UK.

He was told there was no actual cure, and was prescribed an inhaler similar to those given to asthma sufferers. Wilson hated the contraption and only used it when no one was looking. He found it difficult to accept that here he was, a supremely well-toned man struggling like an eighty-year-old to get up a few stairs. Typically, the illness became a catalyst for Charlie's ever evolving 'business' aspirations. As he started to fear that his days might be numbered, he set out to earn even more money than before.

One of his oldest friends later said, 'Charlie became a lot more reckless after the emphysema took a proper hold. It was almost as if he didn't care any more.'

That same year Charlie's close friend Brian Wright was named at an Old Bailey trial as having offered a twenty-thousand-pound bribe to a jockey to throw a race at Cheltenham. Gentleman jockey Jamie Osborne said in court he assumed Wright was behind it because 'he was somebody who had been connected with things … that were corrupt.' He later insisted he did not take the money. By this time, Wright was betting fifty-thousand to one-hundred-thousand-pounds a time on fixed races. In the racing world Wright – now nicknamed 'the Milkman' in the drug world because he 'always delivered on time' – was known as a man of enormous charm, wit and generosity, with connections everywhere. But then he could afford to be kind, with a personal fortune estimated at more than twenty million pounds, and numerous properties spread across the world, including a luxurious penthouse apartment in the Chelsea Harbour complex overlooking the Thames in London.

Charlie Wilson was warned by his old train robber friends that his connections to Pablo Escobar were poison because the tide of public opinion inside Colombia was definitely beginning to turn against the Medellín cartel and its psychopathic chief. Wilson dismissed their concerns as sour grapes. He had given sizeable chunks of his cocaine earnings to help keep those very same train robber friends afloat when they were struggling. They'd been happy to accept that cash from him, so why now bite the hand that fed them? In any case, the cartel were still supplying Narco Charlie with mountains of cocaine and he wasn't prepared to cut off his connections to Escobar when there had been no actual problems between the two of them.

At one stage Escobar himself called Wilson via satellite phone to assure him that, despite rumours he was on an American government hit list, he had no intention of closing down the cartel and he was grateful to Wilson for his continued support. Wilson knew from the tone of Escobar's voice that what he was really saying was that if he, Charlie, ever dared to pull out of their deal then he'd face the consequences: no one turned their back on Pablo Escobar.

With the pressure mounting from Colombia and a wife at home who refused point-blank to go out and enjoy herself, it was perhaps not surprising that Wilson continued with his double-life when it came to romance outside his marriage. In autumn 1988, he was out in his deliberately modest white Toyota Corolla with his North African mistress, driving along the Marbella seafront when he spotted an attractive British-looking blonde woman in her mid-thirties walking along the promenade. 'Casanova Charlie' slowed down – even though his lover was sitting next to him – and introduced himself. The woman's name was Georgie Ellis and she said she was on a 'get-away-from-it-all holiday' on the Costa del Sol, having just fled from her partner in England.

Georgie Ellis later recalled, 'Charlie did a straight pick-up on me and, at first, I didn't want to know. I thought, what the hell is this? Please go away. But he was so charismatic with a terrific personality I weakened and we all met for a drink together. I even gleaned from him that he was running drugs from coast to coast across the Mediterranean, although I had no idea who he was at first. But he had a very strange girlfriend who was a drugs runner from Marbella. But they were good fun, amusing and friendly and, in a nutshell, just what the doctor ordered.'

Georgie was in fact the daughter of Ruth Ellis, the last woman to be executed in the UK, and she was very different from most of the women Charlie had encountered over the years. Ellis had been just three years old in 1955, when her mother was hanged after being found guilty of the murder of racing-driver lover David Blakely. Georgie's own former lovers included film idol Richard Harris and wayward soccer star George Best. She'd also been married three times.

The day after that first meeting, Wilson and Georgie Ellis embarked on an affair. She later summed up her relationship with men like him: 'Unfortunately, my satisfactory relationships have always been with other women's husbands. Charlie was so charismatic and had a terrific personality. Just like my mum, I find these sort of men hard to resist. Money and success is sexually attractive to women and gangsters certainly fit the bill. Charlie took me to Marbella, to gangland paradise and introduced me to lots of people.' And the relationship didn't just involve sleeping together, as Ellis later recalled. 'I remember taking thousands of Irish punts stuffed under my daughter's buggy to a bank in Marbella for him. I didn't know where the money came from and only later realised it was money to launder.'

Wilson adored the tiny heart Georgie had tattooed on one of her breasts and her penchant for rubbing moisturiser on her legs at all times of the day and night. She said, 'The people who are supposedly evil gangsters are actually the more gentle ones. The so-called hard men aren't hard at all – they're soft as butter.' Of Charlie she said, 'I was thirty-seven and he was nearly sixty, but we just clicked. Everywhere we went he was so protective about me. If anything went wrong he'd have been the first one there to protect me and I liked that. Charlie was a nice, happy-go-lucky rogue with a winning smile and a great wit.'

On one night out in Puerto Banus, Ellis was surprised to find that Wilson also invited his North African lover along with them. Ellis later explained, 'We were out in a bar called Sinatra's, having drinks before we had dinner at Silks restaurant when Chas and the girl, well oiled with alcohol, engaged in the mother and father of a row, during which he promised revenge with the loss of her beauty.' According to Ellis, the other woman 'went crazy' and threatened to go to the police and tell them about some money Wilson had hidden in a flat he owned in Marbella. Then she stormed off.

Later that night, Wilson and Ellis were heading to the Marbella apartment when they spotted three police cars outside. Ellis recalled: 'Charlie told me to go off alone, and I reluctantly walked away, looking like any other tourist. That was the last time I saw him.'

In the middle of this domestic chaos, Wilson's emphysema was worsening. As one of his gangster friends later explained, 'Charlie started to look more haggard. He'd always seemed so fit and young for his age. Then I heard he was struggling even to dig a flower bed in the garden at Chequers. We was all worried about him and some of the chaps even wondered if he had cancer.'

But Wilson had other priorities besides his bad health to attend to.

37/

Pablo Escobar was facing intense pressure and scrutiny in Colombia, and it was no big surprise that he was getting increasingly paranoid. By this time, he believed that many of his closest aides might be traitors.

He heard a report about Narco Charlie's efforts to set up heroin and cannabis deals without offering him a slice of the profits. One DEA officer later explained, 'This is when Charlie Wilson made a big mistake. He thought that Escobar was under so much pressure in Colombia that he wouldn't care about his efforts to find drug supplies from other organisations.'

Escobar flew into a rage and demanded that Wilson be told in no uncertain terms that his activities were risking an unpleasant end to their business relationship. He had also been told by his people on the Costa del Sol that Charlie's health was deteriorating and their partnership might well be coming to an end in any case. The same, now retired DEA officer, continued, 'Escobar's cartel was undoubtedly beginning to lose its power and influence. Their rivals in the Cali cartel were attracting more business because they weren't in the public spotlight like Escobar and his Medellín operation. This was hard for Escobar to accept, which made him even more dangerous.'

As a result, Escobar had been killing even more of his enemies and, indeed, his friends, with impunity. No one, it seemed, was safe. For the moment, the Medellín cartel in Spain remained out of firing range. But that would only continue for as long as they brought in tens of millions of dollars for the cartel. These were dangerous times ahead for anyone connected to Pablo Escobar.

In Marbella, Wilson continued to maintain a lower profile than most other British criminals, resisting the temptation to drive around in the expensive cars that were always a big giveaway. One Costa del Sol associate explained, 'We all wondered what Charlie did with his money and most of us reckoned he kept it in that safe in his secret basement at Chequers.'

Alongside the nondescript, white, two-door Toyota Corolla 1.6 sporty hatchback with Gibraltar licence plates 'for the birds', Wilson had a beaten-up, red Datsun estate he called his workhorse. He used it for picking up building materials when rebuilding Chequers and to take the couple's two dogs out for their daily walk.

Businessman Bernie Finch and his wife Liz lived in the house next to Chequers, having moved in just a year after Wilson. Bernie Finch noticed that whenever his neighbour was grafting away in the garden he'd be dressed in shorts and a T-shirt. But at night he'd drive off, on his own, looking very smooth in smart but casual clothes. Finch also noticed that Wilson left the house once a day to walk his dogs, heading either into the mountains behind the development or down on the beach at Las Dunas, between Marbella and Estepona. The Finches became close to the Wilsons through their mutual love of dogs. Often, Wilson would be walking the dogs for hours on end, as he thought through all his criminal activities. Many of his friends later said that he was 'quite a worrier and still obsessed with planning every deal down to the last detail'.

The two couples were similar in age and went out for dinner several times together. Finch later recalled, 'Charlie was always telling us to pop by and keep an eye on Pat when he was away on business. It was strange because they never seemed to go on holidays together. Pat went back to the UK a lot on her own and Charlie did at other times because one of them had to stay behind to look after the dogs.'

During their dinner dates, Wilson drank wine and beer, followed by a huge Spanish-style measure of local brandy at the end of each meal. Finch recalled, 'We were always virtually the last to leave the restaurant but that was typical Charlie.' And it seemed to the Finches that Charlie was well-known wherever they went. 'He was often running across people he knew in restaurants. I remember one time he bumped into this very nasty-looking American but he never bothered to introduce us.' Heavy drinking didn't stop Charlie driving his neighbours home to Las Montanas. 'But luckily he was an excellent driver, even when he was pissed.'

Wilson happily agreed to look after the Finches' pet parrot when they went on a trip to the UK. Pat even told Finch, 'Don't worry, Bernie, I'll make sure Charlie minds his language so the parrot doesn't pick up any rude words.' However, there was one subject Bernie Finch quickly learned not to mention in front of Wilson – his secret basement. 'I'd heard about it from another neighbour but when I mentioned it he went stony silent, so I never made any jokes about it again. I was fascinated by the little window it had. Many times I noticed the light on late at night. God knows what he was up to down there.'

Meanwhile, Charlie continued doing all the gardening and most of the cooking in the Wilson household. 'He mowed the lawn and clipped everything himself, even though most people round here had a gardener,' said Finch. Wilson also let slip to the Finches that he'd travelled to a number of exotic locations around the world since moving to Spain. 'I remember Charlie going on about the aloe vera in our garden and taking a cutting of it and keeping it in his fridge. He said it had great healing powers and might help his emphysema. I asked him how he knew that and he said, "I was told about it on a trip to South America." I didn't like to ask what he'd been doing there.'

Wilson once agreed to run Liz Finch and her elderly mother to Malaga airport when Bernie was away. He waited at the airport while the women said their goodbyes, as Liz Finch later explained: 'Charlie didn't seem to mind at all. Most men wouldn't have wanted to just sit and wait there, but he knew I was upset because my mum was going home.' Finch insisted on taking Wilson lunch as a thank-you for waiting after he'd had to cancel a business appointment. But Wilson paid for the meal.

'Put that money away girl, look at all these men here, they'd hang me if they saw a woman payin' for lunch,' he told Finch. Years later she reflected, 'That was just about kindness. There was nothing in it for Charlie. He knew I was feeling down. I think in some ways he felt more comfortable with women in general because he was so used to an all-female household.'

A few months later, the Finches witnessed another example of the kind and considerate side of their neighbour when their dog Toby went missing. The couple ended up sleeping the night on a local beach while out looking for him. When Wilson heard about the missing animal the next day, he insisted on driving Liz Finch around the places where she believed the dog might have gone. She explained, 'We even went to a local gypsy encampment which he seemed to know well. I didn't ask why. He knew all sorts of strange people and places. Again, there was nothing in it for him. He was just being a kind person.'

But while driving around, Wilson turned to Finch and said, 'Liz, are you afraid of me?'

'What?'

'Are you afraid of me?' repeated Wilson.

'Why the hell should I be afraid of you?'

Wilson didn't reply and changed the subject. Finch later said it was as if he'd wanted to tell her something but had changed his mind at the last moment. When she was talking to him on another occasion, she described the Costa del Sol as: 'A strange place filled with all these criminals.'

Wilson hesitated before replying, 'Yeah, Liz, I know exactly what you mean.'

It wasn't until months later that the Finches heard about Wilson's great train robber background when they attended another neighbour's drinks party. Bernie said, 'But it didn't make any difference to our attitude towards him. Charlie was a good bloke in my book. He was certainly a very good neighbour.'

One rare hint from Wilson about his own criminal connections came when the Finches went round to Chequers for a glass of wine one evening. Finch mentioned he'd had a problem with a man in a local bar the previous evening who'd been rude to him. 'Charlie said, "You should have broken his fuckin' legs,"' recalled Finch.

Pat appeared at her husband's shoulder and said, 'Oh, Charlie, you and yer' jokes.'

That's when Bernie Finch noticed Wilson pat his nose with the tip of his finger and look right at Pat as he did it. 'I realised afterwards that was their sign to each other to be careful what they were saying,' recalled Finch.

The dynamic between Charlie and Pat Wilson fascinated the Finches. Wilson continued to do virtually all the shopping and gardening while Pat sheltered from the sun inside the house. Charlie even bought his wife most of her clothes. Finch recalled, 'He was often popping out on his own. We wondered if Pat had agoraphobia. Then we thought it might all be a control thing.'

But if Pat was indeed suffering from a form of agoraphobia it would be no big surprise. Her inbuilt fear about avoiding places or situations that reminded her of the past was no doubt peppered with vivid, often disturbing memories from so many chilling incidents.

Meanwhile, Wilson used his friendly, cheeky side as a convenient shield to cover up his criminal activities. Finch never forgot the day he found a snapped-off toy doll's hand in the garden while he was talking over the wall to Wilson. 'I waved the hand over to Charlie in the garden and said, "Here, Charlie, d'you want a hand in the garden?" and threw it at him. He loved that joke so much he never stopped going on about it for months afterwards. And he even kept the hand in a flowerbed and would wave it at me every time I passed.'

When Finch first spotted the now infamous toy doll's hand sticking out of the flowerbed he said, 'Now look what Charlie's done with Pat – he's buried her in the garden.' Wilson doubled up with laughter.

The only really significant clue about Charlie's criminal connections came when Liz knocked on the front door of Chequers and asked to borrow a lawn mower. An extremely overweight man in his mid-thirties answered and abruptly asked, 'Who're you?'

An uncomfortable silence followed, which was broken by the sound of Wilson's voice from inside the house. 'Let the girl in. She can have whatever she wants.' Then he appeared with a huge smile on his face.

Another neighbour said that overweight friend was introduced as 'Twiggy'. Wilson said he lived in a newly built block of flats nearby. 'I got the impression Twiggy worked for Charlie and the two men often drove off from Chequers in Charlie's Toyota,' explained the neighbour.

The hardman, criminal side of Wilson came to the surface when he was on the phone in the garden. One neighbour noticed him furiously gardening while swearing and shouting down the phone. 'I've never seen someone snap the heads off dead roses with such venom. It was actually quite frightening to watch,' that neighbour later explained. 'As his voice got angrier, he'd rip them off ever harder.'

But there were other days when Wilson was up at dawn, painting on an easel in the garden he'd so painstakingly created. In many ways, it had become his refuge from crime *and* from Pat. A neighbour later recalled, 'When he was painting, Charlie seemed totally at peace with himself. He'd stand there for hours concentrating on recreating one particular flower or bush. He was a million miles away.'

In the summer of 1988, Wilson bumped into an Argentinian neighbour called Fernando, who was leaving his home with a dog basket full of Alaskan-German shepherd mix puppies. Fernando gave Wilson one. 'I knew he'd give her a good home. He was soon feeding her too much food and getting her fat but he really loved that dog.' Wilson christened the dog Bo-Bo and the two became virtually inseparable when they were at the house together. Fernando was impressed by a little wooden house Wilson built for the dog. 'That showed Charlie liked animals,' explained Fernando, who was struck by the size of Wilson's hands. 'They were the hands of a man used to working hard. I could also see in his eyes and face that he'd been in prison. But he did not have earrings like many criminals or tattoos. I guess that made him a professional in every sense of the word.'

Like many successful criminals, Charlie Wilson was leading not just a double life but a triple one. At home with Pat or interacting with his friendly, normal neighbours, he could be that charming, animal-loving, gentle character. Then there was the drug empire he ran; many law enforcement agents and other criminals were now watching Charlie very closely. And, finally, there was the fun-loving, cocaine-snorting ladies' man who liked to have a pretty girl on his arm. It was a lot for any man to cope with, in addition to worsening health problems. But for the moment Wilson still seemed to thrive on it all.

38/

Towards the end of 1988, Charlie Wilson and two other men flew to London and visited two banks in the West End with suitcases containing money that was later transferred back to Spain.

Scotland Yard were so concerned by Charlie's activities in the UK they went through the complicated formalities of getting new 'letters rogatory', a legal document signed and sealed by the Home Office. This gave the detectives authority to operate overseas. An earlier team of detectives on the Costa del Sol had pulled out of Spain a few months earlier after failing to uncover any actual evidence of Wilson's nefarious activities. The document was essential because without it no formal investigation could go ahead in Spain. In any case, the detectives from the UK would still have to work under the supervision of the local police. That included visiting Costa del Sol banks alongside Spanish officers. There were further claims that Wilson had spent a lot of money buying at least six apartments on the Costa del Sol as investments. Detectives also intended to take a look at the finances behind his principal villa.

While Wilson was still in London, according to one UK Customs source, he was summoned to a meeting with Pablo Escobar's London representative, a beautiful Colombian woman known as 'La Patrona' (the 'lady boss'). She lived in a five-hundred-pounds-a-week apartment overlooking the Thames and had a driver and limo to take her to one-hundred-pounds-a-head restaurants and all the most exclusive designer clothes stores. The Medellín cartel often used London as a base for their people travelling in and out of the UK and Europe. La Patrona's work included providing safe houses across the city for anyone connected to the cartel. She moved her henchmen and teams of couriers to different addresses in the capital on virtually a weekly basis. She had once been a prim, naive teenager who arrived in London in 1978 as a cleaner, and her transformation into a manicured, sophisticated drug baroness was remarkable. La Patrona, who stood just a shade over 5 feet when not in a pair of her favourite strappy platforms, had risen through the ranks, first working for the cartel as a mule in Colombia when she was a schoolgirl.

Wilson knew he had no choice but to meet La Patrona in London, but he was very suspicious of her motives. Indeed, it soon became clear that Escobar was planning to distribute cocaine directly to UK streets, cutting out Wilson. La Patrona said this was only a proposal and that Wilson's cocaine operation would not be impacted at this stage. But Wilson knew that was bullshit, and he confronted La Patrona about the real reasons behind the decision. She admitted that Escobar had heard about Wilson's ill-health and they feared he might have to step away from the cocaine operation sooner rather than later.

Wilson was outraged. He told La Patrona that he would never close down his operation. She tried to defuse the situation by assuring him that the cartel would recompence Wilson handsomely if their plans for the UK went ahead. She even told him, 'You should retire before it's too late. Enjoy your life. Get your health back.'

Charlie Wilson left that meeting with La Patrona with a sinking feeling. He didn't believe Escobar would pay him any compensation. The Colombians were telling him to shut down his operation so they could take over. He also suspected that the cartel had some support in the UK. This meant other London criminals had been lined up to handle all the cocaine from Medellín. The moment he'd been dreading for years was now on the horizon. Wilson needed to work out which way to turn. Did he swallow his pride and cash in his chips or defy the deadliest drug cartel in criminal history?

For the moment, Wilson chose to bury his head in the sand and ignore the approach. But he knew a time would come when he would have to make some very big decisions.

39/

By early 1989, Charlie Wilson was almost fifty-seven years old and his life certainly wasn't as much fun as it used to be. Many of the old faces had left Spain and his initial enthusiasm about living in a sunny climate was now being overshadowed by the difficulties of running his criminal empire on the Costa del Sol.

There was also a growing and constant threat of kidnapping. One old criminal hand in Spain explained: 'There were a lot of lower-end villains desperate to make a few bob and, at that time, there was a lucrative sideline in kidnapping. Most of these cases never even got reported to the police. What usually happened was that a rich villain got pulled by a bunch of desperadoes, a ransom of at least a hundred grand would be paid within hours and then the victim would be handed back to his or her family.'

Because of the various dangers, Wilson was careful to avoid the constant media attention that followed villains like Ronnie Knight and Freddie Foreman. As one friend later explained, 'Charlie was as quiet and careful as ever. Few outside his close circle of friends even recognised him because the photos used by the press were from before he was nicked for the Great Train Robbery more than twenty years earlier.' But the unmarked cars containing UK police detectives still regularly turned up at the end of his street and the British redtops trumpeted 'Gangster wars on the Costa del Crime' every time there was an incident in Spain. It had got so bad that Wilson, who usually took the *Sun*, stopped reading newspapers for the first time in his life.

He watched on as, in July 1989, his friend and Security Express suspect Foreman was asked by Spanish police to help them with their enquiries. He agreed to meet local detectives in a hotel in Marbella, accompanied by his Spanish lawyer. Foreman's passport was found to be false and he was declared a *persona non grata* – an undesirable alien. That was enough to force him on a plane back to London. Foreman and others later described this 'extradition' as nothing short of kidnap by Spanish police. Hours later, the former Krays associate was escorted from a plane at Heathrow airport to stand trial for his part in the Security Express robbery.

The Spanish had become sick of being derided for harbouring UK criminals and felt restricted by the strict terms of their own extradition treaty. The police were accused of outrageously bending the rules to get Foreman home.

However, there were other far more cold-blooded characters waiting in the wings to take the place of the Freddie Foremans of the world. Decades after the first British chants of 'Viva Espana' and the Brits' early morning sorties to bag a sunlounger before the Germans, the Costa del Sol was being invaded by the Soviet Union and other eastern bloc nations as communism began crumbling in their home countries.

The murders of a Muscovite couple and their two young children in Marbella in 1989 heightened fears amongst the remaining British faces that the traditional rules of engagement were about to be thrown out of the window. Gangsters from countries that some British villains couldn't even find on a map were making southern Spain their home. Interpol issued warnings that these characters were about to change the face of organised crime in Europe. Their specialities were drugs, prostitution and money-laundering. Dollar-rich Soviets started arriving in the bars and restaurants of Marbella and Puerto Banus. One old-timer on the Costa del Crime recalled: 'These people were cold, hard, ruthless bastards. They didn't care about reputations. One Russian I met said to me once: "We like to spend all our money quickly because we never know how long we're going to live."'

UK criminals on the southern coast of Spain from Estepona to Torremolinos tried to steer clear of these so-called 'foreign bastards'. But they shared one objective in common – to make the really big money from drugs. The Russians and their eastern European rivals were busy building up contacts in North Africa and South America. Charlie and most other

British faces on the Costa del Crime hoped they'd all shoot each other in the back.

Meanwhile, a few small-time, local crooks also began turning up dead on the Costa del Sol after getting too big for their boots. Hugh Lomax was a thirty-one-year-old odd-job man for a number of British villains. He had been pulled in by Spanish police on a couple of occasions before someone decided he might inform on them. Lomax was taken to a field near Torremolinos and stabbed so many times it took police several days to identify his scarred and bloody body.

The rules on the Costa del Crime were very different to those back home in the UK. Here in the sunshine, the local police weren't that interested in criminals' feuds. Their only priority was to make sure these big, bad gangsters didn't affect the lucrative tourist trade. In the summer of 1989, a massive police operation code-named Diplomat was launched after a tip-off landed a container that had been tracked from Afghanistan via the Soviet Union. Hidden in sacks of liquorice was 'Afghan black', cannabis resin with a street value of £135 million. The haul was the result of the first-ever joint investigation mounted by British customs alongside their Russian counterparts. The hash's former owners were over in Holland: Charlie's old prison mate Roy 'the Lump' Adkins and his boss, the short-tempered Klaas 'the Preacher' Bruinsma – now the proud owner of a £2-million yacht called the *Neeltje Jacoba* – and they were bitterly upset.

Adkins was also wanted by British police over previous offences and his addiction to cocaine was worsening so that, in the words of one Dutch associate, 'he'd become almost as big a monster as the Preacher'. One of Bruinsma's rivals had recently been found upside down in a barrel of cement having had his penis and legs cut off while he was still alive. Perhaps not so surprisingly, Bruinsma and Adkins at one stage even suspected each other of being grasses. This bad feeling boiled over when the two men had a vicious argument in Amsterdam's most notorious sex club, Yab Yum. Shots were fired but nobody was injured. When the police arrived at the scene witnesses wouldn't say what had happened.

Among those arrested by UK police was Charlie's old friend, master-smuggler Paddy, and five members of his gang. Paddy was put under enormous pressure from authorities to name his paymasters and, as a Bermondsey boy of the old school, he knew that unless he wanted to shorten his life expectancy his lips would have to remain sealed. But he had been refused bail and, with his trial back in Britain not due until the following January, he had plenty of time to think about how to reduce his sentence without risking his life in the process. There was no way he could name Adkins in open court but maybe he could throw his name into the ring. What harm could that do? Adkins was already on the run and details of his involvement with the drugs shipment were well-known to many criminals and policemen. But for the moment, Paddy wasn't prepared to upset the highly strung Adkins in case he ended up with a death sentence.

What neither Charlie nor Paddy realised was that Adkins had been working as an agent for the Brink's-Mat robbery gang, who were trying to buy shipments of Medellín cocaine with the gold bullion they'd stolen five years earlier. Worse still, the latest bust wasn't the first occasion on which Adkins had lost product. He owned a share in that shipment of hash which Charlie Wilson's gang had stolen on the Costa Brava a couple of years earlier from a bunch of young British gangsters, including fugitive Danny 'Scarface' Roff. He was now working for Adkins in Holland, having escaped from prison in May 1988, alongside two other hardened, south London inmates, each covered in tattoos and scars. They had beaten up their guards, handcuffed them and hijacked a prison bus en route from jail on the Isle of Wight to Blundeston prison, Suffolk. Scotland Yard had immediately issued a warning: 'Don't go anywhere near them. If you think you see them, just call the police.'

Scarface and a twenty-seven-year-old known as 'Skins' were notorious for the violent nature of their crimes. Roff was inside for armed robbery while Skins had been convicted for supplying drugs and wounding. Both escapees had gone to Holland in search of work from fellow Londoner Adkins. One retired Flying Squad detective who met both Skins and Roff later recalled, 'Danny was a bad, mad bastard. A lunatic. I nicked Skins after some idiot started loosing off a loaded .45 next to a coffee stall in Elephant and Castle. He didn't shoot anyone, but he was up to all sorts of mischief. He even threatened to kill a policeman at one stage.'

In Colombia, Charlie Wilson's refusal to walk away from the cocaine trade meant that the increasingly paranoid Pablo Escobar had some decisions to make. His own power-crazy aspirations had resulted in him having a presidential candidate assassinated in August 1989. A few weeks later he orchestrated the terrorist-style bombing of a local airliner that crashed with the loss of more than a hundred lives. The USA labelled him the world's most evil gangster: he had undoubtedly evolved into the single most divisive figure in global crime. Many said he'd gone 'loco' because of the pressures of being the most hunted man in criminal history. For the moment, however, he remained relatively safe and distant in his home town of Medellín. But for how much longer? Although he wanted Charlie out of the way he didn't want to start a war on UK territory as it was not somewhere his cartel knew how to operate.

Escobar tried another tactic. He got a message to Charlie saying that he had a new plan for them to form a partnership, assuring him that his current profit margins would not be affected. The cartel intended to double the amount of cocaine that went into the coke-hungry UK marketplace anyway. Narco Charlie was highly suspicious, as he'd already presumed Escobar was trying to force him into an early retirement. Now Escobar seemed to be giving him a chance to retain his huge income from cocaine while at the same time allowing the Colombians to operate directly in the UK.

Charlie once again played for time. He knew all about Escobar's mounting problems inside Colombia. With any luck

Escobar would either be dead or in prison before any agreement was finalised. It was a huge gamble but Charlie was determined not to let the cartel destroy him. Charlie's train robber friends, both in the UK and in Spain, once again warned him to walk away from Escobar for good.

One old associate later recalled: 'I told Charlie to quit while he was still ahead. He said it wasn't that easy. He also seemed to think that if he stopped being a villain then life would become boring, and he couldn't stand the thought of that. He thrived on the big risks and just couldn't let go.'

Many of Charlie's old-fashioned, London underworld friends had disapproved of his drugs activities right from the start. But now many of those associates genuinely feared for his life. 'But Charlie didn't seem to give a fuck,' one old friend later said. There was no doubt Charlie needed to seriously consider retirement. He must have known it would help lift Pat out of her almost constant depression. However, Charlie loathed the fact that he'd be seen by many as running away from Pablo Escobar.

Charlie Wilson didn't run away from anyone.

40/

Back in Britain in August 1989, Charlie's train robber pals Tommy Wisbey and Jimmy Hussey were sentenced for their part in trafficking cocaine with a street value of more than £500,000. Hussey had put down a cash investment in a shipment of drugs without ever getting directly involved. The judge told him: 'All you were going to do was pass the drug from one hand to another, not to the ultimate consumer, but the effect would have been the same.'

When Charlie heard about Wisbey and Hussey he thanked his lucky stars he was in Spain, where things still seemed more relaxed, despite recent crackdowns. He'd had enough hassles in the UK during those difficult years after he'd got out of jail following the Great Train Robbery. Charlie sent his two friends handwritten notes telling them to keep their spirits up, fearing that a similar term in prison would have been too much for his bad health to handle.

Former south London gang boss Charlie Richardson was arrested for allegedly trying to bring a container-load of cocaine and 2 tons of cannabis worth millions through Southampton docks. It was further proof that drugs were now the main source of income for many old-school British gangsters.

There was another, even more serious criminal development in Spain in late 1989. ETA announced the end of their ceasefire with the Spanish government and the alliance between the terrorists and drug barons began to look very rocky. Explained one of Charlie's oldest friends: 'Charlie and other European drug barons were locked into bringing most of their coke from Galicia via ETA, who then decided they wanted a bigger fee because they needed to buy even more weapons for their war.' When a Spanish gangster with strong links to a European drug cartel based on the Costa del Sol was killed in Marbella, it was seen as a deadly warning to all criminals to watch their backs when dealing with ETA. A bomb had been planted in a stolen Fiat Tipo and, despite receiving on-the-spot medical attention, the victim was dead within thirty minutes.

In the United States, the DEA's ongoing war on drugs was waged through the Organised Crime Drug Enforcement Task Force (OCDETF). This assisted law enforcement agencies in several countries probing so-called 'heavyweight' druglords, including Charlie and other British criminals on the Costa del Sol. On the basis of those findings, a Florida assistant US attorney, Robert O'Neill, hoped there would be sufficient evidence to force them to go before a grand jury in his district.

The next stage of the OCDETF operation was to get Spanish and UK police to agree to raid homes and confiscate anything that might link the suspects to drug dealing. The DEA intended to prove at least a dozen charges against Charlie and the others, including conspiracy and money-laundering as well as drug-dealing. The DEA arrested a Colombian in Miami with links to Pablo Escobar and his Medellín cartel. He immediately threw three British names, including Charlie's, into the ring when he was being interrogated. It was a classic cartel move. They were offering up a few people not from Colombia in the hope that the US authorities might ease off on their hunt for Escobar and his cronies. This new DEA prisoner – held in the Miami metropolitan correctional centre – stated that Charlie and the others were financing massive cocaine shipments from Colombia.

Despite the misdirection of his associate, Pablo Escobar was irritated that he was 'singing' at all. He responded to the pressure exerted by US law enforcement by stepping up his activities, killing even more government officials and policemen in Colombia's big cities, virtually on a daily basis. He even bombed the headquarters of the equivalent to Colombia's FBI and was also embroiled in a deadly war with his only rivals for the worldwide cocaine market, the Cali cartel. They had thrown down the gauntlet to Escobar because they believed they would soon be running the Medellín cartel's most valuable US territories, including Miami and Los Angeles.

In late 1989, a London criminal called Michael Michael – who Charlie met through his armed-robber-turned-drug-baron friend Mickey Green – became a Scotland Yard police informant, in exchange for a light, eight-month prison sentence. He had been working as an accountant and helping to run a string of massage parlours in Britain with his common-law wife, Lynn, when he was arrested for a three-million-pound mortgage fraud. He was given the pseudonym Andrew Ridgeley, after George Michael's *Wham!* singing partner. He passed information about members of various criminal families and their activities in the UK and Spain to his police handler. His contact sheets named Charlie Wilson, Mickey Green, Brian

Wright, Tony White and numerous other UK criminals as dealing in drugs in Spain.

He claimed to have met Charlie, Green and White numerous times in the country, as well as at expensive hotels in London's West End. Michael himself supervised the UK distribution of massive amounts of drugs, much of them smuggled from southern Spain. Cannabis resin was hidden in drums that were suspended inside liquid tankers and cocaine tended to be hidden in cars because it was much smaller in quantity. Some drugs were regularly hidden inside a secret compartment on a tourist coach, nicknamed the 'Magic Bus' after The Who's song. Michael also laundered vast sums of cash for his contacts through a currency exchange bureau specially set up in west London. Women were usually preferred as couriers to move cash and drugs in and out of Heathrow or Gatwick to Spain, flying out with two-week return tickets as if they were going on holiday, but actually returning the following day.

Michael Michael also claimed he paid tens of thousands of pounds to corrupt police officers on behalf of Charlie and Mickey Green in exchange for information about other criminals and ongoing police investigations. Detectives known to have gambling or drug problems were prime blackmail targets for the pair. He claimed they kept asking for more information from their crooked police contacts, knowing that whatever came their way could also be sold onto the highest bidder within the criminal underworld if it was of no use to them personally.

Charlie Wilson clearly had a lot more enemies than friends in the world by this time. He was now entrenched in no man's land. His biggest and most lucrative cocaine deal with the world's most dangerous criminal Pablo Escobar was up in the air. He'd been named as a drugs baron to police and his health was deteriorating rapidly.

As his oldest friends on the Costa del Crime warned him: 'Watch yer back, Charlie.'

41/

In late 1989, Charlie got a call in Spain from Paddy's wife Julie. The couple knew Charlie well and had been to stay at Chequers many times. She wanted permission for her husband to name the Lump to police in the hope that Paddy might get a lighter sentence at his coming trial. Charlie initially did not get involved.

Julie tried again, explaining that it wouldn't really harm Adkins because he was already on the run from British and Dutch police for other offences. Charlie promised to think it over. He had a soft spot for Paddy and Julie and dearly wanted to help them. Paddy had done him a lot of favours down the years.

Charlie's associates have always insisted Charlie would never have given permission to name Adkins, especially not to Julie over the phone as he already suspected it was being tapped. Yet Charlie did leave a message for another, well-known criminal who was connected to Adkins on the Costa del Crime, something along the lines of 'What harm could it do?'

As another of Charlie's criminal associates later explained: 'It wasn't really grassing up in the true sense of the word because Adkins' activities were already well-known to the police and Charlie hoped he'd understand the reasoning behind Paddy's request.' But Charlie did not realise that the Lump had other scores to settle with him, and any suggestion that Charlie was giving his best mate permission to grass him up could spark vicious reprisals from Adkins. It was said that, a few days after Charlie's message, Paddy told detectives to 'talk to Roy Adkins'. Soon after, Dutch police – acting on information from UK customs – raided Adkins' hideout in Holland and located a small amount of gold from the Brink's-Mat robbery. This infuriated the Lump, who had fled before the police arrived. He immediately connected the raid to Charlie because of the call to his friend. Adkins also knew this development made him look like a risky proposition from the point of view of the Brink's-Mat robbery gang, who were about to use him to handle another shipment of gold to Escobar in exchange for more cocaine.

Adkins had to think fast or else he really would get caught in the crossfire. He made sure that Pablo Escobar was told that Narco Charlie was a police informant. Escobar was already paranoid about all his associates so he didn't take much convincing and he was also angry that Charlie had cost him a large shipment of cut-price Brink's-Mat gold that he could have sold on for an even bigger profit than he made from cocaine. His people on the Costa del Sol were told to watch Charlie even closer. He also decided it would soon be time to force his gringo associate into agreeing to that new cocaine distribution deal. Back in London, the Brink's-Mat gang were also infuriated when they heard that Paddy may have cost them that shipment of cocaine when he grassed.

In early January 1990, Charlie got a call from an incandescent Roy Adkins. Charlie tried to explain why Paddy had named him. 'But Adkins wouldn't have any of it. He accused Charlie of grassing him up,' one of Charlie's oldest friends on the Costa del Sol explained. The fact Charlie and Paddy were such close friends had undoubtedly fuelled Adkins' paranoia. Charlie tried to warn him to be careful what he said in case others were listening. But he had no idea that Adkins had already informed Pablo Escobar of his suspicions or that Adkins had been setting up exchanges of Brink's-Mat gold for Medellín cocaine.

A couple of days later, Paddy and four other men were jailed for almost fifty years after a three-week trial near London. The gang was also ordered to pay back nearly three million pounds' worth of illegal assets. It was the biggest seizure of investments, bank accounts, homes and businesses made under the 1986 Drug Trafficking Offences Act. The court heard that Paddy had set up at least six bogus companies and masterminded further plans to import cannabis resin from Afghanistan and India hidden in cargoes of acid, bleaching powder, mango chutney and liquorice root.

Paddy – now in his early fifties – was described in court by his counsel as a 'company director' although the judge called him 'a drugs baron'. He was given twelve months to comply with the confiscation order or face a further ten years in jail. But it was predicted the sentence would be cut considerably on appeal because Paddy had helped police by naming Adkins. A few days after the trial ended, a British criminal delivered a message from Roy Adkins to Charlie: 'You should not have given that permission to Paddy.' Adkins – who was by then stuffing grams of coke up his nose – and Bruinsma had lost a fortune when Paddy and his gang were arrested with all their hash. Adkins had, as he had feared, also lost a huge sum when the Brink's-Mat gold for cocaine deal hit the rocks. Now, having threatened Charlie, Adkins couldn't back down without losing the respect of the underworld. Reputations were at stake.

Adkins reminded Pablo Escobar and his Medellín cartel that Charlie's actions as an informant had directly led to the cartel losing all that gold. It seemed to Pablo Escobar that Narco Charlie – the man he had once respected and liked – was now a liability. It was time to cut him loose.

Law enforcement agencies from the US, UK and Spain monitored phone calls during which Adkins referred to 'traitor' Charlie, but they chose not to step in. They had no intention of blowing their own cover until they had enough evidence to catch much bigger fish than Narco Charlie. Ironically, Adkins no doubt knew by this time that his threats to Charlie were being monitored. But he didn't care because he believed that the Medellín cartel would eventually sort things out.

At the end of January 1990, Charlie flew to London for another medical check-up for his emphysema. It had got even worse over the Christmas period, not helped by the stress Adkins was causing. Shortly after arriving, Charlie was contacted by one of Adkins' associates, who repeated the threat. Charlie responded by calmly asking the same man to a lunch he was having the following day with Paddy's wife Julie 'so you can find out what really happened'. Neither Adkins or his associate took up Charlie's invitation.

A couple of days later, Charlie was crossing Harley Street when he noticed a man on a motorbike driving very slowly behind him. For the next ten minutes the motorcyclist stayed on his tail constantly. 'Charlie didn't scare that easily but he was pissed off with Adkins for making threats against him and reckoned the motorbike was part of it,' one friend later explained. In fact, the motorbike was being driven by a henchman employed by Medellín cartel London boss La Patrona. Escobar wanted their target monitored before deciding how to deal with him.

Charlie met with one of his closest friends during that trip to London and asked him: 'Would you have let Paddy drop that name in if you'd been me?'

Charlie's friend replied: 'Why not? Is not as if the law didn't already know what Adkins was up to. I don't think it harmed anyone.'

Charlie told his close friend he believed Adkins would eventually calm down and the whole thing would blow over. 'It's nothing to worry about. The geezer's completely out of order on this one,' he said.

The friend later recalled: 'Charlie was more worried about his emphysema than Roy Adkins. Now that was *really* getting him down.'

Charlie held a meeting with three major London criminals in a West End hotel to discuss a drug deal. Undercover police and customs officers flooded the hotel with officers, eight at a time to provide round-the-clock surveillance, and followed the group's every move. Conversations were taped and all participants were photographed. But by the end of the three-hour meeting the police could only conclude that something big was in the air.

It was. Charlie had discovered for the first time that the Lump had been handling the Brink's-Mat gold for cocaine deals with Escobar, which then had to be cancelled after Paddy informed. Now Charlie realised why Adkins was so angry with him. The following day,

Charlie was Brian Wright's guest at his private member's box at Windsor racecourse Wright had also persuaded Adkins, his one-time associate and still wanted by British police, to attend the same meeting to sort out the problems he had with Charlie.

One source, who spoke to someone who was present that day, recalled: 'It was a disaster. Adkins didn't say a word to Charlie and they avoided each other the whole afternoon. I heard afterwards that Adkins had wanted to have a go at Charlie there and then but Brian Wright calmed him down. Charlie complained to Wright afterwards that Adkins' attitude was "completely out of order".'

Charlie expected respect from characters like Adkins, not abuse. He was outraged that Adkins thought he was a grass and just as angry to have discovered that Adkins was doing Brink's-Mat gold deals with Escobar behind his back. That night, Adkins travelled overland to Suffolk, where he caught a ferry to Holland, still brimming with hatred for Charlie Wilson.

Meanwhile, law enforcement agencies from the US, UK and Spain saw this simmering feud with Adkins as the perfect catalyst to help them bring down the world's biggest cocaine cartel. The multi-layered surveillance team on the Costa del Sol had established that Charlie was using a warehouse on a brand new *polígono industrial* (Spanish for 'industrial estate') near Marbella as his unofficial office.

Working hard, they picked up simple 'overhears' – snippets of information – as Charlie walked past members of the team in the street. They also followed Charlie to his house in the Urbanización Montana, but they lacked enough concrete evidence to issue arrest warrants.

42/

On a warm night in late February 1990, two undercover policemen saw Charlie leaving his Marbella house at four in the morning. They followed Charlie to the Atalaya Park hotel, on the road towards Estepona, where Charlie met Brian Doran – the Professor – and three other men who looked like they were all South American. These were Pablo Escobar's representatives in Spain.

Charlie explained that Roy Adkins was stirring up trouble for him. He wanted Doran and the others to convey a message to Pablo Escobar that, as far as Charlie was concerned, it was business as usual. He also asked for confirmation that Escobar had been swapping cocaine for Brink's-Mat gold.

The following day, someone inside Marbella police station told a well-known British criminal on the Costa del Sol that Charlie was under twenty-four-hour surveillance. Alarm bells went off everywhere from Madrid to Colombia. The last thing anyone wanted was to deal with a man who was now being shadowed by the authorities around the clock. The paranoid Adkins believed Charlie was trying to set everyone up for a fall and had convinced himself that Charlie was deliberately exposing himself to prevent Adkins carrying out his threat to kill him. He remained convinced that Charlie was 'a fucking grass' and told the Medellín cartel that he was a liability. He insisted that Pablo Escobar needed to deal with the Charlie 'problem'. Escobar's main concern was that there was no comeback on his cocaine empire. Otherwise, as far as he was concerned, getting Narco Charlie off the scene would make it much easier to directly flood the UK and Europe with Medellín cocaine. Adkins expected the Colombians to send their own people over to deal with Charlie but when it became clear they wouldn't, Adkins said he would handle it all himself.

Law enforcement agencies were content to watch and wait. They were still prepared for Charlie Wilson to walk into a trap set by his criminal associates and were not planning to make an attempt to save him if that happened. Their number one priority remained Pablo Escobar and the Medellín cartel. If that meant a bit of collateral damage, then so be it.

The stress of these weeks left Charlie suffering badly with his emphysema. He'd even stopped taking cocaine, after being warned that it would make his lungs even worse. Neighbour Bernie Finch later recalled: 'I remember seeing Charlie struggling to lift a barrow in his garden because he was so short of breath. He definitely hadn't been like that when we first moved in. He said he'd been back to the UK but there wasn't much they could do to make it any better. I could see in his eyes that he didn't really believe any treatment was helping. Charlie even tried a herbal tea cure. But we all knew he was clutching at straws. After January there was a definite deterioration. He seemed to lose a lot of weight very quickly. We started to wonder if he had cancer. He was coughing all the time and seemed very short of breath.'

The Finches noticed that Charlie and Pat never ventured out anywhere together after Christmas 1989. Bernie Finch said: 'It was as if Pat refused to leave that house. We tried to get them to come out for dinner as a couple, but they both looked exhausted at the very thought of it.' Pat was finding it increasingly hard to face the world. She'd been through so much as wife to Charlie: murders; life on the run; notoriety. Now it felt to her as if the nastiest criminals in the world were hiding behind every palm tree on the Costa del Crime.

As one friend later explained: 'No wonder Pat didn't want to go out. The world had evolved into a scary place for her. She was stuck in Spain, a long way from her beloved daughters and she felt vulnerable and very alone, especially when Charlie went off on his business trips.'

On 26 February 1990, escaped London convict Skins was arrested in Amsterdam after a shoot-out with Dutch police. One week later he managed to escape from his police cell once again. Within days, Skins met up again with Danny 'Scarface' Roff. In early March, the pair were summoned to a meeting with 'the Lump' Adkins in Amsterdam. He had a 'very special job' for them, telling Roff to book himself a holiday on the Costa del Sol with his wife and young child. Roff had connections to some of the Brink's-Mat gold bullion robbers, so he knew all about how the gold for cocaine deals had hit the rocks, apparently thanks to Charlie and Paddy. Roff also had a personal score to settle with Charlie, as one of the British gangsters humiliated by Wilson's gang stealing the hash shipment on the Costa Brava.

Charlie didn't really seem to care, but the net was closing in. Criminals and law enforcement agencies alike were after his blood. He was, in the words of one old Costa del Sol criminal, 'a dead man walking.'

43/

At midday on 23 April 1990, Charlie's cousin Norman Radford and his wife – who'd been staying at Chequers – were driving down to the shops in Marbella when they spotted a youth with blond hair sunning himself on a mini-roundabout close to the Urbanización Montana. A yellow mountain bike lay beside him as he lounged on the grass verge.

Norman didn't give the man a moment's thought until much later that day, when he drove past a second time on his way to Malaga airport to fly back to the UK. He later recalled: 'He was still sitting on the grass verge. We made a joke of it as we passed because we'd earlier thought he'd fallen off his bicycle.'

In the garden of Chequers, Charlie was lighting his barbeque for the special anniversary dinner he planned. Less than 2 miles away, a young south-London man was talking on a payphone, before getting into his van and driving up the hill. After passing the Europa health club the driver came across many larger, detached houses. Some of the properties looked like virtual palaces to the driver who was more used to the crumbling, grey concrete tower blocks and drab, red-brick terraces of Vauxhall and Bermondsey. He passed another block of apartments before negotiating a roundabout where he ignored the signpost north and instead took a smaller turning west on Avenida Nerja, towards the Urbanización Montana. He passed a ten-bedroomed hacienda before reaching the mini-roundabout where his friend was waiting with his bike. Separately, they walked to Chequers.

Pat answered the front door to a man who, in a distinct cockney accent, mumbled that he had a message for Charlie from his boss. Pat told him to put his bike in the porch. 'It might get nicked if you leave it outside,' she said pleasantly. The man didn't answer, but placed the bike between the front door and Charlie's carefully built garden wall.

Pat later recalled what happened next: 'Charlie was busy chopping up food so I called to him and he came in from the garden.' Charlie recognised the man and immediately showed him out to the patio area next to the pool. For some inexplicable reason the legendary sixth sense that had helped Charlie Wilson remain one step ahead of his enemies for a lifetime failed to ring the alarm bell. As the pair walked into the garden, Pat heard raised voices. 'I remained inside. Charlie and this man must have been talking for at least five minutes. Perhaps he was telling Charlie about someone he knew back in London – giving him a message or something. He must have told Charlie something which caught his attention, otherwise they wouldn't have been together so long.'

The visitor was delivering Roy Adkins' message of hatred and contempt and, once concluded, he began to attack Charlie and the dog who tried to help his master. Charlie's cousin Norman Radford later said: 'Bo-Bo must have tried to defend Charlie. He could never have fought back anybody on his own. His lungs were so bad.'

The messenger took out his Smith & Wesson 9mm pistol. Pat heard the two loud bangs from where she was in the kitchen. 'I heard Bo-Bo screaming. I came out and saw Charlie ... He just pointed his finger to his open mouth. Blood was streaming from it.' Charlie then tried to point towards the back wall, which the gunman had just climbed to escape. 'As I looked at him struggling everything went into slow motion. I couldn't do anything.'

As slow motion snapped into real time, Pat screamed over the back wall to the Finches, trying to raise the alarm. When no one responded, Pat rushed back into the house and telephoned their close friend and Chequers architect Marti Franco, who later recalled: 'Pat just said, "Shot Charlie. You come!"'

The shooter had planned the escape well, having gone over the wall at precisely the right point: on the other side was a 20-foot drop into a dry river bed that was tangled in thorny scrub and strewn in litter, except just to the left of the barbeque. In that area alone, the earth was banked up on the other side of the perimeter to within 6 feet. After jumping down, the killer ran to the front of the house and took the mountain bike, free-wheeled down the hill to the mini-roundabout and met his accomplice, who was waiting in the white van. They stowed the bike in the back of the van and drove off at a modest speed to avoid attracting attention, back to the big roundabout and then towards old Marbella and Avenida Cascada Camojan.

The evident careful planning suggested that this hadn't been a fully-fledged cartel-style execution. If it had been, Pat would almost certainly have been killed as well, since she was the only person who could identify the killer. But the shooter had strict orders: 'This row's with Charlie, OK? Leave Pat out of it.'

Approximately six minutes after shooting dead one of Britain's most famous criminals, the two men parked their small white van up next to a petrol station opposite the Hotel Don Pepe, took out the bike and went their separate ways. It was 5.45 p.m.

44/

Marti Franco arrived at Chequers minutes after Pat's call. She recalled: 'When I saw Charlie he looked already dead. But what surprised me most was that there seemed to be no bullet wounds and Pat had told me she heard a gun. There was a swelling on the side of Charlie's neck, so tiny it seemed like it was made by a small blade or scalpel.'

Other neighbours alerted by Pat's shrieks also quickly arrived at the house. They saw a 20-foot trail of blood where Charlie had clawed his way across the grey marble patio with two bullet wounds in his head. Paramedics attempted to revive Charlie, even though it was obviously already too late. Marti Franco recalled: 'I couldn't take my eyes off Charlie. Everyone was rushing around the house but my eyes were on Charlie.'

Pat turned to Marti and said: 'Can you go to the hospital with him, please?'

Marti was stunned to be asked but agreed. It was only later she realised Pat didn't want to leave the house because it was swarming with police and she was worried they might find incriminating evidence that could link Charlie to crimes. Marti later recalled: 'What could I say – "No"? Pat didn't want to leave them alone in the house.' Despite all those years of doubt and insecurity about her marriage to Charlie, Pat was still covering for him, even after he'd been murdered in their back garden.

The Seat ambulance was the size of a standard estate car and Marti had to sit next to Charlie's corpse. His legs were up in the air because his 6-foot frame was too long to fit in the back of the vehicle. 'It was awful. There I was sitting next to the dead body of a friend. It was the most traumatic thing I've ever had to do in my life,' she said. Marti took a taxi back to the house as soon as Charlie's body was delivered to the Marbella Clinic hospital, 5 kilometres away.

The Wilson's best friends on the estate, neighbours Bernie and Liz Finch, had just driven back from a shopping trip and they found their street buzzing with police and paramedics. Bernie recalled: 'I saw the Guardia Civil and said to my wife, "I'm going up to see what's happened. There must have been a break-in." She said, "Don't get involved." I ignored her. By the time I got to the house Charlie had already been taken away, but the dog was still lying in the garden. He was alive, so I phoned the vet to come and put him down. It was a terrible scene. Pat was crying. There were police and neighbours everywhere.'

Liz later recalled: 'Just after we'd walked in and found out what had happened, Pat said to me, "Liz, I've got something to tell you. Did you know who Charlie was?" I said, "Yes, Pat, but it made no difference. You were just Charlie and Pat – our friends."'

A look of relief came over Pat's face. She said, 'He always said you knew. But I always felt so embarrassed.'

'It's nothing to be embarrassed by, Pat,' replied Liz Finch. She later recalled: 'Even as distraught as she was, I think Pat still felt she had to explain.'

The Finches stayed with Pat until late that night. Their dog Chico even leapt over Charlie's wall and spent the night with the Wilson's surviving dog, Dino. The Finches were to take in Dino rather than see him be put down. 'It was strange to think that Charlie wouldn't be there any more to cook those dogs a whole chicken and feed it to them like he did so often,' remembered Bernie. That evening, he walked out onto the blood-splattered patio area and noticed that it hadn't even been cordoned off by the police. 'There was a big monkey wrench lying nearby on a flower bed close to the barbeque, which no one seemed to have noticed. It might have been used by the killer to break the dog's leg or maybe even smash Charlie in the face.'

Pat was consoled by Charlie's cousin Norman – who'd been contacted at the airport on his way home and returned immediately to Chequers – as well as Liz. Pat kept saying that Charlie had nothing to do with drugs. But as Liz Finch later said: 'I never believed it.' Pat insisted on talking about Charlie's escape from Winson Green prison more than twenty years earlier. 'She kept saying he'd broken out against his will. That he didn't want to escape,' recalled Bernie. It was as if Pat was on automatic pilot after being briefed time and time again by Charlie about how to react if the police ever came to the house.

Charlie was still telling her, 'Deny everything, love. You understand?' She always nodded her head nervously when he said those words.

45/

The criminal fraternity on the Costa del Crime were asking many questions in the wake of Charlie's death: why wasn't the killer worried that Charlie might fight back? Why was he so relaxed when the young south Londoner appeared at his house? Did he know there was a threat? If Charlie had been expecting trouble, he would surely never have invited the killer into his house.

It seemed as if the assassin had been ordered to deliver a message:'I want Charlie to know he was out of order before you blow him away.'The use of the mountain bike was in itself an act of careless bravado; it stood out because young people tended to use mopeds in Spain. It would have been easier and safer to kill Charlie with a sniper's rifle from the cover of a new apartment block being built on the other side of the small pine wood. It had an excellent view into the Wilson's back garden.This was an unusual hit for all these reasons.

'If you think there's gonna be a row you deal with it outside on the street,' explained one criminal shortly after the murder.

At the Marbella Clinic hospital on the east side of town, Charlie's corpse was the subject of an immediate post-mortem. This concluded he was killed by the first bullet which entered the right side of his neck and lodged under his left shoulder blade. Charlie's beloved dog Bo-Bo was also due to be examined. Pat and Charlie's cousin Norman Radford informed Spanish police that the family wanted Charlie's body brought back to south London and buried in their plot in Wandsworth.

Police began removing boxes, papers and plastic bags containing Charlie's belongings from his house. Neither Pat nor

Norman Radford mentioned there was a basement to the house. It was only discovered by police after one detective asked why there was a small window at ground level. A senior Marbella magistrate was appointed chief investigator and ordered police not to issue any comments before they could establish a clear motive. Spanish authorities hoped the crime would fade away as quickly as possible because it was bad for the tourist trade on the Costa del Sol. They had no idea at this stage that a multi-national law enforcement task force had been watching Charlie for some considerable time.

At Chequers, Marti Franco was now acting as interpreter for the policemen asking Pat questions about her husband. The widow also helped a Spanish police artist put together a photofit image of the man she said had shot her husband. The picture was to be immediately published in all newspapers and broadcast on Spanish TV.

Dozens of Spanish and British reporters gathered at the scene and noted the bars on every window of Chequers and the 6-foot wall that Charlie had spent so much time building. They all concluded that the Costa del Crime had finally caught up with Charlie Wilson. Unable to talk with Pat herself, journalists turned their attention towards neighbour Bernie Finch. He said: 'Charlie would do anything to help. He was always doing odd jobs and running errands for people. We knew who he was, but this is grotesque.' Almost as grotesque was the behaviour of one small group of London tabloid reporters that Bernie Finch saw trying to climb over their back wall to get into Charlie's house. 'I had to hosepipe them down in the end. They were like animals.'

Inside Chequers, a tearful Pat phoned her three daughters in London, who all pledged to fly over to Spain immediately. Pat also called Charlie's old train robber pal, Gordon Goody, who immediately set off from his home in Mojacar, 200 miles east of Marbella. Goody openly loathed reporters and refused to be interviewed when he turned up at the house five hours later. He was furious the following day when one newspaper wrongly reported that he was awaiting trial on a £70,000 marijuana smuggling ran.

Pat – chain-smoking and looking haggard – insisted to police that Charlie had left his life of crime behind long ago. She said: 'I can't think who would want to kill my Charlie. But I can tell you this, it is nothing to do with drugs. Charlie didn't like drugs of any description.'

Early next morning, Charlie's cousin Norman Radford invited a group of British reporters into Chequers and helpfully retraced the killer's steps through the entrance gate and past the swimming pool. 'That's where they stood talking,' he said, pointing to the barbeque area. 'There was a handprint there. It trailed back to the pool where Charlie finally collapsed. I wouldn't allow anyone to clear up the congealed blood. I did it myself with a shovel. It was ghasty. I felt sick to my stomach.' Like Pat, Radford dismissed all talk of a drugs motive. 'When police searched the house they found no drugs. There was no shotgun, no weapons of any sort. Not even a pickaxe handle which, if Charlie had feared for his life, he would certainly have had at the ready.' Radford floated the idea of two men being involved in the killing. 'I think the murderer jumped over the back wall after shooting Charlie,' he said. 'Then he removed the mountain bike and they met at the end of the road in a car, taking both him and the machine away.' Radford said that Pat was going into hiding. 'Pat doesn't seem frightened – all she's concerned about is getting the killer. But we're concerned for her safety.' Radford then added chillingly: 'The murderer must have had an ice-cool temperament to have carried out the killing with such precision. It's like something out of *The Godfather*.'

Spanish police had no doubt that an underworld feud had led to Charlie's murder. Back in London, Fleet Street used the killing as the perfect excuse to drag up details about the Great Train Robbery that would have infuriated Charlie. Newspapers made a point of saying how Charlie had been labelled 'the silent man' after saying so little during his original GTR trial.

In Medellín, news of Narco Charlie's assassination was met with a shrug of the shoulders by Pablo Escobar. He knew who'd done it. But he'd managed to avoid being directly involved, even though he'd given permission for the hit to go ahead. Escobar wasn't one to dwell on such things. He had his own pressures mounting back home in Medellín. The Narco Charlie problem had now been solved, which meant he could earn tens of millions more from his cocaine by having his own people run the distribution throughout Europe and the UK.

People like Narco Charlie were surplus to requirements. Pablo Escobar had a multi-national business to run and no one could get in the way of that.

46/

Nearly 5000 miles south of Medellín, in Rio de Janeiro, Brazil, the only Great Train Robber still on the lam sent a message of condolence to Pat and the couple's three daughters.

Ronnie Biggs said: 'Charlie was a fun-loving kind of person, devil-may-care, good company.'

Even Charlie's old enemies in the police were saddened and surprised by his demise. Jack Slipper – the intrepid Scotland Yard detective who'd spent years tracking Biggs – said: 'Wilson had a strong character and physique. No one deserves to go like this.'

In Spain one of Charlie's oldest criminal associates said: 'I don't think Charlie believed Adkins would do him for such a stupid reason, until he heard about the Brink's-Mat gold for cocaine deals. That's when Charlie realised he was in dire trouble. But if anyone was going to cop it, it should really have been his mate Paddy.'

News of the World veteran reporter Trevor Kempson had known Pat for twenty years, ever since Pat had sold her story for thirty thousand pounds, just after Charlie's recapture in Canada. Pat told Kempson she believed a London underworld boss with a long-time grudge had hired the hitman. Clutching Kempson's hand, she sobbed uncontrollably and said: 'I'm absolutely sure this murder has something to do with Charlie's past back home. The murderer was about twenty-two years old, far too young to have known Charlie in those days. He must have been paid to do the killing by an older man, possibly one of Charlie's old associates from his criminal days.'

Many of Charlie's pals in Spain remained baffled by certain aspects of the killing, which simply didn't add up. One of Charlie's smuggling team on the Costa del Sol later explained: 'The karate business was a classic Russian calling card because all their killers are trained in martial arts in the military. They have the balls to do it. They don't come behind you, they don't shoot you in the back, they want you to see it coming.'

It was hardly surprising that Spanish detectives encountered a wall of silence when they tried to interview some of the ex-pat criminal fraternity on the Costa del Sol. As one British detective – unnamed – told the *Daily Mail*: 'This is a British mafia killing. The British mafia here knows who did it, but they're not going to help the police.'

Inspector Juan Lorenzo at Marbella's 'international delinquency' squad was appointed lead detective in charge of the police investigation and he had no doubt that Charlie's death was linked to drugs, despite Pat's denials. He was quick to note that Charlie had no visible source of income, yet had spent considerable sums of money renovating and rebuilding his house. Lorenzo – a stocky, quietly spoken, neatly dressed character in his mid-thirties – soon heard about some of Charlie's 'business trips' around the world. Less than forty-eight hours after Charlie's death, Lorenzo said: 'We are under no illusions that the British underworld is just as keen to find Wilson's murderer as we are and they may get to him before us.'

The file on the Wilson murder case was held in a small, bare office on the first floor of the old Marbella police station, a shabby, overcrowded two-storey building tucked away in the dusty back streets behind the city's Moorish castle and a world away from the ritzy piano bars, nightclubs and pricey restaurants of tourist Marbella. Outside were rows of cars impounded from drug dealers, each one vandalised, every window smashed. One was a brand-new Mercedes, recently set on fire by street urchins. Lorenzo's office contained just two desks, an old typewriter, a single telephone that worked erratically and a battered filing cabinet. On the brown walls were a couple of plaques from visiting police forces. A faded map of the town of Marbella, the street names just legible, covered half of one peeling wall. The squad, comprising the inspector and two sergeants, was responsible for investigating all crimes involving foreigners, from bag-snatching all the way to murder.

Lorenzo already had a full caseload: a few months earlier, the body of an American drug-trafficker was found, shot, like Charlie, twice in the head in a burnt-out car that bore traces of cocaine. The corpse of a Frenchman who had been tortured and killed had also recently been discovered in a chalet in nearby San Pedro. A man out walking his dog in Marbella centre spotted the arm of a corpse, the rest of which had been covered in quicklime to prevent identification. Only a couple of days before Charlie's murder, police arrested fourteen Turks and seized 210 kilos of heroin. Two foreigners carrying 175 kilos of cocaine were also arrested later that same day, in a separate raid.

Bernie Finch was invited to Inspector Lorenzo's office to be interviewed. He later recalled: 'There were two Scotland Yard officers there. They turned round to me and said, "Charlie was one of the good old boys. The younger ones wouldn't think twice about shooting their own mum."'

On 27 April, a judge prevented Charlie's body being repatriated to the UK and called in a second pathologist to carry out a new post-mortem as a precaution because of the immense public interest in the case. At Chequers, Norman Radford told reporters: 'Pat's in a dreadful state. She'd hoped to be taking Charlie home this weekend and the unexpected delay is causing further anguish. We have no idea what is going on.' She was refusing to leave the house at all, although she had already assured her family she'd quit Spain permanently once she got her husband's body home.

That same day, UK newspapers carried reports that Scotland Yard and the National Drugs Intelligence Unit had extensive dossiers on Charlie's contacts and criminal dealings over the previous couple of years. One source from Scotland Yard said: 'The criminal community here knows who is behind this and we have our own very strong suspicions. The type of people who did this stick to the old-fashioned ideals of not hurting women. How else can you explain the fact that Wilson's wife was not killed?'

Speculation that Colombian drug barons were angry about an unpaid shipment of cocaine and had killed Charlie was dismissed for that reason. 'They wouldn't have left Pat standing,' said one of Charlie's friends.

A member of Charlie's smuggling gang, who still resides on the Costa del Sol, later said: 'There were lots of theories flying around at first. Some people said a delivery of cocaine was due to take place but for some reason it didn't show up. And when that happens everyone's in trouble. That could have made Charlie vulnerable. Then there was ETA. Some of us wondered if Charlie had upset them. There was a story going round at the time that a British criminal had double-crossed them over a drugs deal. We all started to wonder whether that criminal was Charlie.'

But any suggestions that Charlie was a police grass were dismissed out of hand. 'No way. Charlie was from the old school and they never told tales,' said another of his former smugglers in Spain.

In London, many of Charlie's oldest criminal associates were deeply upset by his death. Long-time pal Joey Pyle said: 'I was stunned. I knew Charlie didn't work well with people. He was a loner but that didn't mean he deserved this, for Christ's sake. I'd heard he was depressed that all his train robbery cash had gone and he'd had to keep on working to keep things going.

Charlie was a hero with ninety per cent of south London. No one wanted it to come to this.'

Security Express blagger Ronnie Knight, whose wedding Charlie had attended just three years earlier, said: 'Charlie's death just made no sense. We all wondered what he could have been up to get shot like that. Charlie and the boys used to go down to the port [Puerto Banus] now and again but he never mentioned anything about these sort of heavy characters. Most of the time him and Pat kept themselves to themselves.'

Charlie's murder had put up the backs of a lot of British criminals because it implied that the old guard was losing power and influence. It seemed as if the up-and-coming, younger gangsters were sharpening their weapons and gaining a stronger grip on the Costa del Crime. There were also genuine fears that Charlie's death could spark a deadly cycle of violence. Scotland Yard had known for some time that Charlie was up to his neck in drugs, along with Mickey Green, Tony White and others. But was a bloodbath now inevitable?

Back in England, Charlie's one-time lover Georgie Ellis read with shock about his death in the newspapers. She'd heard nothing from Charlie since their last date together, except for a Christmas card a few months earlier with a simple message 'From Charlie'. She recalled: 'I took a deep breath when I saw the story in the paper and looked at Charlie's smiling face staring at me from a photograph. I just hoped he was as happy where he was now as when I'd met him.'

At Scotland Yard, supergrass Michael Michael was, as they say, still singing like a canary. Just days after Charlie was killed, he told his police handlers that the two young hoods Scarface and Skins had carried out the hit on behalf of Roy Adkins. The Yard were initially sceptical about the statement but passed the names on to Spanish police. Michael made no mention of Pablo Escobar's involvement because he knew – like everyone else – that if he so much as breathed the name of the Medellín cartel then he'd be the next name on their list.

A few days after Charlie's death, Bernie Finch was helping dismantle the doghouse Charlie had so carefully built out of plywood for Bo-Bo when he noticed the doll's hand that Charlie had found so amusing still sticking out of a nearby flowerbed. Bernie said: 'I looked down at it, smiled and wondered what sort of crazy joke Charlie would have cracked if he'd been there. Then I bent down to remove the hand, but stopped in mid flow and left it exactly where it was just in case Charlie was watching over me.'

'The Lump' Adkins, for his part, believed he had killed at least three birds with one stone by arranging the shooting of Charlie: he'd got revenge on Charlie for being an informant, for costing him a fortune on the Brink's-Mat gold-for-cocaine deals with the Colombians and for stealing the hash on the Costa Brava. He just hoped that, despite everything, he still had an in with the Medellín cartel. Being in their good books could help him towards earning millions for handling their cocaine in the future.

But Roy Adkins was ignoring the bleedin' obvious. He was the only link between Pablo Escobar and the murder of Wilson, as well as those disastrous dealings with the Brink's-Mat gold bullion robbers. That made Adkins a liability in the eyes of the Colombians. His days were already numbered. And then there were Charlie's old friends. They wanted a word with Adkins as well.

47/

The legal difficulties in getting Charlie's body released added to Pat's distress over the shooting. She still insisted to family and friends she'd never set foot in Spain again once she'd accompanied him home to London. She also asked the staff at Wandsworth cemetery to leave room for her to be interred next to her dearly departed husband one day.

The second post-mortem on Charlie's body was completed on 29 April and no extra injuries were uncovered. His body was released for embalming and laid in a zinc coffin at a Marbella mortuary. But the funeral continued to be delayed, because legal papers dealing with his death had to be translated into English before his body could be shipped back to the UK. Another obstacle was that of Westminster coroner Dr Paul Knapman, who decided that the violent nature of Charlie's death qualified for an inquest to be held in London. The funeral could not go ahead until that inquest had been officially opened.

Eight days after the murder, Charlie's body was finally released by Spanish authorities and Pat gave the Chequers' house keys to a neighbour and asked them to keep an eye on the place – although she 'forgot' to include the key to Charlie's secret basement. Another neighbour, Bernie, drove Pat to Malaga airport in Charlie's white Toyota behind a hearse carrying the casket. Norman Radford followed in a rental car. Bernie later recalled: 'It was a nightmare journey because the paparazzi followed us on motorbikes. They were chasing us up the motorway and then overtaking and firing off shots with their cameras. I nearly crashed Charlie's car, it was so chaotic.' Bernie had forbidden his wife Liz joining them because there were fears that Pat might still be the killer's next target, as the only witness to her husband's murder. 'The police protection was pathetic,' said Bernie. 'One squad car accompanied us to the airport and they did nothing to even stop the journalists stalking us.'

At the departure terminal, two armed Guardia Civil officers accompanied Pat and Charlie's cousin on an electric buggy that was waved through the check-in desk and passport control. Out on the sizzling hot tarmac, the casket containing Charlie's remains was wrapped in a plain green tarpaulin with a red airline label unceremoniously stuck on the side as it was pushed by four airport workers into the cargo hold of a British Airways Boeing 737. Shortly afterwards, Pat and Cousin Norman boarded the BA jet that was filled with holidaymakers bound for London's

Heathrow airport. Pat said virtually nothing during the two-and-a-half-hour flight and refused all offers of food and drink. On the tarmac at Heathrow, there were no flowers to put on Charlie's coffin as it was efficiently checked through customs before being driven away in a hearse belonging to the undertakers who were to officiate at Charlie's south London funeral.

The following day, Charlie's closed coffin was laid out in the front room of Norman's three-bedroom council house home in Lidiard Road, just off Wandsworth Common, less than half a mile from where he was to be buried. Pat had accepted Charlie's cousin's invitation to stay at the house until after the funeral. Many of her husband's old associates came to the house to pay their respects including, on 5 May, three well-known members of the underworld, who asked Pat about rumours that Charlie had whispered the name of the man behind his shooting as he lay dying. No one knows what Pat said to those criminals, but they went away muttering about 'taking measures' on behalf of Pat and her daughters.

Even Charlie's traditional enemies at Scotland Yard were keen to help solve the murder. Pat let it be known she was comforted by their efforts, while others wondered whether it really was in anyone's interests for the killer to be found. No one seriously expected anyone else to be at risk because the murder had all the hallmarks of an old-fashioned hit in which there was just the one target.

On 9 May, an inquest at Westminster Coroner's Court into Charlie's death was opened and adjourned until 6 June so that formal identification and the funeral could go ahead the following day. Detective Inspector Alec Edwards was appointed by Knapman to carry out investigations into Charlie's death on his behalf. Edwards worked for SO11 (Special Operations 11) otherwise known as the Organised Crime Group of New Scotland Yard.

At Norman Radford's home that same afternoon of the ninth, the day before the funeral, wreaths and bunches of flowers filled the triangular garden of the white semi as the last of the visitors paid their respects. In the morning, Charlie's coffin was carefully removed from the front room and placed in a hearse to lead a funeral cortege of eight cars. Behind the glass sides of the hearse was a flower wreath spelling 'Chas'. Other floral tributes alongside the coffin included a small white dog, a chair and miniature archways. Five limousines were fitted with roof racks that were awash with huge flower baskets. Pat was in the first car rocking with sobs. Her daughters Cheryl, Tracey and Leander held onto their mother.

A few minutes later, Bruce Reynolds watched as Pat struggled from the undertaker's Daimler at Wandsworth cemetery. Norman Radford helpfully explained to the dozens of assembled reporters that some of the characters attending 'might not appreciate having their photos taken.' Spritely Reynolds was fifty-nine, one year older than Charlie would have been, and looked a million dollars in a navy-blue mohair suit, slim and distinguished, less a great train robber than the CEO of a City bank. Former colleague Roy 'the Weasel' James was approached by a reporter but denied his identity at first. 'I'm not Roy James,' he said. 'You've made a mistake, you've got the wrong guy.' Then he whispered, 'OK, Charlie was one of the best.' The pair, along with two more train robbers, Bobby Welch and Buster Edwards, joined Pat and her daughters behind the coffin as it was carried towards the chapel of remembrance in the grounds of the cemetery.

Buster Edwards' hair was now snow white and he had left his flower stall under Waterloo station to attend. Reynolds walked alongside him and Welch, who had struggled in with the crutches he needed after a cartilage operation had gone wrong in prison. Reynolds' arm was ready to stop him falling. Roy James – looking much heavier than in the good old days – was bringing up the rear. His hands were clasped in front of him and his head was low in mourning. As cameras probed through the crowd the train robbers turned away once again.

The coffin had the big family wreath as it was carried into the chapel behind the minister, the Rev Kevin Parkes, from

St Anne's church, just down the road in Tooting. His hair was in a ponytail with a blue ribbon. 'The family liked the way he handled Charlie's Aunt Nellie's funeral so they asked for him again,' undertaker Roger Gillman explained afterwards. As the coffin was carried past the mourners, Kevin Parkes chanted, 'I am the resurrection …' The service featured Charlie's favourite song, 'My Way,' sung by Frank Sinatra. To close, Pat's choice was 'When Your Old Wedding Ring Was New', crackling over the speaker system. The crowd parted to let her and her daughters through to follow the coffin out to the graveside. Pat was supported by Charlie's cousin.

Charlie was to be laid in the same ground as his father Bill, flowers strewn around him with cards signed by many from the history of late twentieth-century crime. 'Charlie, from Reg and Ron' was written on a ticket taped to a wreath of red-and-white carnations from the Krays. There was a rumour that one of the twins might turn up, but it wasn't likely since they were both still in prison. Several other ageing criminals were also unable to attend in person but sent flowers, including Ronnie Knight, still fighting extradition from Spain on those Security Express robbery charges, and great train robber Tommy Wisbey, in jail for cocaine trafficking.

The wreaths included a large dog sculpted in white chrysanthemums to resemble Charlie's beloved Bo-Bo. It had come with the message: 'I'll make you proud of me. I will always love and remember you – David, grandson.'

Pat, Tracey, Cheryl and Leander looked down as the mahogany coffin, polished like a mirror, was lowered into the ground. Pat held a single red rose tightly in her hand as still more tears streamed down her face. 'We have entrusted our brother Charlie to his keeping,' Reverend Parkes said, Bible in hand. Pat kissed the rose and let if fall on the coffin. Her daughters did the same.

Pat was led from the graveside and the other train robbers stood aside to let Welch on his crutches wobble to the graveside. He reached down for some earth and let it trickle through his hand onto the wooden casket below. Only Bruce Reynolds was seen to look down. He quietly muttered his own epitaph to Charlie. 'He never left anyone behind.'

It was left to Nosher Powell to sum up how high emotions were running: 'The murder was all so unnecessary and whoever did it is now the walking dead. Someone will get him.'

Another man chipped in: 'They'll get somebody for doing this to Charlie. They'll have him, you watch.'

The old men who'd robbed that famous train and spent scores of years in jail soon vanished from the cemetery, leaving a couple of Scotland Yard's finest, complete with raincoats folded over their arms. They'd already given Pat the names of the alleged assassins following the statement made by supergrass Michael Michael, although they weren't making anything official yet. One of Charlie's criminal friends said to a reporter at the funeral: 'It's given her a lift to know they think they know who did it.'

Four men with shovels then slowly started filling in the sandy grave. A few days after Charlie's funeral, police in Spain released the body of Charlie's beloved dog Boo-Boo and his ashes were scattered on Charlie's grave in south London. In one way, it was the end.

But the story of who murdered Charlie Wilson, and why, was about to take a very strange twist.

48/

Three days after Charlie Wilson's funeral – on 13 May 1990 – the *News of the World* blasted a banner headline across their front page: WE NAME TRAIN ROBBER MURDER SUSPECT.

The *NoW's* 'sensational crime scoop' claimed that jailbreak fugitive Danny 'Scarface' Roff was the police's prime suspect. The paper said that, after a number of leads from 'crime intelligence sources', one of their reporters had obtained photos of Roff from their own library and showed them to Norman Radford. After carefully studying the photos, he picked out Roff and said: 'It looks like the man I saw sitting on the grassy bank with his bicycle near Charlie's villa. The man I saw had spiky, bleached-blond hair and was thinner in the face, but everything else looks identical.'

Pat picked out the face of a second man from another set of photographs and said it was he who'd actually shot dead her husband. That man, also twenty-nine, was not identified by the newspaper at the time but it was 'Skins' from south London, the man who'd gone on the run with 'Scarface' in 1988 after hijacking a prison van in Norfolk. The *NoW* reported: 'Tears welled in Patricia's eyes as she studied the photo: "That's him. I'm ninety-nine per cent sure of it. The lips are pursed and bow-shaped. The nose is the same – so too is the jawline and bone structure."' The paper had shown Pat a new photofit sketch of the killer wearing a baseball hat. She said the artist had drawn a perfect likeness and declared: 'That's him. I'll never forget the way those eyes stared at me.'

Pat and Norman Radford claimed that just one hour before they'd met the paper's reporters, they'd received a separate tip-off from an underworld figure also alleging Roff was one of the men involved. All this conveniently ignored the fact the police had actually already told her the identity of both men after the tip from supergrass Michael Michael. But the *News of the World* also claimed that they'd received further information alleging that Roff was part of a drug-smuggling team in Spain. They alleged that Charlie had been killed because he double-crossed a gang over a lorry-load of cannabis. But Pat insisted her beloved husband was not involved in drug trafficking. 'My Charlie hated drugs,' she said.

The reference to cannabis wasn't entirely accurate, although it was certainly true that Charlie's gang had stolen a shipment of hash on the Costa Brava from a gang that included Roff.

In Medellín, Colombia, Pablo Escobar and his cartel henchmen were delighted to hear that other British criminals were being blamed for Narco Charlie's death. However, this also reminded Escobar that Roy Adkins was the next problem that needed solving. He ordered his people in Holland to track down Adkins and then he'd decide how he should be dealt with.

49/

In early June 1990, Inspector Juan Lorenzo and one of his detectives flew to the UK to interview a British businessman suspected of involvement in Charlie's death. The tycoon, who lived in a luxurious house in the suburbs of south London, was linked to an international drugs ring believed to have smuggled tens of millions of pounds worth of narcotics into the UK. His name was never disclosed by Inspector Lorenzo, but the suspect denied all knowledge of Charlie's killers, even though Scotland Yard had strong evidence linking him to the two alleged hitmen, Scarface and Skins.

While in the UK, Inspector Lorenzo also interviewed Charlie's family and associates as his team tried to uncover more clues as to why Charlie was killed. With assistance from Scotland Yard, but little or no intelligence from the other international law enforcement agencies who'd been watching Charlie, the two Spanish detectives believed that their five-day trip to England had been worthwhile. Besides Scarface and Skins they now had a suspect in Holland, Roy Adkins, whom they believed had ordered the hit. They'd also established the chain of events that seemed to lead to his death. But they still had no idea that the trail would lead all the way back to Pablo Escobar in Medellín.

When two Scotland Yard officers flew out to Spain a few weeks later they energetically tried to cover all aspects of the case. They visited Chequers to examine the location of the actual shooting but weren't allowed inside the house itself because of a problem with the locks which seemed to have been changed.

Meanwhile, British newspapers published stories naming other criminals besides Scarface and Skins as 'new suspects' in Charlie's killing. In July 1990, the *Sun* named a man known as 'Scots Willy' whom the paper claimed Pat had identified. His name had originally been put forward by an anonymous underworld tipster. One of Charlie's oldest mates branded the story as 'a load of fuckin' lies. Either that or Pat was fingering any old photo that was put in front of her.'

On 15 August, Danny Roff and his wife Tina were arrested by Dutch police when they swooped on a flat in the small town of Naarden. Roff was still wanted in the UK after his escape in 1988, when he had served less than twelve months of his thirteen-year sentence. The Dutch police had been tipped off by Flying Squad officers in London who'd tracked Roff through Europe. Roff was held in a Dutch jail, pending his extradition to the UK. Spanish police were expected to apply for permission to interview him in connection with Charlie's murder. The other prime suspect, Skins, remained on the run.

Neither suspect knew that Adkins had been encouraged by Pablo Escobar to kill Charlie. Adkins had been careful not to tell anyone because he knew the Colombians would come after him if they thought he'd been 'indiscreet'. What he himself didn't realise was that this would not be enough to prevent there being a bullet with his name on it. By the late summer, it was being rumoured in the London underworld that some of Charlie's oldest friends were tracking Roy Adkins across Europe. They'd been tipped off by relatives of Scarface and Skins that Adkins had commissioned the hit.

At least two of Charlie's friends had promised Charlie that they'd 'sort out' any potential killer if he ever got taken out. 'Charlie was pretty open about his likely fate,' one of his oldest friends later recalled. Charlie had given many of his friends a great deal of money when they were down on their luck. They owed him dearly. Charlie had even told two old friends the location of a vast stash of money and jewellery in the mountains behind Chequers. 'Charlie told us to use that to pay for taking out his killer. He talked about it as if it was a given. As if he knew it was going to happen.'

When forty-two-year-old Adkins was gunned down by two men in the fashionable Nightwatch bar in the American Hotel, Amsterdam, on 28 September, it came as no real surprise. He was shot in the head five times and the murderers escaped on foot. Two men drinking with Adkins, thought to be his minders, also disappeared. Detectives presumed that Adkins' death was an act of revenge for the killing of Charlie. Pablo Escobar was delighted. His plan to kill Adkins did not even have to be put into action because Narco Charlie's friends seemed to have done the job for him and the cartel.

Escobar's own reign as the world's most successful drug baron was under threat. He was no longer the powerful gangster he once was. Many in Colombia loathed him for nearly sparking a civil war, as well as a host of atrocities. A new president had been elected on a wave of anti-narcos sentiment and he promised the law-abiding citizens of his country that Escobar's days were numbered. 'The tide had turned against Pablo. After years of his bullying, the people of Colombia had had enough,' one Colombian politician later recalled.

On the domestic front, Escobar's wife Tata had taken a leaf out of Pat Wilson's book and started refusing to leave the family home in Medellín for fear that they might both be gunned down. It would be fair to say that Pablo Escobar anyway had bigger things on his mind than the murders of Narco Charlie and Roy 'the Lump' Adkins. To Escobar, they were just another couple of greedy gringos who'd crossed the cartel and paid for it with their lives. Meanwhile, Escobar had the DEA, right-wing death squads and an entire national army trying to bring him to justice by this time.

A few days after the Adkins slaying, Spanish police seized 1,200 kilos of cocaine, the largest single amount of the drug ever found in the country, worth at least £300 million on the black market. The cocaine had been hidden in a van parked in the north of

Madrid. It was found just as the driver – a Colombian called Juan Carlos Morales – was about to start the engine. At the same time, in the northern region of Galicia, five more people were arrested. The ripple of this success of the police could be felt as far afield as Medellín and London. These drugs were part of a consignment Charlie Wilson might well have invested in if he'd still been alive.

On 14 December, the Madrid-based daily newspaper *ABC* published an extensive investigation into the Charlie Wilson murder in which they revealed that Danny 'Scarface' Roff had taken his wife and child to Spain with him as cover for the hit. The paper talked of a drug-traffickers' vendetta and questioned Pat's ability to identify either Roff or Skins because she was short-sighted. *ABC* also claimed to have been told by a criminal informant on the Costa del Sol that Roy Adkins only paid five thousand pounds for the hit on Charlie (most criminals had presumed a fee of at least four times that amount had been involved). There were also claims that Charlie had actually told friends he was worried about 'that nutter Adkins'. But, if he was taking the threat seriously, why didn't he take any extra security precautions in the months leading up to his death?

By the end of 1990, Pat still hadn't sold Chequers, having asked £200,000 for it. Many believed that Charlie's murder had scared people off. Pat hadn't stepped foot in Spain since accompanying Charlie's body back to London, although June Hackett, a former neighbour in Spain, was still handling inquiries on her behalf. In addition, not much progress had been made in the investigation into Pat's husband's murder. The weapon, the bicycle and the getaway van had still not been recovered and no arrests had been made.

By February of 1991, British and Spanish newspapers were claiming that the investigation into Charlie's murder had been 'wound down' by authorities because of a lack of evidence. Inspector Juan Lorenzo later explained: 'We'd tried everything but could not find enough evidence to prove Roff and Skins did it.' In any case, the man who commissioned the hit, Adkins, was now dead. Scotland Yard were 'somewhat surprised' by this attitude. 'We had Roff back in the UK, serving his time for that earlier offence and we were expecting the Spanish to ask for his extradition but it never happened,' said one Flying Squad detective.

But the ripple sent out by Charlie's cold-blooded murder, now one year earlier, had not yet faded.

50/

In June 1991, Roy Adkins's business partner, Klaas 'the Preacher' Bruinsma, was assassinated by two hitmen in front of Amsterdam's Hilton hotel. He was thirty-seven.

The Preacher had been under intense police surveillance and become a liability to his own organisation. A former Dutch policeman was later convicted of carrying out the hit. Meanwhile, the flow of drugs through Holland continued uninterrupted as two of Bruinsma's former lieutenants took over his empire.

Charlie's Marbella house Chequers finally sold for the full asking price in September. A Danish man bought it on behalf of a wealthy client after seeing a sale sign outside the property. It was only when a surveyor inspected the house after Pat had shipped her belongings back to England that the new owners realised there was a basement with a safe in it. Chequers was quickly re-sold for a £20,000 profit.

In Kent, Charlie's one-time prison mate, 'Mad Mickey' Blackmore – who'd worked closely with Roy Adkins in Holland – was released from Maidstone prison. He had served a lengthy sentence for arms offences and attempted murder. He claimed he was owed £250,000 by Adkins for going to prison without squealing and believed he could still collect on the debt, even though Adkins was now dead. Mad Mickey was so furious he began threatening the men who had murdered Adkins. One of Charlie's criminal associates later explained: 'Blackmore decided to go to Holland to collect his money from the Preacher's team but that could only end one way.' Blackmore was never seen alive again and his body eventually turned up in an Amsterdam canal. According to one story that did the rounds, he was shot in Marseilles and his body taken to Holland. His family publicly denied his involvement in Charlie's death because many newspapers were incorrectly naming him as the man who commissioned alleged hitmen Roff and Skins.

As one villain explained recently: 'They'd missed the point. Mickey had to go because he was threatening to bring down the fellas who'd avenged Charlie's death by getting Adkins topped.'

In November, the inquest into his murder was finally heard at Westminster Coroner's Court. DI Edwards told the inquest there was clear circumstantial evidence linking Charlie to some major drug deals. He said:'MrWilson is thought to have been connected in some way with drug dealing, and he upset a member of a rival gang and an execution was ordered against him.' Edwards said Charlie was alleged to have given permission for Paddy to name Adkins to police 'which upset Adkins enormously'. But the policeman did not name Roff and Skins in case it prejudiced any subsequent criminal proceedings.

Home Office pathologist Dr Rufus Crompton told the court that the first bullet to hit Charlie entered through the side of the neck and lodged inside. As it passed through his larynx it caused heavy bleeding and, inhaling blood, he was unable to speak or cry out, which seemed to contradict earlier claims that he had muttered the name of the man responsible for his murder. The verdict was that Charlie had been shot by persons unknown.

Outside the court, the Wilson family solicitor insisted: 'The drug allegations are strongly denied.'

Pat remained as determined as ever not to let Charlie down. No one will ever know if she was aware of the full truth about Charlie's involvement with drugs. But she'd clearly chosen to defend her husband's reputation after his murder. It was ironic in many ways because, while Charlie had been alive, she'd been desperately unhappy at times and even admitted that divorce had crossed her mind. But she'd always concluded that, despite everything, Charlie was the one whom she loved and couldn't live without. Now he had gone – and she'd been left to pick up the pieces

The morning after the inquest, Pat returned to Westminster Coroner's Court to hear the details of the last moments on Earth of Roy 'The Lump' Adkins, the man everyone was saying had commissioned the hit on her husband. Connections between Charlie's assassination and the death of Adkins were made public during the opening to his inquest. DI Edwards told the court: 'There was much speculation and some evidence to suggest the link between the two high-profile deaths. The connection with the killing of Wilson is Adkins.'

Shortly after the two inquests, it was announced that police commissioner Sir Peter Imbert was to receive a cheque for £1.5 million on behalf of the Met from a grateful US Drug Enforcement Administration. It was the UK's share of more than £200 million in assets, seized as part of the Anglo-American-Spanish operation that had 'rolled up' a worldwide web of crooked deals. These had been uncovered by detectives investigating the Brink's-Mat gold bullion robbery and 'other crimes'. Legislation had to be passed in the US to enable the UK authorities to receive the money. All the relevant law enforcement agencies claimed that 'international agreements' were starting to be effective when it came to beating the drug barons and that this would spell even bigger problems for major criminals.

However, one of Charlie's oldest criminal associates later said: 'I'd call it bounty money for Charlie being killed. One-point-five-million pounds is peanuts, so why else would they bother paying that? It's a bloody disgrace.' The cash award was also the only public hint that a massive surveillance operation had been underway on the Costa del Sol for years. But the reality was that the drugs business – then estimated to be worth £70 billion a year worldwide – was still making huge fortunes for certain individuals. With the stakes so high, murder had become virtually a daily occurrence.

There had been outrage and dismay amongst Charlie's train robbery associates over his cold-blooded murder. Now they took it upon themselves to probe further into the circumstances behind the killing because they believed Adkins was simply carrying out orders. 'We all knew Adkins was too far down the pecking order to have personally green-lit that job,' one of Charlie's criminal associates later explained.

In the middle of 1992, a London criminal well-known to Charlie Wilson and his associates was arrested by Scotland Yard on suspicion of drug running. One of Charlie's criminal associates later explained: 'This fella was told by the police that Pablo fuckin' Escobar had encouraged Adkins to carry out the hit on Charlie. In fact, he'd given Adkins permission to do Charlie because he thought Charlie was becoming a bit of a liability. We was outraged by this and felt we owed it to Charlie and his family to make sure that something was done about this. Charlie hadn't deserved to die. He got himself caught up with a bunch of South American killers because he liked doing a bit of business. But that didn't need to cost him his life.'

When Charlie's associate demanded evidence from the police, he was shown transcripts of phone conversations between Escobar and his European associates. 'The police had got these transcripts from the DEA,' explained Charlie's former associate. 'And Escobar clearly mentioned the Charlie "problem" and how pleased he was that Charlie was no longer around.'

On 2 January 1993, another victim of a hit was linked to the Charlie Wilson case. Scotland Yard detectives believed businessman and property developer Donald Urquhart invested in some of the same drug deals as Charlie. Urquhart was shot dead in broad daylight in London's West End by a man on a motorcycle. It was a method usually only used by South American *sicarios*. On the Costa del Sol it was claimed that Urquhart might have been killed in revenge for Charlie's death. Urquhart himself was considered something of a criminal eccentric because most of his business deals were carried out in the back of his stretched chauffeur-driven Rover that contained several phones and a fax machine.

Despite this latest death, some of Charlie's oldest friends were still fuming about the way that the former train robber had been abandoned to his fate.

51/

By the summer of 1993, it had become clear to Charlie's friends that law enforcement agents did not warn him he was in danger because they were more interested in gathering evidence against Pablo Escobar. This was intended to help the DEA extradite the Colombian drug lord to the USA.

'Charlie's death just wasn't that important to those bastards,' one of Charlie's associates later told this author. 'Their priority was finding Escobar and taking him to the US to face justice – or killing him.'

Charlie's associates also knew that, while the Adkins problem had been easy to resolve, nailing Escobar would be nothing short of a suicide mission. His chilling attacks on innocent civilians reached new heights of depravity when his henchmen exploded a bomb outside a Bogota pharmacy owned by his Cali cartel rivals. Twenty people – including four children – were killed. One of Charlie's oldest criminal associates later recalled: 'Escobar was murdering kids. Somebody had to do something to stop him. He was fuckin' psychotic.'

Charlie's old-school gangster friends put the feelers out to try and find out who Escobar was still connected to in London and Spain. 'It was crunch time,' explained one of Charlie's oldest associates. 'Sure, we was sickened by what Escobar was doing, but none of us was stupid enough to think we could just pop over to Medellín, ice him and then jump on a plane back to Blighty.' A group of Charlie's friends decided to find a professional hitman prepared to kill Escobar. The same associate later explained: 'We eventually found this half-English, half-Spanish fella who reckoned he could plant a bomb under Escobar's car and blow him up. He made it sound simple and claimed he'd done it many times before. But he wanted a million pounds in advance to do it. Well, that was a fuck of a lot of dough and there was something about this fella which seemed too good to be true. A couple of the lads then checked him out very carefully and found out he was a complete conman. He'd planned to take the million quid and scarper. We let him know we knew what he was up to and he disappeared.'

Charlie's old friends decided it was time to turn from poachers to gamekeepers. Charlie's mate later explained: 'All of us prided ourselves on being old-fashioned operators. We'd never grass up each other. No matter how much pressure we was under. But it was time to break the rules. We needed to track Escobar down and then let others do the dirty work for us. But, of course, we had to find him first.' La Patrona – Pablo Escobar's right-hand woman in London – was having an affair with a well-known British gangster who'd grown up with many of Charlie's criminal contemporaries in South London. 'So we had a chat with this fella and persuaded him to start pumping La Patrona for info about Escobar.'

On 1 December, the gangster lover of La Patrona contacted Charlie's friends. 'He'd found out from her the area in Medellín where Escobar was hiding at that time,' Charlie's one-time associate later recalled. 'We had no choice but to grass him up.'

Were a bunch of old-school London gangsters really about to help bring down the most wanted criminal in history?

52/

By the beginning of December 1993, Pablo Escobar knew the authorities were closing in on him as he moved from safe house to safe house in Medellín. A task force had been looking for the drug lord for sixteen months, ever since he'd escaped from house arrest at La Catedral, the prison he'd been allowed to build for himself.

The DEA – in Medellín as part of the task force – were given information, via their London office, that Escobar was hiding out in Los Olivos, an area on the outskirts of the city. The DEA agents refused to divulge who'd provided that tip. But they were obliged to then inform the Search Bloc, a Colombian unit made up of crack national police troops who were dedicated to locating and taking down Escobar. Within hours, a Colombian electronic surveillance team working from a nondescript van that was circling the suburbs of Medellín intercepted a call from the Los Olivos district. Officers immediately recognised the voice of Pablo Escobar calling his son, Juan Pablo. In fact, Escobar had a feeling that they were onto him, so the call was cut short.

Minutes later, members of Search Bloc burst into a small house where Escobar and his bodyguard, Alvaro de Jesus Agudelo, known as 'El Limón' were hiding. A gunfight ensued as Escobar and El Limon clambered out of an attic exit onto the roof above. As they aimed bullets at the authorities while scrambling over crumbling roof tiles, Search Bloc marksmen returned fire, shooting El Limón and Escobar as their backs were turned.

Pablo Escobar died from gunshots to the leg, torso, and a fatal shot through the ear. 'Viva Colombia!' a Search Bloc soldier screamed into his walkie-talkie moments later, as he stood proudly over Escobar's corpse. 'We have just killed Pablo Escobar!'

The gory aftermath was captured in images that have long since become infamous. A group of smiling Colombian police officials, along with members of the Search Bloc, stand over the bloody, limp body of Pablo Escobar splayed across the barrio rooftop. Pablo 'El Doctor' Escobar had finally met his maker in Medellín. Details of his last few minutes of life have been reported many times across the world. But the complex truth, the story of how he really came to be tracked down, has never before been disclosed.

As one of Charlie's oldest associates later explained: 'Charlie would have turned in his grave knowing that we grassed Escobar up to the police. I remember Charlie once told me that he'd rather die than ever help the cops with anything. But this was a matter of honour. Pablo Escobar never played by the rules, so why should we? He made billions out of Charlie and then dumped him like a dead dog on the roadside to hell. We had to send a message out to his people that Charlie Wilson was an important character in all our lives and we could never have stood by and done nothing.

'Now at least we could all rest in peace.'

DEATHSCRIPT

In a surprise move in early May 1995, Inspector Juan Lorenzo returned to the UK and tried to interview suspected hitman Skins. Aged thirty-four, he was by this time in Durham prison and serving a long sentence for wounding, assault and possession of drugs.

One of the Scotland Yard detectives who accompanied Juan Lorenzo on his trip to the north of England later said: 'Skins went crazy in the interview room and turned the furniture over and insisted he had nothing to do with the Wilson hit. Juan was shocked by his response and Skins then refused to answer any questions.'

The police had no doubt that Skins' behavior further implied he was guilty of killing Charlie. Yet Juan Lorenzo still failed to get either Skins or Scarface Roff extradited from the UK to Spain. Scotland Yard remained baffled by the Marbella detectives' failure to bring the two men to justice.

Visited during that same trip made by Lorenzo, Pat Wilson was asked to re-identify Skins from a piece of recently filmed video footage. Pat now said she was only 'seventy per cent' certain this was the man who'd killed her husband. Why was she backtracking? Skins' parents – who were interviewed by this author at their south London home in 2003 – claimed Pat Wilson deliberately identified their son to take the attention away from the real killers of Charlie. 'He didn't do it. I swear,' said Skins' father.

While still in London, Inspector Juan Lorenzo also questioned Paddy's wife, Julie. She admitted to Lorenzo she knew the Wilson family, but insisted she had no recollection of phoning or seeing Charlie in January 1990 or asking 'permission' for her husband to name Roy Adkins to police.

Skins was transferred to Whitemoor prison, Cambridgeshire, shortly after Inspector Lorenzo's visit to the UK. He constantly feared for his life because of his alleged link to the Charlie Wilson hit. 'He knew Charlie had a lot of mates in Whitemoor and we was really worried,' explained his father. They included Charlie's old south London friend, Joey Pyle, who'd run that illegal gambling club the Charterhouse with Charlie in the early 1960s. Pyle had been sent to Whitemoor in 1995 after being found guilty of drugs charges he later insisted were 'a fit-up'. He soon heard that the man rumoured to have 'done' his friend Charlie was housed in a cell on a neighbouring wing.

Pyle later recalled: 'I said to another inmate I didn't want him coming anywhere near me 'cause of what he'd done to Charlie. But then this geezer went and told Skins I had the hump with him and he insisted on coming to meet me. I thought he was mad, but gave him the benefit of the doubt and agreed to see him. He swore on his grandmother's grave that someone had wrongly picked him out of a photo album and he really didn't do it.'

Another of Charlie's oldest friends told this author that Charlie's murder 'will never be forgotten'. He said: 'Skins, or whoever did it, will have to watch their backs for the rest of their lives. These sort of jobs are never cancelled. They're never forgotten. It doesn't matter how long ago it was. Payback can come at any time. They could be in their seventies before they get 'em.'

Meanwhile, the spiral of violence that began with Charlie Wilson's death continued. At 3 a.m. on 10 February 1996, Danny 'Scarface' Roff was in an upstairs bar at the Passport Club in New Cross, south-east London, when a gunman walked in and sprayed the crowded bar with bullets, smashing Roff's spine and hitting a girl of sixteen in the arm. Miraculously, Scarface survived, although he'd suffered life-changing injuries. But the incident raised serious questions about why he'd never been charged with Charlie's murder by Spanish police. Scotland Yard had no doubt Roff was targeted to avenge Charlie's killing. One detective said after the attack: 'Roff knows who shot him but he's too terrified to tell us.'

A few weeks later, the now crippled and wheelchair-bound Roff and his family moved into a new house in Wanstead Road in Bromley, Kent, and promptly tried to turn it into a fortress. Workmen even installed 10-foot high lattice fencing. Roff's Mercedes was specially adapted for him to drive because of his injuries, although as the months passed he left the house less and less frequently. Then neighbours noticed he even stopped going in the garden with his two young sons. 'He looked terrible, pale and shaking and hardly able to stand because of his injuries,' said one neighbour.

Just under a year later Roff had a short spell in prison. Within an hour of being released he was pulling into the driveway of his home in his Mercedes. The front garden was littered with toys belonging to his two young sons. Scarface was about to heave his crippled frame into his wheelchair when a dirty-white Ford Escort van pulled up outside the house. The rear doors swung open and two masked gunmen opened fire, shooting Scarface in the head and chest and leaving him sprawled on the tarmac. They sped off down the neat, tree-lined residential road with the van's back doors flapping open. The vehicle was later found abandoned half a mile away.

Roff's wife, Tina, rushed out of the house on hearing the gunshots and within minutes police had sealed off the area. An air ambulance helicopter landed nearby and took Scarface to the Royal London hospital in Whitechapel, where he later died. Detectives quickly announced that Scarface's death was linked to the feud started by Charlie's murder, which had already cost at least half a dozen other people their lives. Police hoped Tina might shed some light on the murder but it was always more likely she'd take the same attitude as Pat Wilson to assisting them with their enquiries.

In October 2003, DI Juan Lorenzo – now a neat, tidy, and stockier man with greying hair – met this author. He got out

Charlie's file and began talking about the killing in his tiny office at the newly built Marbella police station. Incredibly, those notes consisted of just two pieces of A4 paper with a couple of sentences written on them. Lorenzo said: 'Yes, Roff and Skins were not extradited because the extradition was not sought by the court, which means that the court decided there was not enough evidence to guarantee a prosecution. The trouble was we had no actual evidence that they were both in Spain at that time.' Lorenzo admitted that it was strange that Skins had never suffered the same fate as Roff. 'Maybe that means he is innocent. Who knows?'

Charlie's murder appears to have sparked one of the deadliest feuds in British underworld history. At the centre of this struggle was control of the cocaine being shipped from South America into the UK. An international law enforcement task force had witnessed this spread of cold-blooded violence with apprehension but appeared to have done relatively little to prevent it because of their obsession with catching the world's most evil criminal – Pablo Escobar. Experts at Scotland Yard's elite criminal intelligence unit, then called SO11, have admitted that they can't predict how the international drugs business will eventually pan out.

But one thing is for certain: Charlie Wilson's favourite song perfectly summed up his life and crimes – he did it his way.

BIBLIOGRAPHY

Ronald Biggs (1994), *Odd Man Out*, Pan, London

Mark Bowden (2002), *Killing Pablo*, Atlantic Books, New York

Duncan Campbell (1996), *The Underworld*, Penguin, London

Frank Cater and Tom Tullett (1990), *The Sharp End*, Grafton, London

Georgie Ellis with Rod Taylor (2000), *A Murder of Passion*, John Blake Publishing, London

Ronnie Knight, John Knight, DS Peter Wilton with Pete Sawyer (2002), *Gotcha!*, Pan, London

Tony Lambrianou (1992), *Inside the Firm*, Pan, London

Duncan MacLaughlin with William Hall (2002), *The Filth*, Mainstream, Edinburgh

Howard Marks (1998), *Mr Nice*, Vintage, London

Graeme McLagan (2002), *Bent Coppers*, Orion, London

Bruce Porter (1993) *Blow*, HarperCollins, 1993

Joey Pyle, *Notorious: The Changing Face of Organised Crime* (2003), Virgin, London

Piers Paul Read (1978), *The Train Robbers*, W. H. Allen, London

Bruce Reynolds (2003), *Crossing the Line: Autobiography of a Thief*, Virgin, London

Bruce Reynolds, Nick Reynolds and Alan Parker (2000), *The Great Train Robbery Files*, Abstract Sounds Publishing, London

Mel Williams (2000), *Nearly Famous,* self-published